(un)selling

14 (un)conventional principles to reduce
sales anxiety and increase sales

KEVIN CASEY

(un)selling
14 (un)conventional principles to reduce sales anxiety and increase sales

For Mom

My mom had a wish.
She wanted just one of her four kids to grow up and be a doctor.

I would have made a terrible doctor.
People would have died.
From something as simple as an ingrown toenail.

So, I ended up being a sales guy.
And whaddya know?
She still loves me.

I don't kiss and tell... but they do

Like so many of us, Kevin 'fell into sales' and he gets what it feels like to be used and abused as a salesperson. He lived it and he battled hard to fix it. Who better to learn from than someone who's been there."

Benjamin Dennehy
The UK's most hated sales trainer
Bournemouth, England

The principles and tactics inside the (un)selling process relieve the pressure off both me and the customer during the sales process. My goal has always been to make prospects feel at ease, not pressured. I have been able to make that happen by using Kevin's (un)selling method.

Danny Graf
Sales Leader, Viernheim, Hesse, Germany

I've partnered with Kevin for the past 20 years to drive sales and revenue for our portfolio companies and never once did I ever feel like I was being sold to or pressured. He always brings an angle that no one else had the courage to share. Never the hard-sell.

Dean MacDonald
CEO | Deacon Sports & Entertainment, Canada

Your (un)selling strategies have already helped me double my sales goals, and that's just reading your free stuff. Starting to feel guilty. Is there paid stuff coming soon?

Dermot Kearney
CEO | Kildare Renovations, Kildare, Ireland

Kevin has been a true mentor to me. Although I've been in a number of leadership roles over the course of my career, I rely on Kevin to challenge my thinking and kick me in the ass when needed. I truly value his no-nonsense methods of connecting with clients and prospects and his generosity of sharing all the "secrets" of being a fulfilled and successful salesperson and/or leader. A very special human being with very special skills!!

Heather Stamp
Senior Advisor, MC Advisory, Atlantic Canada

This book transforms selling into natural, authentic conversations that convert—a necessity for anyone with something to offer. It's a game-changer for those seeking to promote what they sell with confidence and authenticity. It's not just a must-read; it's a must-study.

Jeremy Bennett
Author, Business Mindset Coach, Canada

If you love your business but hate the idea of selling it's time to get out of your own way and serve the people you can help. This is the book to get you there.

Justin Michael
Executive Coach and best-selling author
Los Angeles, California

Kevin Casey is a consummate professional who genuinely cares about his customers, putting their needs first. He excels in providing thoughtful feedback, wisdom, and guidance, making him a valued leader. Inclusive, enthusiastic, and kind, he invites others into his world, fostering strong and loyal business relationships.

Pegret Harrison
Southern Health Partners Inc.
Florida, USA

For all you reluctant sellers, this is a game-changer.

Mike Herberts
Creator Of The *UPSP System, UK

Take everything you learned about selling and toss it in the can. Just refer to Kevin's work when you get that unpleasant salesy feeling before a call.

Pete Durand
CEO | Entrepreneur
Host of the Eating Crow Podcast
North Carolina, USA

Kevin has really figured out how to take the 'selling' out of sales. His relationship-driven approach focuses on the person and the organization first, he really understands how to build relationships, and promotes the fact that business will naturally happen once there is an established rapport and trust. It is refreshing.

AnnMarie Boudreau, Chief Executive Officer
St. John's Board of Trade, Canada

It's time to sell.

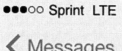
I resign!

You can't. You're the boss.

Shit! Now what?

Read this book.

CONTENTS

PART 4: (UN)TAPPING

PART 5: (UN)CORKING

Blatant Praise

Nonfiction books typically start with the author ~~pleading~~ begging, asking some industry titan to write a 1,000-word gushing review they can slap at the front of the book. There's a secret Amazon bestseller community where they go tit for tat: you write me a blurb, and I'll punt you one back.

I'm not in that club.

Instead, I asked one of the most fearless sales leaders around: My mom. Here she is, 87 years ~~old~~ young:

She single-handedly raised four kids, plus the biggest kid of them all, my late dad. I was the youngest brat.

One particular Wednesday night, in 1978 when I was 10, something happened during our weekly goulash dinner that changed our family forever. With a look in her eyes that was less Mom and more like Rocky's stone-cold stare when he faced Ivan Drago, she revealed something she had been secretly planning behind our backs for months:

"I'm ditching my secretary job and becoming a real estate agent. I won't be home cooking suppers and washing your clothes anymore."

The family was speechless. I'm betting we all shared the same inner fear of starving to death and being found by the police weeks later in dirty clothes. Thankfully, I'm happy to report that none of my brothers and sisters died of starvation, and we even managed to master 43 ways to spice up Kraft Dinner.

That day was "Mom's Breakout Day."

Over the next 35 years, she became one of the top real estate producers in the region, snagged awards left and right, and was invited to RE/ MAX's head office in Denver more than once to meet the head honchos. Mom juggled her rise to the top of her sales career while simultaneously wearing the crown of the family matriarch. Like so many moms I know, she was a superhero without the cape. Mom retired from real estate at 70 years old, and there's nobody on this planet I would rather have featured up front in my book.

But asking my mom to write a few words about me comes with a real risk. You see, while my mom was a remarkable sales professional during her era, she did so at a time when people weren't glued to their smartphones. Her weapons were a landline telephone, a hip pager the size of a box of matches, and a battered Day-Timer. She hates tech.

We gave our mom laptops, smartphones, and iPads as gifts over the years. Every time she smiled and put them in a drawer, where they remain—untouched.

Mom still keeps track of everything in her old Day-Timer book, still sends handwritten notes and Christmas cards in the mail, and still has a Motorola flip phone with the lowest data plan on planet Earth.

So, you can see why just handing over my laptop and asking my mom to write a few words for this book is like orchestrating a NASA space shuttle mission. I did everything I could to make this easy. I set up a blank page on my laptop and carefully explained the basics: "Touch these keys. Don't touch these keys." Then I left so she could write a few words without me breathing down her neck.

After 94 minutes and 12 tech support calls, I'm happy to share these words from my mom:

HELLO.

THIS IS KEVIN'S MOM. ELEANOR.

KEVIN JUST PASSED ME HIS COMPUTER AND ITS ALREADY CONFUSING.

HE KEPT POINTING TO A MOUSE, BUT HE MAY BE A LITTLE HIGH. I THOUGHT HE QUIT THAT.

I HAD HOPED ONE OF MY FOUR KIDS WOULD HAVE GONE TO MEDICAL SCHOOL TO BE A DOCTOR, AND KEVIN WAS MY LAST HOPE.

HE ENDED UP A <u>SALESMAN</u>.

IT JUST TOOK ME EIGHT MINUTES TO MAKE THAT UNDERLINE THINGY HAPPEN.

IT COULD HAVE BEEN WORSE.

HE COULD HAVE ENDED UP A POLITICIAN.

NOT MANY OF HIS TEACHERS GAVE KEVIN MUCH OF A CHANCE.

ESPECIALLY MRS FIRTH. SHE WROTE ANTICHRIST ON THE FRONT OF HIS FOURTH GRADE REPORT CARD, AND HE TRIED TO SCRATCH IT OUT.

KEVIN JUST LEFT MY CONDO AND PLUGGED IN THIS TYPEWRITER SO I COULD FINISH. HE GETS IMPATIENT SOMETIMES. HE CAN BE A BIT OF AN ANTICHRIST.

———

THAT LITTLE LINE WAS EASIER; THAT ONLY TOOK ONE MINUTE.

ANYWAYS, I LOVE YOU, KEVIN.

I AM PROUD YOU ARE WRITING A BOOK. I MEAN, YOU'RE NOT SAVING LIVES LIKE I HOPED YOU WOULD, BUT YOU ARE MAKING PEOPLE SUCK LESS AT SOMETHING.

I TOLD THE BRIDGE CLUB LADIES ABOUT YOUR BOOK AND THEY WILL EACH BUY A COPY, BUT MRS. HENDERSON WANTED ME TO REMIND YOU TO KEEP THE LETTERS BIG AND THE PRICE LOW.

MAYBE YOU'LL GET FAMOUS FROM THIS BOOK AND BECOME RICH. KEVIN, IT'S NEVER TOO LATE TO BE A DOCTOR, YOU KNOW.

THANK YOU FOR READING THIS. I'M GLAD I JUST DIDN'T

WRITE THE WORDS KEVIN LEFT FOR ME TO USE.

I LOVE SURPRISING HIM.

I ALWAYS TOLD HIM TO USE YOUR OWN WORDS, NOT SOMEONE ELSE'S.

LOVE, MOM

P.S. I'M NOT SURE WHAT THIS P.S. BIT IS FOR, BUT I SEE IT A LOT.

A very (un)foreword by Justin Michael

Kevin Casey is a kindred spirit when it comes to a no-BS approach to doing deals. High-pressure, old-school tactics from the '80s and '90s are ineffective, yet what's very popular now is more arrogant and self-aggrandizing than ever. Record scratch…

Think about the "modern" best practices. It's cathartic as hell to listen to Alec Baldwin barking at reps in *Glengarry Glen Ross* because the reality is not quite different these days, with our blowtorch sales managers applying ever more pressure to hit insane targets set up by corrupt VCs in the "not quite recession." If you work for yourself, you feel like Willy Loman in *Death of a Salesman*, desperate as you slowly slog it out and might even face losing your business.

Ninety percent of new businesses fail, after all… but that doesn't have to be you! Because now you have Kevin Casey in your life, sharing timeless truths and wisdom in these pages.

So what are people smoking? What's happened to the pursuit of becoming a "trusted advisor?" Everyone wants to be "Insta-famous." Sellers are encouraged to "build their personal brand." Translation: obsessively post about themselves on LinkedIn, Twitter, and Instagram. All day and night. This leads inexperienced reps to offer cohort courses with a ridiculous guarantee like "Learn the Secrets to Earning 100K for Just $7 or Your Money Back." But you just started in sales?

Salespeople are pushed to dial 10 phone numbers at a time, do 1,000 dials a day, and send 300–1,000 emails daily. But there's no training on what to say if, God forbid, someone picks up or starts responding. Then they're told to apply "personalization at scale," spending 3-30 minutes researching every prospect.

Frazzled and with a stunning array of technology, they are *over*selling, *over*thinking, *over*blasting, *over*selling (again), and the cardinal sin: *over*closing the close. We are even blowing up deals with our overzealousness that would have closed.

Enter (un)selling.

Salespeople must slow down and have one conversation at a time. As Kevin Casey brilliantly puts it in *(un)selling*, 80% of the time you're not going to close, so you need to "sift," not sell.

ABC ('always be closing') morphs into ABD ('always be disqualifying').

I built my similar selling style based on Mike Tyson meets a honey badger—insane patience, persistence, vigilance, and readiness to take the punches. I also agree with Earl Nightingale and George Costanza. "Opposite Land" is where all the revenue lies. Do you want to thrive in life? Think and act differently. Differentiating yourself from the next 999 sellers is the name of the game. Move from war-like to empathy; walk a country mile in their shoes, Forrest Gump.

Kevin lived it, rebuilt it, and teaches you how to not only not suck, but how to make this an art form available to anyone.

But it's a chilling portent in another way. Sales is *Groundhog Day*. Millions of sellers send trite emails that open with "I hope you're doing well." Opening cold calls with "This is a cold call. Wanna roll the dice?" Gimmicks, templates, tactics, and the Hollywood media are inflating Vin Diesel's magical manipulation in *Boiler Room* or *The Wolf of Wall Street's* DiCaprio with his perfect sequence of scripted subterfuge.

The gold is in studying people like Seth Godin (*Purple Cow*), and Chris Voss (hostage negotiation tactics), and—humbly speaking—my work (the Justin Michael Method), because they are fundamentally juxtaposed to the common sales thought. To work, strategies and tactics must be based on pattern interrupts.

The (un)expected.

Customers don't expect you to be real, act in their interest, serve, and be human. If you do that, you'll win... and big. The effort, the pressure, and the slog fade away.

What I love about Kevin's new book is he breaks down how to stand out as an everyman and everywoman. This book will resonate with 400m small business owners. Section by section, he shows you what's broken—aka what not to do—then lays out a simplified path forward: how to think about sales, how to get your mind right, how to deal with your self-induced sales anxiety, and a suite of Yogi Berra-style techniques that make this dark art, cursing you as you tear your hair out, great again.

Sell without selling. Sell without selling out.

We don't need to be desperate with commission breath. We don't need to sell to survive. It's not a dire profession. We need to slow down and serve others—one at a time. This means simply: putting their needs first and diagnosing them like a doctor who is concerned. You wouldn't want your oncologist to jump for joy when he sees you, so why do you get so "people-pleasing" the minute someone answers the phone? Just be you.

Just help people and get real. That's the overarching message of the book. It's all about "(un)learning" everything you know, because the methodologies that you've embraced are turning you into a commission-seeking automaton clone. Prospects are put off by this and tune you out.

I suggest reading this book's five sections over four to five weeks. Soak it in. Make it a lifestyle. Take a section and apply it to your life. Peel away the layers of the onion of your mediocrity each time. When you finish, sit down, and read it all again. You can love to sell again or enjoy it for the first time. (I know you just threw up a little bit in your mouth.)

This grand profession will no longer be a dirty word in your vocabulary. Kevin is a Canadian insurance sales mastermind, who is unassuming like Columbo, with a rare sardonic wit and willingness to be "(un) PC" and tell it like it is when the industry is preventing anyone from coming along and slaughtering the sacred cows.

Remember, great sales trainers love to sell sales training. Kevin is like me and you, decades in the arena, looking for an honest way to help good people. He has no pyramid scheme or empire, no incentive to lie. It's a wooden carpenter's cup, not a golden chalice. "Only the penitent man shall pass," intoned Sean Connery.

What if everything you're doing in sales now is expected and wrong? But the majority are telling you it's right? Kevin joins me in revealing the Matrix. That darn black cat just keeps crossing our path.

Don't you ever wonder if you're living in a bad dream, a sales delusion? A simulation where everyone thinks it's somehow OK to hammer prospects, hunt them with walls of noise, constantly check in and follow up, persuade, do white-knuckled last-minute discounts, and then manipulate everything and everyone until you scare away all the fish?

Sales is the engine of the economy. It's alive and well. None of the channels are dead. But the way sellers all do it the same is why it feels that way. You need a new way, and that way is fundamental.

(un)selling.

Embrace these pages. Kevin's simple words and ideas are potent. You have in your hands a hidden gem: a guidebook to transform your life and business.

(un)selling will fill your bank account, give you back your time and peace of mind, and you'll get a real kick out of reading it.

Take my word for it. You'll feel awkward doing this stuff, but geniuses like David Sandler can't be wrong. All the gold is in the lonely extra mile, the road not taken, the (un) of life. This book will change your life. Getting to know Kevin Casey has changed mine—validating my work and shared mission: to cut out the BS from sales so honest people can make a good living with the world's second oldest profession.

Justin Michael, three-time best-selling author
Los Angeles, California
November 2023

A Rude Awakening

On April 18, 2012, I was in for a rude awakening. Fancy tech like Zoom didn't exist yet, so we used this kind of awkward-looking contraption to host conference calls:

The vibe of our call was light, celebratory, and upbeat as I anticipated one of the biggest wins for our team of 16 talented misfits. There I was, all by myself, basking in the praise from the four decision-makers on the other side.

Verbal confetti was falling all around me:

"Kevin, we love the way your team approached this project. Brilliant..."

"Sounds like your team is up for the challenge to make this campaign happen under the pressure of tight timelines. We feel like your crew is 'all-in'."

I remember wishing that everyone on my team could hear how much the prospects appreciated their hard work and extra effort, and why it was about to pay off.

And that's where this story takes an ugly turn.

We were saying the usual goodbyes, and even though the panel did not officially say "Congratulations," anyone who could read between the lines and energy would know the call was just a formality and our team had closed the sale. I was grinning from ear to ear as I casually reached over and pressed the red "hang up" to end the call:

But instead, I accidentally pressed the "mute" button:

Remember this story from the back of the book? A harmless mistake, right? With that slip of the finger, all hell was about to break loose.

The four decision-makers continued talking. They thought I had gone. But there I was, a fly on the wall. I realized what had just happened. "Shit, I hit the wrong button."

My index finger hovered over the "hang up" button, but something stopped me. Curiosity got the better of me. Would I get some insider intel? Were there more five-star reviews I could lather myself in?

No. And my life was about to change forever. The same four people who had been singing our praises just 30 seconds ago were now trash-talking like a bunch of schoolyard bullies:

"Listen, Kevin's team is wildly creative, perhaps more than what we got... but we've got a lot of shit on the go, and I'd rather deal with the devil we know than an agency we don't know that's 1,500 miles away."

Then a second voice spoke up. "When you get back to Kevin, pump him to get some more details on production costs—we can use that to save a few bucks with our agency."

And then a third voice and a final roundhouse kick in the teeth, "Helluva team, but I don't think it's really enough to move things."

My heart sank. I was 43 years old, but felt like a defeated six-year-old kid. I felt small, ashamed, and unfit to be a leader. I couldn't believe what I was hearing. I hung up and sat there alone, frozen.

I wondered how many times this exact same shitshow had happened to me without me noticing. Suddenly, memories flashed in my head: the sure-shot wins over the past decade that never materialized. The promising opportunities that vaporized. The relentless chasing around trying to get prospects to call me back, email me back, or *just show me some sign of life.*

I finally realized the harsh truth:

I had wasted most of my sales life chasing lies, not leads.

But in that moment, as low and empty as I felt and trying to find any ray of light in the darkness, I wondered if pressing the wrong red button was my path to something more.

The fork in the road

I had a decision to make.

Wrap myself in shame, quit, or pull up my big boy pants and figure out a different way to sell. I mean, it couldn't get any worse. If I was going to survive another 20 years, I couldn't go on selling and living like this.

A lot of sleepless nights and soul-searching took place over the coming weeks and months. On one of those nights, I stumbled upon an old episode of *Seinfeld*, which is one of my all-time favorite TV shows. It was the episode where George Costanza did the opposite of everything he "should" have done. We'll discuss George more in Part 1.

But for now, the lesson is this: Every time George did the *opposite* of what he would normally do—what logic and common sense dictated—he "won."

And you know what? In a lot of ways, it's the same with selling, too. Almost all the outdated sales advice that's out there can leave you feeling rejected and emotionally exhausted. But doing the opposite of everyone else can give you a big "leg up" in the carbon-copy world of salespeople.

Even though I know *Seinfeld* is a fictional piece of work, the lesson of doing the opposite wasn't lost on me. I started secret little experiments with "opposites."

Over the next eight years, I nerded out and spent well over $50,000 to enroll in sales training programs around the world. I went down rabbit holes and read every book I could find on sales, behavioral psychology, and negotiation. I worked with and learned from the experts:

♦ Benjamin Dennehy, the self-proclaimed "Most Hated Sales Trainer in the UK." He was brutally honest, the nuclear version of a sales trainer. Ben embraced "the opposite" as much as any sales trainer I've ever met, and he leveled up my game.

♦ Christopher Voss, a former hostage negotiator for the FBI. I thought that if he could calm things down and get these crazy criminals to trust him, it had to work in my world of sales, where the only thing that dies is your pride.

♦ The great Justin Michael, one of the most renowned sales executive sales coaches who has an uncanny ability to solve, paired with a rare willingness to share his work. His open-source CODEX guides have driven an astounding $1 billion in qualified pipelines and he has advised over 200 tech companies. Over the past two years, we somehow collided digitally and ranted for hours on end around sales and the future. Justin has dropped me advice and validated so many of my thoughts for this book without once asking for anything in return. Out of nowhere, he offered to write the foreword for this book. In my excitement, my fat thumbs typed "no" instead of "go," but I fixed it one millisecond later. Justin, you are my first stop in LA.

♦ Seth Godin, who is the best marketer and thought-provoker on the planet and author of 20 bestsellers in 37 different languages. I landed an interview with Seth in 2021 and if that wasn't enough (it was), his off-camera advice gave me the courage to step up and write this book.

The change from selling to (un)selling and embracing the art of the opposite was not a straight line and, in the beginning, it was more of a hot mess; I had some epic failures. I got tongue-tied and backed out of trying new things more times than I care to admit. It took eight years of trial, error, eye rolls, and fighting my "inner critic" before I figured it all out, then it all came together and good things began to happen:

♦ I chased less and closed more.

♦ I no longer felt used and abused by tire-kickers and info hogs and I became really good at weeding out the prospects from the pretenders.

♦ I stopped winging it and created a process I could repeat like clockwork.

As I write this, I'm one of the owners of a $90 million insurance brokerage in Canada. Since 2016, we've added $21 million to the market cap value. I know many of the techniques and ideas I share in this book helped fuel that rapid growth. OK, that's enough about me.

Soul-sucking sales books

Perhaps you can relate to my story. Do any of these signs of sales anxiety ring true in your world?

♦ You get this icky feeling inside when you think about selling or promoting yourself.

♦ You "white-knuckle" through networking events, reaching out to strangers, having sales conversations, or even asking for the sale.

♦ You repeatedly put off getting in touch with prospects or don't do it at all. You catch yourself doing other "busy work" and tell yourself you'll start looking for new business tomorrow. But tomorrow never comes.

◆ You're afraid of coming off as too pushy or too aggressive and being seen as someone you never wanted to be.

◆ The night before a big sales opportunity, you can't sleep because you're worried about what you're going to say.

◆ You get completely tongue-tied when it comes to discussing your fee or closing the deal.

If you have two or more of these signs, this book is for you. But it's not really a sales book, because the last thing you need is another sales book. There are thousands of hard-sell books that will unlock 101 soul-sucking ways to convince, persuade, cajole, pitch, crush, and win over prospects. Some of the titles are as cringeworthy as their content.

I'm not making these titles up; these are the actual titles of real sales books you can find on Amazon in just a few clicks:

10X Selling.

Sell or Be Sold.

Ninja Selling.

Pick Up the Damn Phone!

If You're Not First, You're Last.

It's no wonder people are afraid of salespeople. Now, if any of those titles sound interesting to you, I am 100% sure you will hate this book, so now would be a good time to leave. No hard feelings.

Soul-sucking selling

So, why should you listen to me? It's a fair question. First and foremost, I'm not a professional book writer. Maybe that's why it took me almost three years to finish this book.

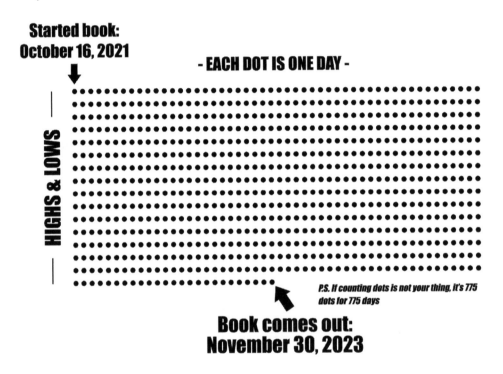

I'm not sitting in Los Cabos overlooking the ocean writing my fifth book about how I used to sell in the 1970s, 1980s, and 1990s. I've been an entrepreneur since 2001. I still sell, every day.

Think about it. If you had a ruptured appendix and found yourself wheeled into an emergency room, do you want an enthusiastic newly qualified surgeon standing over you, or a surgeon on his 412th appendix? Like the dexterous surgeon, I have two decades of experience.

Plus, discovering a low-pressure sales process that is frictionless, repeatable, and predictable was the key to reclaiming my dignity.

Hustling, grinding, and hoping everything works out when it comes to selling is a terrible situation, and I suffered with sales anxiety for years. Back then, selling felt like a millstone around my neck. I could never just take it off and leave it at the office.

Whenever I arrived home and had dinner with my young family, I was never really present. As my young daughter told me about the best part of her day, I nodded but never heard a word. I was zoned out, replaying the crappy 3:00 p.m. meeting and how I could've done things differently. Selling was a wrecking ball in my work life, my home life, and everything in between. The hard sell I was using was draining my emotions and I was ready to quit the business for good.

Yes, I was making a living, but *I was failing to make a life*.

But this is not just my story. I believe it's the story of millions like me who fall into two groups:

1.   Salespeople who had no choice but to learn, adopt, and apply the pushy and sleazy techniques conceived inside the dinosaur age of selling and who now find themselves emotionally worn out and don't even recognize the person they've become.

2.   People who need to sell for the survival of their business but suffer from bouts of sales anxiety around selling and just can't seem to take that first step.

To both of these groups, I want you to breathe a sigh of relief and open your mind. Because no matter what your skill level, you can sell *without selling out* and I'd love to have you come along for the journey.

My promises to you

The journey inside this book is going to open your eyes to seeing sales in a whole new light. It can work for anyone. You don't have to:

♦   Rewire your personality

♦   Become an extrovert

♦   Manipulate people

♦   Pretend to be someone else

And you will never lose your dignity chasing people around.

If you read this book with an open mind, get your reps in by practicing the techniques, and you still feel like this book failed you, just email me at kevin@kevincasey.ca, and I'll refund the price you paid for the book.

And in case you think there's a catch, there isn't. You don't need to show me your work, prove the pages are battered, or do any of that small-print nonsense. We're all grown-ups here.

Queasy to easy: The journey ahead

Here's a little sneak peek of the contrasting selling styles we'll be tapping into inside this book:

~~Always be closing (ABC)~~ Always be disqualifying (ABD)

We can thank Hollywood for glorifying the hard sell. Hollywood can't make movies about someone selling ethically; it's too boring. *Wall Street*, *The Wolf of Wall Street*, *Boiler Room*, and *Glengarry Glen Ross* convinced millions of salespeople that it was OK to show up as back-slapping, product-pushing jerks that only a mother could love. Thanks, Hollywood. For nothing.

And while most hard sellers are hustling and grinding to make more dials and persuade more people, you'll be making fewer dials and disqualifying people as your first move.

~~Selling~~ Sifting

Selling creates pressure. Sifting creates no pressure. And less pressure means more truth.

~~Seeking the sale~~ Seeking the truth

It's worth repeating:

✘ traditional selling = seeking the sale

✔ (un)selling = seeking the truth

Can you imagine how much less pressure you'll feel if your only goal in every conversation with a prospect is to find out the truth?

~~Pitching~~ Diagnosing

When you don't care about the result (the sale) and only care about a predictable, repeatable sales process that you control, everything that makes you queasy about selling just floats away.

◆ You get to be you, not pretend to be someone else.

◆ You are seen as a problem-solver, not a product-pusher.

◆ It feels more like a casual conversation than an interrogation.

♦ You control the sales process, so you know exactly when to continue or when to walk away.

You'll always be in control without being controlling. And you get to call the shots, not be the one taking the shots.

~~Winning more~~ Losing faster

The world of sales is about more. More dials. More closing. More wins.

I want you to flip the script on the destructiveness of being obsessed with "more" and shift your thinking to "losing faster." I know this sounds so counterintuitive but hear me out.

About 70–80% of the prospects you meet in the world of sales won't be a good fit for you for a number of reasons. Knowing this, wouldn't it make sense for you to "get to no" as quickly as possible?

When I learned to lose faster, all the anxiety and pressure around selling vanished for me.

The road map for this book

This book is split into five parts that flow in a very intentional order. You can't get ahead by skipping chapters, because each one builds on the one before it. The five parts:

Part 1: (Un)Learning. We'll cut right to the chase and obliterate some of the myths and head trash that's keeping you from selling. We can't get to the fun, shiny tactics if we don't first fix your worldviews and mental blocks about selling.

Part 2: (Un)Tangling. In this section, we'll talk about the sad state of affairs between buyers and sellers and how to end the chaos. I'll introduce you to the idea of "Building Your Core Four," a powerful lever for the rest of the book.

Part 3: (Un)Veiling. In these chapters, we'll lift the curtain on "The Zero Pressure Selling Sequence" (ZPSS), which is a simple but powerful five-step process that took me eight long years to get just right.

Part 4: (Un)Tapping. Inspired by the sheer brilliance of the aforementioned FBI hostage negotiator, who uses tactical empathy to save people's lives in high-pressure situations, I'll show you five FBI-proof techniques to help you lower the sales pressure, make the prospect feel at ease, and get to the truth.

Part 5: (Un)Corking. At this point, you'll have finished the book, and be ready to continue on your (un)selling adventure, fully equipped with everything you need for success.

Fair warning

This book will, at times, make you uncomfortable and challenge your long-held beliefs around selling. Your "inner critic" will try to fight you on it because it's so counterintuitive to everything you think to be true when it comes to selling.

Earl Nightingale gave us these wise words:

> "If you're in a situation where you don't have any clear way forward and want clear advice, look around and see what everyone else is doing and do the opposite."

The art of (un)selling is really about embracing the art of the opposite, with the goal of making selling feel more comfortable and effortless— for both you and the prospect.

If this idea intrigues you, then let's begin our journey into (un)selling.

I stumbled upon a video that effectively illustrates how our upbringing, environment, and even our inherited traits from less-than-perfect ancestors can hinder our aspirations to become improved versions of ourselves. I highlighted this concept in my "Fix in Six" series for our community. It's surprising how impactful a video involving fleas in a jar can be.

You can watch it at www.kevincasey.ca/fleas or simply scan the QR code below.

PART

1

the
(un)learning

1

Selling Isn't a Dirty Word

S elling. Is there any activity inside a business that more people seek to avoid? Imagine a bookkeeper not keeping the books. A doctor not seeing patients. A baker not baking. But there's something seemingly awful about selling. Even salespeople avoid selling!

So it should come as no surprise that if "selling" has never really been your thing, you have every right to feel anxious around it. And overcoming that anxiety and queasiness is exactly why you're here.

And I'm here to tell you that "selling" isn't a dirty word. If sales don't happen, a business fails. Selling is where the juice lies. Whether you're a small business owner or a freelancer running things from a kitchen table, it doesn't matter. Sales is the lifeblood of any business, and sales anxiety can be the silent killer inside any business. Even if you have the world's best solution to a problem and a line of eager buyers waiting outside your door, you won't be in business for long if you can't come out of the shadows and sell them the solution they need.

What makes selling feel radioactive and scary? Selling is about upending the status quo, making a change happen, and intentionally creating tension. Why would anyone in their right mind sign up for that?

(Un)Comfortable truths

Let's get some of the ugly truths out of the way. These are the harsh realities most people don't want to talk about but ignoring them won't make them go away.

1.   People are afraid of salespeople.

2.   People lie to salespeople.

3.   Even salespeople lie to other salespeople.

And there's a fourth unspoken truth I need you to own up to:

4.   You lie to salespeople.

I'm not talking about big lies that amount to perjury. I'm talking about the small, harmless lies you tell salespeople. Am I wrong? By the way, I am just like you; I also lie to salespeople.

This photo was taken at a baseball game in 2016 with my dad. Sadly, he died three years later. My dad was one of the kindest people on Earth, and we all miss him every day.

But even Dad lied to salespeople. Yes, my dear old dad was a liar too. Thankfully, the late, great David Sandler told us, "You can lie to a salesperson and still get into heaven." His words give me peace of mind because I know Dad is in the right place.

However, most salespeople can't handle the truth, which is why prospects (and you and I) have no choice but to resort to telling "little white lies" just to escape the situation.

Also, let's face it, it's easier and more polite to tell a little white lie than to hurt someone's feelings by being direct and honest. This is why the most important job you have as a salesperson is to make people feel safe. When you figure out how to create a low-pressure environment for selling, you will not even feel like you are selling. In fact, selling will feel as easy as having a conversation with a friend at a pub.

Yes, if you do it right, selling can feel that easy and calm.

Creating "buyer safety" is really the underlying foundation of what you'll discover inside this book. But you won't be able to create that comfort on the outside if selling makes you feel uncomfortable on the inside. If you're uncomfortable, so is everyone else.

Selling is broken

Traditional selling is about talking people "into" things. But the problem with talking people "into" things is that if prospects believe they are being pushed and their freedoms are being threatened, they push back, and sales resistance is triggered. For instance, tell someone they can't smoke, and they'll smoke even more.

What's causing all this sales pressure? Attachment to money. You can only keep a business alive by getting more meetings, closing more deals, and making more money. Because of that vicious cycle, most salespeople have a bad case of "commission breath."

The point of this book isn't to teach you how to convince, sell, or persuade, because if that's your goal and mindset going into a conversation, you'll always feel under pressure. Your thoughts will dictate how you act.

Now, imagine if your only goal in any sales conversation was to get to the truth and not stress about making the sale? Can you see how the pressure would immediately drop?

Hopefully, you're beginning to see how (un)selling turns the old ways upside down. (Un)selling is:

- The relentless focus on seeking the truth instead of the sale.

- Letting go of the things we can't control (other people) and only focusing on one thing you *can* control: yourself.

- Letting go of expectations and assumptions.

Most likely, you believe you can help someone and you are passionate about your product or service being just the solution they need.

But here's what's also possible *and* out of your control:

- *Maybe* your timing is off, and the problem isn't big enough yet to make them want to change how they do things now.

- The kind of problem they have is not the kind you solve, and you'd be better off sending them in a different direction.

- They're the kind of person who would drain your energy and make you wish you had never let them into your world.

- When you call someone, they just had a big fight with their kids 10 minutes ago, and you caught them in a bad moment.

Or maybe they simply don't have the budget to afford your solution.

When you let go of things you can't change, the pressure goes down because that's no longer your intention.

Making this subtle mindset shift from "seeking the sale" to "seeking the truth" will be your superpower for overcoming your fear and anxiety about selling. You're sifting, not selling. And you're no longer thinking like a salesperson, you're thinking like a scientist.

An (un)fair advantage

Here's an odd truth: *non-salespeople and reluctant sellers have an unfair advantage.*

Huh? How can that be? Let's imagine the following two people:

1.   The reluctant seller who is anxious about selling
2.   A seasoned salesperson with 15 to 20 years of experience under their belt

If I could pick one to teach (un)selling to, I'd choose the reluctant seller every single time. And I'm not feeding you some kind of early Tony Robbins motivational rah-rah-rah. So, if you're a reluctant seller, you already have a big edge, and here it is:

You have far less (un)learning to do.

The sales veteran has to unlearn 10 to 20 times as much as you do. They have strong beliefs and habits that are hard to change because they are built into their muscle memory. Most of the ideas in this book will be hard for them to accept, and I don't have the time or energy to convince them otherwise.

When I try to teach experienced salespeople the principles and techniques inside this book, they usually water everything down and then yell at me about why it doesn't work. It would be like trying to teach someone who has played tennis for 24 years and uses a two-handed backhand to switch to a one-handed backhand like Roger Federer. It doesn't go well.

They'll start out with a lot of enthusiasm, but after hitting 30 balls over the fence they'll give up and go back to using their old two-handed backhand. But you've never hit a backhand with only one hand, so I don't need to break you from the two-handed backhand you've been using for 24 years. I can teach you the basics of the one-handed backhand from scratch, and then you can follow and practice the small steps—the footwork, the contact point, and the racquet angle—with the right attitude and willingness to make that one-handed shot look smooth and natural like Federer.

Roger that. *(See what I did there?)*

Everything I say in this book about selling is ethical and is designed to sell the way people really buy, not work against it. You won't find any high-pressure tricks or techniques, and you'll never have to sell in a way that requires you to pretend to be someone else. Because, again, this isn't a sales book about conquering your prospects. It's a book about conquering yourself. And by that, I mean:

♦ (Un)learning all those damaging beliefs around selling that create sales anxiety.

♦ Discovering a new set of beliefs and techniques reserved for the most ethical and noble sellers.

Let's begin your (un)learning.

2

The 14 (Un)Selling ~~Commandments~~ Costanzas

If you don't know George Costanza, you're missing out. George was one of the most memorable characters in *Seinfeld*, one of the most popular TV shows of all time, which ran from 1989 to 1998.

During episode 86, George is down in the dumps because nothing he ever says or does seems to go right. He is 40-something, unemployed, still shacking up with his mother, and not seeing a whole lot of action on the dating scene. One day, George is sitting with his best friend Jerry in a local diner, moaning about how his life stinks and every move he makes is always the wrong one. Jerry can't take any more of his whining, so he decides to use some "tough love" advice to rescue his pal.

He delivers a harsh dose of direct but sage advice, saying, "George, if every move you've made in life has been wrong, then doing the complete opposite would have to be right." George stares back in amazement, as if the first caveman had just discovered fire.

First, he changes his normal order with the waitress. Then he decides to raise the stakes when he spots a beautiful lady eating alone at the counter. George puts the "opposite theory" to a bigger test. He nervously accepts the challenge, slowly stands up, and whispers to himself like a gladiator about to face death:

> "If every instinct I have is wrong, then the opposite would have to be right."

George gingerly walks up to the woman who is clearly out of his league and finds the courage to say, "Excuse me. I couldn't help noticing you were looking over at our table." He gulps. "My name is George. I'm single, unemployed, and live with my mother." He braces for impact. Everyone in the diner braces for impact. Three million people watching this moment unfold on TV brace for impact. Two seconds pass.

Finally, she smiles and says playfully, "Hi, my name is Victoria."

Holy shit, it worked!

Doing the opposite was about to change George's life forever. You can find this two-minute clip on YouTube if you'd like to see it for yourself.

Thus, as homage to George and his courage to embrace the opposite, I will be replacing "Commandments" with "Costanzas." In this chapter, I will introduce you to the 14 Costanzas that make up the (un)selling method. But more than just a play on words, Costanza is a great metaphor for the ideas and methods you will learn as we move through the (un)selling method.

Check out this clip from *Seinfeld* called *The Opposite*. In this episode, George Costanza decides to change his life by doing the opposite of his usual actions, which gave me the idea to test the 'law of opposites' in the world of sales.

Watch it here: www.kevincasey.ca/theopposite or simply scan the QR code.

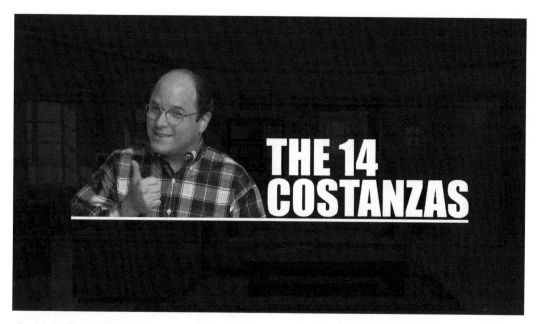

(Un)Selling: A strange combination of opposites

The 14 Costanzas are not random; they work seamlessly together to make selling more straightforward and dignified. Don't be alarmed if they feel counterintuitive and downright uncomfortable; they *should* feel that way.

As we go through the book, the Costanza opposites will come up again and again. They might seem strange now, but by the time you finish this book, they will be part of your new sales DNA.

Here's a snapshot of the opposites:

The Conventional Way	The Costanza Way
Seek the sale	Seek the truth
Qualify prospects	Disqualify prospects
The money is the prize	You are the prize
Lead with solutions	Lead with problems
Be attached to the outcome	Be detached from the outcome
Be 5 stars	Be 4.2 stars
Be liked	Be respected
Be enthusiastic	Be "Aw shucks, whatever"
Use $50 words	Use five cent words
Buying is logical	Buying is emotional and logical
Fear the no	Celebrate the fast no
Humor is unprofessional	Humor is a sales superpower
Control is being manipulative	Control is about being a pro
Be a pest	Be a welcome guest

In the next chapter, we will look at each of the 14 Costanzas in high-definition detail using lots of examples and stories to help make it clear.

3

Zooming in on the 14 (Un)Selling Costanzas

L et's zoom in on each one of the 14 commandments er... Costanzas.

Costanza #1

Conventional: Seek the sale.

Opposite: Seek the truth.

Think of the last time you went to the doctor. They don't start writing a prescription for what's wrong with you until they've asked you a lot of questions—even some uncomfortable questions—to get to the bottom of what's wrong.

The doctor calls the shots, not you. They won't prescribe until they're convinced they know the problem. So even if the most defiant patient begins by demanding a prescription, a doctor doesn't just hand it over without asking any questions, because that's not the way a professional does things—pros have a process.

Doctors don't talk about how "great" their medicines are, hoping it will convince you to buy them. They don't aim to please. They don't strive to be liked. The doctor has one goal: *to diagnose and prescribe.*

The typical salesperson has one goal: *to persuade and make the sale.*

Which feels better to you? This mindset shift of "diagnosing like a doctor" versus "persuading like a salesperson" was the big idea that changed my sales career more than any other idea in this book.

My job was to ask questions, even uncomfortable ones. My job was to get to the truth. But what's the truth?

You can't help someone unless you get a clear yes to three questions:

1.   Do they have a problem I can solve?

2.   Do they accept it's a problem?

3.   Do they have the willingness to make the change and the time and money to make it happen?

When you think this way, it changes how you act and what you say. You won't be looking for the sale, but for the truth, eliminating all that inner pressure and anxiety you feel around selling.

Costanza #2

Conventional: Qualify prospects.

Opposite: Disqualify prospects.

There is hard math behind how sales work, and your business is no different.

According to HubSpot and Salesforce research, an estimated 70–80% of the people who raise their hands won't be a good fit for your business. So, doesn't it make sense that your job as a seller is to get rid of the pretenders and tire-kickers as quickly as possible? You bet it does.

Time is one thing in life you can't get back or buy back, even if you're a billionaire. Knowing this, you simply can't waste time and burn sales calories with the wrong people. All the elite sellers I know are incredibly stingy with their time and insist that if they are going to get a no, it has to happen now, not later.

And that's the power of the second Costanza: *Disqualify First.*

You should go into every sales conversation with the goal of getting rid of the wrong prospects as fast as humanly possible. And yes, you can do it without being rude. The harder you qualify, the easier the sale will be. The easier you qualify, the harder the sale will be. So, disqualify first.

It's unexpected and liberating.

Costanza #3

Conventional: The money is the prize.

Opposite: You are the prize.

Let's play a little game. Pretend you are a billionaire and you don't need to work, but you work a couple of days a week selling something to kill some time. If you were independently wealthy, do you think you'd put up with the crap that salespeople go through every day, like getting lied to, hung up on, and ghosted? Do you think you'd be afraid of hearing no?

Nah. You wouldn't give a rat's ass because there's no risk—you still have a billion dollars in the bank.

This exercise exposes the root cause of all our weak behaviors and anxiety: we are attached to *money*. The need for money causes all the pressure, whether you like it or not. The prospect knows you want their money, so they use it to their advantage.

Let me introduce you to "frames," which we will talk about in more detail in the upcoming chapters. Frames are simply the perspectives or lenses through which we view the world. So, when I say, "Control the frame," all it really means is that you stay in control of the way *you* see a sales conversation.

Let's look at an example. Salespeople often use supplicating and weak language, like:

"Just touching base."

"Just following up."

"Just circling back."

These are low-status frames that will make you look desperate and make it easy for the prospect to control you. Weak language like this puts you in a perpetual state of chase-and-beg mode which sucks up your time and your dignity.

The opposite frame is the prize frame. You go into the conversation with the mindset that the prospect needs your solution to their problem more than you need their money.

Imagine you meet someone in the Sahara Desert and they are out of water. If you have a Thermos full of fresh water in your backpack that you can afford to share, then you should feel like they need you more than you need them. *That's* the prize mindset you need to have when you are selling. They need your solution more than you need their money.

When you use this "prize" frame, you always believe that the prospect needs you more than you need them, and you act accordingly. It is not always easy to own this frame, especially when you have payroll to meet or you truly do need money in the bank. But this is a crucial way to behave, even when things are bad.

If it were easy, everyone would be practicing the prize frame, but most aren't. That's what makes it so powerful and liberating.

Costanza #4

Conventional: Lead with solutions.

Opposite: Lead with problems.

In 2014 a Russian newspaper, *City Reporter*, decided it was sick of all the doom and gloom, and the editors decided to cover only positive news. They flipped all their headlines to put a positive spin on things. Within one day, they lost 66% of their readers.

You can bet that the top story on the eight o'clock news won't be a feel-good story, but rather, a bunch of stories involving some kind of pain and suffering. In other words, the bad news. It's just the way it is.

Humans are attached to problems as part of the human condition. It's no different when it comes to selling. Highlight or make note of what I'm about to say:

Prospects don't care about you or what you do. They only care about what you can do for them.

Put yourself in the prospect's shoes, and ask yourself:

♦ Does this really grab me?

♦ Does this really compel me to want to hear more?

♦ Does this really make me feel something?

If the answer to any of these is no, then why bother? What's interesting to prospects is their problems. Your product or service? Sorry, it's a conversation killer. The prospect doesn't relate to "what you do," and this is why you need to stop talking about your solution.

Consider Valentine's Day, for example:

✘ "Dazzle your loved one with our handmade Valentine's Day gifts."

✔ "Get back into your loved one's good books by dazzling them with our handmade Valentine's Day gifts."

Start with their problems, how those problems affect them, and how much it will cost them if they do nothing about the problem. Capisce?

Costanza #5

Conventional: Be attached to the outcome (the money).

Opposite: Be detached from the outcome.

Helen Klein Ross is a former copywriter/creative director and the author of *Making It: A Novel of Madison Avenue* (2013) among others.

I love Helen Klein Ross's take on the concept of not being attached to the outcome and just sticking to your process. Her hilarious chart below really hit home with me.

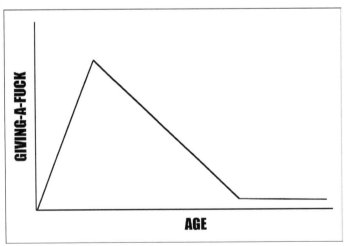

Not giving a flying fuck about the outcome is truly a sales superpower. With (un)selling, you can't control the outcome (the sale), but you *can* control how you sell (the sales process).

Remember the doctor and how they handle things? They have a process they follow, and they call the shots. But it's up to you whether you take the doctor's advice and eat better or go to the pharmacy and get the medicine.

The doctor can't control that part of the experience any more than you can decide whether someone will pay you for your product or service. Thus, the principle of being detached from the outcome will reduce the pressure and anxiety you feel when it comes to selling.

Be detached from the outcome, like the doctor.

Costanza #6

Conventional: Be 5 stars.

Opposite: Be 4.2 stars.

Rewind to the 1960s at Harvard for an Elliot Aronson-led experiment.

This experiment involved a game show. Aronson fed a "contestant" the answers before the show, and the guy got 90% of the questions right and won by a long shot. When done, the contestant makes a small "mistake": a cup of coffee spills on him when he gets up from his chair.

So, Aronson took that recording and played it one of two ways for the people in his experiment:

1. They see the whole episode with the coffee spill.

2. They see the whole episode without a coffee spill.

People who saw the mistake thought the contestant who spilled the coffee was much more interesting and likable. Here's what that lesson means for you:

Stop trying so hard to be perfect if you want the other person to feel more at ease.

There's so much bragging out there in the sales world. So much BS and fake five-star reviews from your mom, friends, family, and co-workers. More Botox? Please, no. Flaunt a flaw and do it early in the conversation. Be OK with being a little un-OK.

It sounds ridiculous, and you shouldn't just believe me. It's proven, and it's called "The Pratfall Effect." You might think that customers will trust you more if you only have five-star reviews or if you show up in your best Hugo Boss power suit. Think again.

The Pratfall Effect is when people perceive others as more likable and relatable after witnessing a minor mistake or vulnerability. It means showing a little imperfection can actually endear you to others.

In the sales world, this could mean that salespeople who are willing to admit a small mistake or share a relatable story of a blunder can build rapport and connect with their prospects on a deeper level.

For example, I once gave a presentation to a full boardroom of serious prospects who were all wound tighter than a golf ball. As I pulled up my presentation, I accidentally clicked on a "prank video" I had made with a Donald Trump impersonator for my best friend's wedding, where I was the emcee.

Instead of getting flustered, I said, "Oops, looks like you all got a sneak peek at my video for my best friend's wedding."

This moment of vulnerability and humor actually worked in my favor. The mistake eased the tension in the room and the head decision-maker asked if I wouldn't mind playing it for them because they were intrigued. Of course, I played it.

So, falling on the sword a little and not trying to be so squeaky-clean perfect will work in your favor. Embrace saying things like:

"I might be completely wrong here, but…"

or

"I might be overstepping my boundaries, and I might be out to lunch, but…"

One final piece of supporting evidence in proactively showing some "imperfections" to build trust comes of Dr Robert Cialdini, author of *Influence*. He says, "Your credibility goes up whenever you say something bad about your product." Showing prospects that your solution is not perfect is a pattern interrupt and makes them feel more at ease because it feels different than other salespeople pitching their "perfect thing."

Successful brands also embrace the Pratfall Effect. You can tell when a brand creates leverage out of what seems to be a weakness and uses it in their favor. Here are some fresh examples:

Guinness

Weakness: Pours slower than other beers.

Flip it and use it to a positive: Good things come to those who wait.

KFC

Weakness: Imagine this—in 2018, KFC briefly ran out of chicken.

Instead of fighting it, KFC took accountability and threw some shade at themselves, replacing "KFC" on their buckets with "FCK."

Buckley's

Weakness: Tastes awful.

Flip it and own it: Tastes Awful. And It Works.

There was a funny ad I came across for a boat. It read:

> "I'm selling it because it was purchased without proper consent of loving wife. Apparently, 'do whatever the f*** you want' doesn't mean what I thought."

There are so many (un)selling ingredients: radical honesty, relatability, and dealing with objections up front. I don't want a boat, but if I did, this ad would get my attention. Don't be flawless. When everyone else is bragging, do the complete opposite.

What's your flaw? How can you flip it?

Costanza #7

Conventional: Be liked.

Opposite: Be respected.

Willy Loman was a fictional character in the 1949 Broadway play, *Death of a Salesman*.

Willy believed sales were about fakery: looking good, charming people, cracking jokes, and always trying to be "likable." If you try to sell like Willy Loman, you will be emotionally drained and show up with a smile but not much else. I should know. I was a people-pleaser for many years, and it can destroy your self-worth. Willy Loman would have hated this book, even though it's just what he needed.

It's fitting to end this point with a soul-sucking quote from Willy Loman's son, who followed in his father's footsteps and, at the height of his own misery, said, "Pop, I'm a dime a dozen, and so are you."

Do you need to be liked to sell? Here's my take.

John Maxwell, author of *21 Irrefutable Laws of Leadership*, says, "All things being equal, people do business with people they like." I don't fully believe that statement, however. Whether you are equal or not, I don't think people do business with you because they like you. Rather, they do business with you because they trust you and believe you are "the one" who can help them solve their problem.

If "being liked" is your top priority, you will become subservient or needy, and back off from asking challenging questions for fear of upsetting the prospect.

Respect is more important for salespeople than being liked because it shows credibility, professionalism, and trustworthiness. While being likable can create initial rapport, respect goes deeper and fosters a long-lasting business relationship. When prospects respect a salesperson, they are more likely to take their recommendations seriously and trust their expertise.

Building trust and credibility should be your top priority, which is far more important than "being liked." Let me demonstrate through an example:

Pretend you're buying a car, and there are two salespeople: Likable Larry and Knobhead Kyle. They are selling the exact same car, price, and financing.

Likable Larry is helpful and nice, and you could see yourself having a beer with him. However, he just told you he can't get the car you picked for at least four weeks because of inventory delays.

Knobhead Kyle is true to his name. He's a little too smart for his own good, and the kind of person you want to hide from at a party. But Kyle knows his products well from a technical point of view and, unlike Larry, he does not have stock problems. The car you love is ready to drive off the lot today. So, what do you do? Right, I thought so.

Don't get me wrong. Being liked is nice, but it is not a must-have. Instead of trying to make everyone your best friend, you should work on building credibility and trust.

According to a 2019 *Harvard Business Review* study, an analysis of 450,000 salespeople found that 89% of elite salespeople—those with the best records—said they do not need to be liked. But 86% of the weakest sellers said being liked is necessary. The weaker their sales records, the more likely people were to believe that their ability to make friends was their greatest asset.

It's a natural human inclination to want to be liked. Learning to let it go can seem like a monumental challenge. But customers care far more about what they're buying than the salesperson.

Embrace the mantra I use constantly when training sales teams I work with: "Be an expert first, and a friend second."

Costanza #8

Conventional: Be enthusiastic.

Opposite: Be "Aw shucks, whatever."

I still love buying physical copies of books I can feel and mark up, and I love supporting bookstores.

Every time I go to a new city and have some time to kill, I love to find bookstores, big and small. I remember walking around the streets of New York and coming across a charming little bookstore with a pale, worn-out door sign that got lost between the bright colors and big signs of a McDonald's and a Starbucks. The owner, let's call her Sara, was clearly a book lover with a lot of passion and was determined to share that full-throttle passion with every customer who came through the door. On this day, that unlucky target was me.

While you might think that passion and enthusiasm are good things, all this hyped-up energy doesn't sit well when it comes to selling to strangers.

I escaped the busy streets of New York and went into a bookstore, where I thought I would go on a relaxing journey of what I love most: books. The hope that this little store would be a quiet place to browse did not last long. Sara appeared behind me three seconds after I walked in, and she could not hold back her excitement.

Sara didn't greet me or even ask me what kinds of books I liked. Instead, she was like that Slap-Chop infomercial guy who ambushed me with sales pitches. While hardly taking time for a breath, she waterboarded me about the 34 genres of books inside, then explained—in painful detail—why a book she was now waving in my face was her "Top Pick of the Month." She then went on to inform me about her loyalty program, which apparently *everyone* in New York loved, yet here I was, alone in the store.

I no longer felt like I was in a bookstore. It was more like a trap and my eyes darted around the room for the exit. I pretended to answer a fake call, excused myself, and walked out of the store. Of course, I never went back there again.

This story illustrates a real problem. So much of the old sales training tells people it is important to be "passionate and excited" about what they are selling. However, as a salesperson, being too enthusiastic can actually backfire and turn off potential customers, and science backs this up. When we encounter someone who is excessively enthusiastic, it can trigger a phenomenon called "the contrast effect." Basically, our brains compare that level of excitement to what we think is normal or expected, and if it is higher than we expected, it triggers skepticism and sales resistance. Studies have shown that when salespeople display extreme levels of enthusiasm, it can make prospects question their sincerity and credibility.

When I first started selling, my energy and tone sounded like I had just chugged a case of Red Bull, which meant I came into the conversation "too hot" and it was a turn-off for the prospect. My unbridled enthusiasm was one of the big reasons why I was getting ghosted so often back then.

Again, Hollywood did us no favors by bringing alpha sellers, like *The Wolf of Wall Street* to the big screen. Just think about your own life.

Whenever you meet a salesperson who is too enthusiastic, do you move away or get closer?

Imagine a used car salesman coming up to you with a big smile and saying, "Nice to meet you! I hope you are doing well today!" You know deep down that he doesn't really want to meet you, doesn't care about how your day is going, and wants nothing but your money.

Overly enthusiastic tonality triggers sales pressure and lowers trust. The more enthusiastic you are, the more you lose. The more "Aw shucks" you are, the more you win. As one of smartest sales trainers, Josh Braun, reminded us, "sound more like a TED Talk speaker and less like a hyped-up CrossFit instructor."

The moment you feel excited is the moment you start to lose.

Let's revisit our doctor analogy. Does a doctor get all amped up when issuing a prescription, or are they more matter-of-fact?

Behave like a doctor, not a hyped-up salesperson.

Costanza #9

Conventional: Use $50 words.

Opposite: Use 5¢ words.

"How stupid are our leaders?" he said. "How stupid are they?" These were the phrases of Donald J. Trump as he ran for President of the United States in 2016. Trump's speech was easy enough for a fourth grader to understand because he used simple words and short sentences.

The Global Language Monitor looked at the words that 19 Democratic and Republican presidential candidates used when they announced their campaigns for the 2016 election. The review used a common algorithm called the Flesch-Kincaid readability test, which looks at the choice of words and the way sentences are put together to rank them by grade level. The results were very surprising.

> Note: The story I am about to tell has nothing to do with my political views or preferences, either for or against the person. But it makes a great case for why you should use five cent words (simple language) when selling, instead of $50 words (big words that make you sound smarter).

Trump spoke using words and phrases at a fourth-grade level that most people could easily understand. He did much better in the polls than his opponents, who used a lot of big words. Political speech experts say that in an age of 140-character tweets and 10-second TV sound bites, simpler language is more likely to reach a wider range of voters. Mike Huckabee and Jim Gilmore, who failed miserably, both used words and sentences above a tenth-grade level, according to the algorithm.

In every way the algorithm looked at it, Trump's speech was easier to understand. He used fewer characters per word and fewer syllables per word than any other candidate, and his sentences were shorter.

His vocabulary is filled with words like "huge," "terrible," and "beautiful." *Not* "gargantuan," "abysmal," and "resplendent."

Whether Trump was talking about his campaign slogan ("Make America Great Again"), reminding everyone how rich he was ("I am really rich"), or how bad Washington is ("It's a rigged system"), Trump used words regular people would say when talking with friends over coffee or "shooting the shit" at the local pub. He did not get caught up in using terms related to the state of international affairs. It's Trump. It's simple.

Paul J.J. Payack, president of Global Language Monitor, which studies trends and language, says, "It doesn't matter if you are talking to a Harvard professor, a farmer in the Midwest, or a member of a motorcycle gang. The words in 'I Have a Dream'—and all the other great speeches throughout history—are always simple and to the point. They use words that everyone understands. They give a big message, but they're not grandiose."

Like him or not, Trump knew how to communicate to his audience, and he did so by using raw, everyday words that made people feel something, whether it was good or bad.

Most salespeople use big words because they think that doing so makes them look smart and they come off like experts. But, sad to say, it has the opposite effect. Most of the time, using these "Harvard-like" words turns people off, sounds too complicated, and it's just too much work for people's tired brains.

Let me ask you a weird question. Did you ever like the smartest kid in class? Probably not—unless it was you.

People do not like being around "one-uppers" and "know-it-alls" because they are annoying.

For salespeople, it's the kiss of death. When it comes to the words you use, it's better to talk to other people like you would talk to a friend at a bar or over a cup of coffee.

Here are some examples of before and after rewrites:

✘ "We can help you streamline your logistical operations in real-time with an integrated API tech stack."

✔ "I'm getting the stink eye from pissed-off truck drivers showing up to grab their stock, while my team is empty-handed and pointing fingers at each other." (Real, gritty, emotional words.)

✘ "Our forensic specialists can identify and extract inefficiencies in your operations to enhance operating margins and increase long-term EBITDA."

✔ "We're burning cash—our supply chain has more holes than Amber Heard's testimony." *(This uses simple, emotional words.)*

Marketing legend Jay Abraham gives us this brilliant advice: sometimes, the best way to sell a horse in an ad is to simply say "Horse for Sale." And sometimes, it works for more than just horses.

Speak as you would to a friend. If you use words like "streamline," "cutting-edge," "synergy," and "robust" every day, other people will avoid you. Every time you use "$50 words," you risk making people stop and think, which is not what you want. You don't want people to think, you want people to feel. And it's hard to feel something when you are thinking about what the words mean.

But, there's an exception to this rule.

The exception here is if you know your prospect communicates using specific lingo or shorthand unique to their industry. Then it is a good idea to use their "technical lingo," which can boost your status and show that you are an insider who "gets" their business.

So, if you are selling to accountants and CFOs, using terms like "EBITDA" and "Market Cap," which are $50 fancy words, is the right strategic move to put you on their level.

The same exception would also apply if you were selling to a gym owner who specializes in CrossFit, and you decided to intentionally use insider language. CrossFit uses the acronym HIIT for "high-intensity interval training." If you are in the CrossFit world or have done CrossFit, you know this acronym because it's a central idea in CrossFit. So using HIIT would be a smart way to position yourself like an insider. In such a case, *not* using their "inside lingo" might make them suspicious and question whether you really understand their space.

So, depending on who you're talking to, using complex words and phrases can help you seem more credible and trustworthy. But it's important you understand when and where this exception applies.

That's my two cents on using $50 dollar words and five cent words.

Costanza #10

Conventional: Buying is logical.

Opposite: Buying is emotional and logical.

My pal David is 58 years old and bought a super expensive sports car. It turned heads, made him feel young again, and made him a bit wilder and edgier. It was a reward for years of grinding it out and showed his ex, who broke his heart, that she missed out on the good life.

But when I asked Dave why he bought the sports car, he rationalized his big-ticket purchase with 100% logic.

He cited factors like excellent gas mileage, JD Power ratings, and "It's a short Canadian summer, I want to enjoy it."

That's bullshit, Dave.

And he knows it deep down, but he won't say it because we all want to think we buy things that make sense and are well thought out. But that wasn't true for Dave, and it isn't true for humans. With logic, Dave can easily hide the truth about how he feels and explain his investment to his friends, family, coworkers, and even his wife.

Gerald Zaltman, a well-known professor at Harvard Business School, came up with a fascinating theory that we make 95% of our purchases subconsciously. The common belief is that people usually make smart decisions based on a careful analysis of a product's features and benefits. But that isn't the case in the early stages of the buyer's journey. Maybe this is why most average salespeople start too early with logical bullet points and features like ROIs and case studies, when they should be using curiosity and intrigue to stir more emotion early on.

One emotional trigger salespeople can use is the fear of missing out (FOMO). By emphasizing that a product or service is rare or limited, salespeople can make customers feel like they want it and need to buy it right away. This emotional trigger can push individuals to make impulsive buying decisions driven by the fear of missing out on something valuable.

Another emotional trigger that salespeople can use is the desire for social acceptance. Most people, including you and me, have a natural desire to fit in and be liked. Salespeople can use this to their advantage by showing how their products or services can help people improve their social status or get more attention.

For example, they can talk about how a certain item can make the customer more attractive, successful, or respected by their peers.

Now I think of it, why did I upgrade and start driving BMWs back in 2016? It wasn't the gas mileage or the engine performance. Deep down, I wanted to show people that "I've made it." Is it a bit vain and shallow of me? Of course. I'm human.

But as a salesperson, it's important to know that most people are just like you. That is why I am so obsessed with thinking like the buyer and not acting like the average salesperson. But which emotion should you tap into when dealing with the prospect? Sales expert Geoffrey James explains that all buying decisions come down to one or a mixture of these six emotions:

> Greed: "If I make a decision now, I will be rewarded."
>
> Fear: "If I don't make a decision now, I'm toast."
>
> Altruism: "If I make a decision now, I will help others."
>
> Envy: "If I don't make a decision now, my competition will win."
>
> Pride: "If I make a decision now, I will look smart."
>
> Shame: "If I don't make a decision now, I will look stupid."

The point is no matter what you're selling, you must start with emotion and then add logic to help people explain it to themselves and to others.

The late great Dale Carnegie, the guru of corporate communications trainers, confirmed that 85% of our decisions are emotional and only 15% are logical. Your job is to make someone "feel" something. Logic doesn't convince us to buy, emotion does.

Costanza #11

Conventional: Fear the no.

Opposite: Celebrate the fast no.

I was recently looking for recording software that would help me coach my sales team better by letting me record and analyze their sales calls and measure things like talk time, tone, and sentiment.

I signed up for a 30-day trial. After kicking the tires for a few weeks, I received a call from Sam.

> Sam: Hi Kevin, this is Sam from Tapin-Tech. How are you doing today?
>
> Me: Doing OK, Sam. How are you?
>
> Sam: Doing well, Kevin, thanks for asking. The reason I'm calling is to see if you have any questions about our recording software to monitor and better coach your reps' sales calls.
>
> Me: Nope, no questions here, Sam.
>
> Sam: Good to hear. Hey, I just wanted to let you know that since it's the end of the year, we are running a promotion that will give you 15% off the annual license. But you have to register by the end of the month.

Do you see the problem here? I can smell Sam's commission breath through the phone, and it's clear that all he wants to do is move the sale along by making it seem like time is running out.

But making prospects feel like time is running out can sometimes make them back away, because it takes away their freedom to choose and backs them into a corner. A psychological barrier known as reactance.

For instance, if someone warns you that you can't have coffee, you want it more because your choice is being restricted. Nicolas Guéguen and Alexandre Pascual, both behavioral scientists, looked into how to overcome a prospect's reactance. In the study, the researchers dressed up as homeless people and begged for money on a busy street. When the "panhandlers" ended their request with a sign saying "You're free to accept or refuse," the levels of reactance were reduced, and donations increased by 400%.

Here's the point:

Giving people permission to say no creates much more comfortable and truthful conversations. Let's revisit the conversation with Sam.

Before (zero freedom to say no)

> Sam: Hey Kevin, I just wanted to let you know that since it's the end of the year, we are running a promotion that will give you 15% off the annual license. But you have to register by the end of the month.

After (freedom to say no)

> Sam: Hey Kevin, before we go, would you mind if I ran an idea by you? I'm not even sure this would interest you, but you never know.

> Me: Yeah, OK, fire away.

Sam: For the next 10 days, we are having a flash sale where anyone who wants it can earn an instant $200 discount on an annual license. You're probably going to tell me you're not interested and by the way that's totally cool.

Feel the difference? When Sam gives me permission to make a choice and say no, it makes it all feel more comfortable to me.

I have to say the "going for no" principle was hard for me to understand. Even when I knew it was true, it was hard to put into practice. Maybe because for years and years, every sales training I took talked about the 32 clever and sneaky ways to "get to a yes," and all of a sudden, I was flipping the script and going into every conversation "going for no."

And it's not just me, brain science backs this theory. Our prospects' brains are set up to be careful and skeptical, especially when it comes to making decisions about what to buy. By "going for no," salespeople can actually make prospects feel less pressure, reduce their resistance, and oddly, by going for no, you increase the chances of getting a yes in the end. Here is an example of where you should "go for no."

The Scenario: You sense the prospect is holding back on how badly they really want the problem solved, and your instincts tell you it's not a "now" problem, but more like a "later" problem.

This isn't the time to hide from a possible no. Rather, you need to stress-test the truth. Here are some questions to use to tease out the no:

♦ I mean, why fix this now and not six months ago?
♦ What's changed in your world that's suddenly made fixing this more urgent?

◆   What happens if you do nothing?

◆   Why not just stick with your current partner? It sounds like things are going pretty well with them.

These kinds of questions show the prospect that you do not really need the sale, and indifference and a gentle push away gives you instant status and trust. The strangest thing about all these small pushes is that prospects often stand their ground and fight back, and then they use their own words to convince themselves.

Let me give you something you can use right away. When I listen to and watch sales calls, one thing I always notice is how long salespeople spend building rapport at the beginning. It's like two people on a date who aren't sure who is going to kiss whom first. It's all very awkward.

An "Up-Front Agreement" is one of the best tools I can give you to start a sales meeting in a way that makes everyone feel more open and comfortable.

I like this for several reasons:

◆   It creates a break in the conversation, so you can stop talking about sports scores and the weather for longer than you need to.

◆   It makes you look like a trusted expert because you show up with a plan and a method to help make the process more certain, which prospects will like.

◆   It lets you be very clear about how the process works and sends a strong message that you are not like other salespeople. This is because you openly explain that there are ways for both of you to stop the conversation and agree it is not a good fit without any hard feelings or the need to tell little white lies to be polite.

♦ But the most powerful thing about this is you take away all the mystery and pressure. The prospect knows exactly how things will go in the future, and there are only two possible outcomes. Basically, you never have to close the sale at the end because you are closing *at the beginning*.

I encourage you to follow and modify this "Five-Step Up-Front Agreement" to help you start meetings with more confidence.

These are the steps, which you can make more conversational, so you don't come off as robotic:

1. Time
2. Their right to say no
3. Your right to ask tough, challenging and uncomfortable questions
4. Your right to say no
5. Commitment to move forward with the next step

Here is an edited transcript of a recent sales meeting, but the flow could be for any meeting I lead, because I always want to start with a process I can control and not tap-dance around, waiting for the prospect to come up with their own agenda.

Me: Dean, I'm glad we both found time to talk about whether I can help. We agreed on 45 minutes. Is that still OK?

Dean: Yes, all good.

Me: OK, before we get started, can we agree on a couple of things?

Dean: Sure, go ahead.

Me: First of all, I'm not for everyone. Some people find it uncomfortable to do what I teach, and others don't think I'm the kind of person they could see themselves working with long-term. If you feel like it isn't really sticking with you and it just doesn't feel right, are you OK with telling me no today?

Dean: Hmm… no one's ever said that to me before. Yes, I'm comfortable telling you no.

Me: Got it. I also wanted to be up front and let you know I'll need to ask you a lot of questions to figure out if I might be able to really help you. These questions might even feel a little uncomfortable. Of course, you don't have to answer if you don't want to, but I wanted to let you know it isn't that I want to play a game of 21 Questions. I need to ask these kinds of questions to make a proper diagnosis of the situation. Are you OK with this?

Dean: Yes, I'm cool with that.

Me: OK, good to get that on the table. And if, based on your answers, I don't think I'm the best one to help you and we aren't the right fit, would you be terribly upset if I told you no?

Dean: No, not at all.

Me: Good stuff. And if we don't say no to each other by the end of this meeting, we will take a few minutes to talk about what happens next. Does that sound fair?

That's it.

That is the Five-Step Up-Front Agreement, and now you and the prospect both know how the meeting will go. This makes everyone feel less nervous. And there's another big benefit that comes with the Up-Front Agreement: you won't have to worry or stress about "closing" a prospect because you've already told them if neither of you says no, you will take a few minutes to figure out what the next step should be.

So, you essentially deal with the dreaded close at the beginning.

Costanza #12

Conventional: Humor is unprofessional.

Opposite: Humor is a sales superpower.

Have you ever said "I love you" to a complete stranger on a sales call?

Well, I did.

This non-Hallmark-sponsored card moment happened just as I was finishing up a short phone conversation with a fella in his 50s who was the owner of a mid-sized construction business. Let's call him Mr Hammer. He was a referral, and this was a mini-triage call to see if there was any common ground.

Now, Mr Hammer had the "gift of gab" and was clearly in the mood to talk. My iPhone screen kept lighting up as my daughter, Olivia, kept trying to call through. Not once, not twice, but three times in less than two minutes. Mr Hammer was still yakking. He took a rare breath. I had a millisecond to squeeze in some airtime and say, "I gotta run, someone is waiting on me."

As I was about to make my clean break, my Dad-brain drifted, as the fourth incoming call now popped up on my screen. Mr Hammer bids farewell, "Look forward to Wednesday. So long, Kevin." With Olivia squarely on my mind, I reply and utter the words, "Love you, bye now," and hung up.

Two minutes later, I called Mr Hammer back. I thought he probably wouldn't answer and I could hardly blame him. "Hello," he answered. I gulped, and explained what happened, as it really happened. He laughed loudly and I breathed again in relief.

I was out of danger, so I playfully said, "I mean, it was too early anyway, it was only our first phone date, right?"

Silence. Oh shit, I'd pushed my luck.

But then he laughed again and I breathed again. He eventually became a great client. Mr Hammer's story illustrates that even in the really, *really* awkward sales calls, no one dies.

(In case you were wondering, Olivia's "urgent" calls were to confirm that I wouldn't be around the house that night, because she was having a bunch of friends over, and I promised to give her some space with her friends instead of trying to be "that Dad who fits in with the cool kids.")

If you have a natural sense of humor, don't hide it. People told me for a long time that sales is a serious business and that you can't use humor because it isn't professional. That's dead wrong. Humor is a *powerful* way to ease tension.

Here's an example:

The scenario: You call a stranger you believe could be an ideal client. The prospect barks, "I hate sales calls." This kind of objection threw me off and made me tongue-tied for years.

However, because I'm now fully detached from the outcome, I just take a deep breath and say something like, "Not as much as I hate making them!" or, "I understand that. Can you imagine being in my chair and having to make sales calls all day? Did you want to hang up now, or give me 30 seconds and then decide?"

The scenario: You call a prospect who is already with your competitor. The prospect says, "Yeah. We're all set, we use the folks over at Acme." I respond, "Ah, right, nice folks, I know a few of them. How long have y'all been dating?" Huh? Say what?

Salespeople can't say something that flippant to a stranger. But why not? It releases a good hormone called oxytocin, which makes both of you feel better and brightens the moment for most people. Oxytocin is released during a "feel-good" moment in a conversation, and it helps build connection and empathy, according to a lot of research on sales.

Ninety-five percent of salespeople would rather try to defend, convince, persuade, and overcome the objection like they're playing tug-of-war with the prospect, rather than use some light humor and just be more vulnerable in an awkward moment.

Which one do you think a prospect would react better to?

Let's resume the Acme example after I ask how long they've been dating.

Prospect: *(chuckles)* Dating? A few years, maybe five or six, I think.

Me: Right. Is it like, happily married? Or more like living together as roommates?

Can you see how a little detachment and a dash of humor turned these awkward struggles into conversations instead of tug-of-war battles? And more comfort means more truth when it comes to sales.

I'll leave you with this great quote from Anthony Burgess: "Laugh, and the world will laugh with you. Snore, and you sleep alone."

Costanza #13

Conventional: Control is being manipulative.

Opposite: Control is about being a pro.

Picture this: your appendix burst, and now you are on the operating table in a cold sweat and about to be put to sleep. But you put your hand up to stall things, as you have some last-minute instructions. Just before the anesthesia is given, you gather the doctor and nurses around your pillow, motion for them to come closer, and whisper in a very firm voice how you want the surgery to go from start to finish.

Huh? No one in their right mind would ever act that way when they were in such a weak position. You are the patient, you are in distress, and the doctor is the one who calls the shots.

Sales is a different situation, but the same deal. But salespeople let prospects control the process all the time because they are afraid to take charge and ruin the "good chemistry." But letting the prospect decide how things will go is a recipe for disaster and misery.

The buyer says, "Jump." The seller says, "How high?" This is how most sales conversations roll out—with the prospect treating the salesperson like some kind of animal act at SeaWorld. If you don't have a clear, repeatable sales process, prospects will take over, and you'll feel out of control, and be used, abused, and "ghosted" by prospects.

Embrace this fact: control is not an evil concept.

Control is not a form of manipulation; it's about having a process you stick to that makes you a professional. I have met a lot of seasoned salespeople who do not have a sales process and say they need to "feel it in the moment." This is nonsense, and most sellers who act this way are mentally exhausted from chasing more lies than leads. "Winging it" is not a sales strategy; it's a race to the bottom. The worst thing about that race is you might win.

Whenever I ask a salesperson to sketch their sales process on a whiteboard, 98% of them get infected with a sudden case of writer's block. Your sales process should be so simple you can write it in 15 seconds. That's what you'll have in your hands by the time you finish this book.

HubSpot's recent research shows that 86% of sellers couldn't do that whiteboard exercise because, well, they're just "winging it."

So here are eight reasons why you need a defined sales system that has clear steps from beginning to end:

1.   It gives you control.

2.   It gives you direction.

3.   It allows you to learn and track mistakes.

4.   It gives you a marker of where things went wrong and allows you to isolate it.

5.   It gives you a place to move forward, end it, or nurture it.

6.   It enables you to teach and mentor others.

7.   It creates predictable outcomes and takes away all the chaos of what sales can feel like day after day.

8.   It makes you feel like a professional.

Tom Brady doesn't think about the plays at the two-minute warning. Instead, he just goes through a process that has been drilled into him for 20 years. No wasted energy. Repeatable. Predictable. Almost boring.

Be a pro, not a Joe.

Costanza #14

Conventional: Be a pest (persistent).

Opposite: Be a welcome guest (stop chasing).

Ever seen the movie *Dumb and Dumber*?

An irresistible cult classic from the 1990s, starring Jim Carrey and Jeff Daniels.

Carrey plays Lloyd Christmas, a good-hearted but very stupid character. Jeff Daniels plays Harry Dunne, who is also good-hearted and also very stupid. In a memorable scene, Lloyd, who has a huge crush on Lauren Holly's character, Mary, is about to make a desperate pitch to ask her out on a date. He moves right up to her face, ignoring her personal space, as she leans back and braces herself for his awkward pitch.

Lloyd: So, what are my chances?

Mary: Not good.

Lloyd: Like one in 100?

Mary: No, like one in a million.

Lloyd pauses. How will Lloyd take this dose of honesty and rejection? Is he so focused on the end goal (a date with Mary) that he can't see what is right in front of him? Slowly, a huge smile starts to spread across his face, as if he had just won the top prize in a lottery, and he screams:

"So… you're telling me there's a chance!"

Like so many salespeople with happy ears, Lloyd was looking for any sign of hope and chances to close the deal, and ignored the clear signs in front of him.

The final Costanza principle is about never behaving like Lloyd in this situation and chasing prospects who aren't ready to buy. The "stop chasing" principle says that you need to set your own ground rules, so you do not fall into this trap.

Think about the sport of baseball. When a baseball player gets three strikes, they are out. There is no wiggle room, the rules are clear, and both sides know it up front.

You should also have a "three strikes" rule, especially for prospects who do not respect your time or boundaries and are obviously not ready to buy. What counts as a strike?

♦   Cancels a meeting in the last 48 hours because they had a competing priority. Strike one.

♦   No show with no warning. Strike two.

♦   Won't return emails or phone calls within three to four business days. Strike three. They're out.

And your final email should be something direct and assertive, but not hostile:

> John, it seems the timing is off for this project, so let's put this one on ice. If things change, you know where to find me.
>
> Best of luck,
>
> Kevin

If you don't hear back, it's a gift. You now have more time to start conversations with people who want to talk with you.

Remember, it takes two people to make a sale. Don't invest time with people who don't invest time with you. Chasing destroys your self-worth. The more you chase, the more the prospect runs and hides.

When a prospect is interested, they will:

1.   Talk openly about their situation.

2.   Respond to your emails.

3.   Show up to meetings.

4.   Commit to the next step.

5.   Keep their word.

If, at any point, your prospect stops doing these things, they're not interested. That's OK, you didn't do anything wrong. It's not your fault, they're just not ready yet. They're making progress without you and getting from point A to point B.

It is not your job to persuade or push people from "not looking" to "buying."

Here are four signs you might be dealing with someone who wants to play a horrible game of "hide and seek" with you:

1. **They're not honest and open to sharing information.**
    If they are unwilling to answer your questions openly and honestly, they may be playing hard to get or just kicking tires.

2. **They're not willing to engage and return your calls and emails.** If they avoid you, do not get back to you, are vague, or do not show up when they say they will, that is a red flag. You might need to get rid of them.

3. **They're not willing to take the next step.** You both agreed at the start that if neither of you said no, you would take a few minutes to figure out what to do next. All of a sudden, the prospect tries to change the rules you both agreed to. Here is where you need to show some backbone without being rude and remind them of the plan you agreed to earlier.

4. **They're not willing to ask and answer tough questions.** If you ask hard questions that they are not ready or willing to answer and they get angry, they are probably trying to hide their true intentions or using you to get free information. Tread carefully.

Always remember, the best way to stop chasing is to never start chasing in the first place. So, there you have it: the 14 Costanzas of the (un) selling protocol.

You will see all these guiding principles throughout the book, and before you know it, they will feel as natural to you as the answers to your multiplication tables did when you were in school.

CHAPTER SUMMARY

My life changed when I went against the grain and did the opposite of the old-fashioned and tired sales techniques that so many people learn from out-of-date sales training programs.

I do not think bad salespeople are bad people. I think they got bad training and are trying to make a living and feed their families. I don't like math, but the equation looks like this:

Good Humans + Bad Training = Broken Salesperson

There are ideas and methods in this book that go against everything you thought you knew about selling. At first, your inner critic will fight you tooth and nail, and many of the ideas in this book will seem scary. Push through that resistance and start trying out some of the ideas on low-risk prospects or a practice partner, just to get some reps in.

The 14 Costanzas are not chosen at random; they work together to make selling easier and more dignified. As we go through the book, the Costanza opposites will come up again and again. They might seem strange now, but by the time you finish this book, they will be part of your new sales DNA.

Here's a quick recap to keep things simple:

The Conventional Way	The Costanza Way
Seek the sale	Seek the truth
Qualify prospects	Disqualify prospects
The money is the prize	You are the prize
Lead with solutions	Lead with problems
Be attached to the outcome	Be detached from the outcome
Be 5 stars	Be 4.2 stars
Be liked	Be respected
Be enthusiastic	Be "Aw shucks, whatever"
Use $50 words	Use five cent words
Buying is logical	Buying is emotional and logical
Fear the no	Celebrate the fast no
Humor is unprofessional	Humor is a sales superpower
Control is being manipulative	Control is about being a pro
Be a pest	Be a welcome guest

EXERCISE

Consumption scratches an itch, but action makes the change stick.

What "opposites" in this chapter really made you think? Since you're just starting out, which ones could change the way you sell?

4

Shattering the Big Four Sales Myths

L et's put an end to these harmful myths once and for all, because ignoring them will not make them go away. Now let's debunk the four myths.

Myth #1: I've never sold anything before

Almost every time I am invited to a business, the same thing always happens. Before I start, there are always a few people who come up to me and have a quick chat. They tell me they are not in sales and have nothing to do with it, but they were asked by the company's leaders to be part of the workshop.

Every time, the moment they say, "I'm not in sales," I always smile and say the same thing, which usually freezes them like a deer in headlights, "Oh, yes, you are. You sell every day without realizing it. Stick around."

In their defense, I could see why people might think they are not in sales. One in nine people in the US, UK, and Canada have a job related to "sales." But this statistic is completely misleading. I believe that the other eight people are also selling and just don't realize it.

You see, at its most basic level, selling is the art of "making change happen." And if that simple definition makes sense to you, then congrats, you just admitted you are already selling.

I call it "unconscious selling" and here are some everyday examples of non-sellers selling:

◆	Getting the kids to do their homework

◆	Getting the kids to do chores

◆	Landing a first date

- ◆   Landing a second date (more selling)
- ◆   Finding a job
- ◆   Talking your way out of a speeding ticket
- ◆   Needing to return something but not having the receipt
- ◆   Picking your Netflix show over your spouse's
- ◆   Persuading a colleague to embrace your concept
- ◆   Having dinner at the restaurant of your choice
- ◆   Getting money for your new business
- ◆   Negotiating a better rate on your mortgage

The big revelation is, whether you like it or not, you're in sales. But there is a second part that should really calm your queasy stomach. When you get your friends to go to your favorite restaurant, it doesn't seem like you are being pushy or manipulative, does it?

You know why?

You don't think of it as selling; you just see it as something you do every day. A conversation, not a pitch. You're not freaking out or thinking too much about it; you're just being yourself. Going through life, one conversation at a time. No pressure, friction, racing heart, or sweaty palms.

Imagine talking to a stranger in a sales situation with the same level of calm and confidence you use to get your way and choosing your favorite place to eat lunch with a group of friends.

It's not as hard as you might think.

Myth #2: Salespeople are pushy, manipulative, and borderline evil

I bet you don't have to try too hard to remember a time when a salesperson was pushy and tried to sell you something you didn't want. You know what it feels like, and it's not pleasant. It feels like a tug-of-war, and you can almost smell the commission breath coming from the mouth of the sales savage.

Consider the zombie salesperson at the mall kiosk trying to sell you the miracle facial scrub, or the telemarketer at dinnertime who sounds like a robot as they read word for word from a soulless script about the 84 reasons why you need the newest credit card. It's hard to ignore a hard seller, just like it's hard to shake off a bad nightmare.

But selling doesn't have to involve this kind of blunt force trauma and manipulation. People love to buy, but hate how they are sold to. People buy stuff all the time. Every day, Amazon boxes are delivered to 1.6 million homes. Over 6,500 cars are sold every hour around the world.

But selling isn't about persuasion; it's not your job to talk people into things. This is the myth about selling that's so important for you to break.

Let go of assuming you're for everyone. Shift from persuading to guiding people to persuade themselves. You can't do that with the traditional sales approach. And that's why the way to sell more isn't more selling, it's (un)selling.

Myth #3: I'm not one of those "born" salespeople

Jerry Seinfeld wasn't born to create one of the best sitcoms in television history. His comedic genius and rise to fame were things he learned.

Clearly, Jerry didn't come out of the womb telling jokes and one-liners. He worked on his comedy craft repeatedly, often in half-empty nightclubs, until he became "funny."

Jerry got a lot of serious reps in.

Before he was famous, Jerry would take out a calendar and put a red X on the days he wrote a new joke to remind himself to keep coming up with new material.

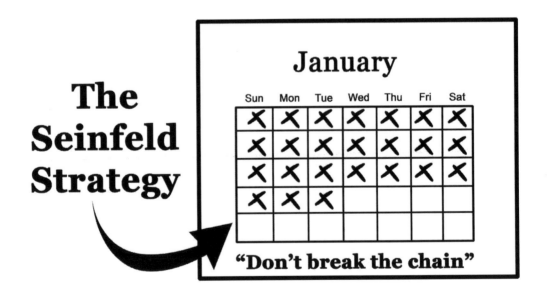

Back then, Seinfeld's goal wasn't to be the best comic, because that was something totally out of his control. But Jerry could control his actions. So he built the daily scoreboard of Xs. His goal was to earn as many red Xs on the calendar as possible, without skipping a day. At the end of the month, it was easy to see which squares were empty.

Jerry's method of using a calendar isn't fancy, but it's a great way to get better at writing jokes, and having more jokes in your back pocket makes you feel less stressed about running out of jokes. Being better isn't natural; it's a byproduct of having fewer empty squares on the calendar.

Getting the reps in is not a laughing matter.

Was LeBron James born a natural basketball player? Was Tom Hanks born to play the role of Forrest Gump? Claiming their success is due to some kind of inherent talent or destiny is an insult to LeBron and Tom. Riding a bicycle, giving a speech, helping a patient, juggling three balls, writing a poem, leading a team, and selling are all learnable skills, not born talents.

Here's one more example: Tom Brady was born at 8 pounds and 7 ounces. Do you think his family cheered for him because they knew he would be one of the best quarterbacks in NFL history? Hardly.

In fact, things were not looking so good for Tom as late as 1996. During the Scouting Combine, he was called "slow and clumsy," and he was the 199th pick in the sixth round of the NFL draft, long after everyone had gone to bed. He was invisible to the football world.

But being overlooked and ignored only made Tom Brady work harder. He got his reps in. He knew it took practice to go from good to great, so he worked harder than anyone else. And, as they say, the rest is history.

So, there you have it: sales is not something you are born with, it is something you learn. Which means you need to do more than just read this book. You need to "do it" and get your reps in.

Myth #4: You need to be a back-slapping extrovert to be good at sales

First, there are three types of people: extroverts, ambiverts, and introverts. An extrovert is someone who gets their energy from being around people. They love socializing, meeting new people, and being the life of the party. Think of extroverts as those outgoing, bubbly individuals who thrive in social situations and have the gift of gab.

An ambivert is like a mix of both extroverts and introverts. They can enjoy hanging out with others and having a good time, but they also appreciate their alone time. Ambiverts are like those cool cats who can adapt to different situations, whether they're in a lively gathering or cozying up with a good book at home.

Introverts are the ones who gain their energy from spending time alone. They value solitude and prefer quieter settings. Introverts are like those chill souls who enjoy their own company, find peace in solo activities, and need some downtime to recharge their batteries after being in a social setting.

Now, there is this false belief that extroverted people do better in sales. It seems logical, right? But it's dead wrong. Extroverts won't like this next part, but don't just take my word for it.

Adam M. Grant, a professor at the University of Pennsylvania's Wharton School of Business, challenged the theory that extroverts would not be the best salespeople. Instead, he had a hunch that ambiverts, who are equal parts extroverted and introverted, by definition, would be better salespeople. This was a pretty bold idea at the time, and it went against what most people thought.

Grant did a survey of people's personalities and then spent three months looking at the sales records of more than 300 male and female salespeople. The results showed that strong introverts weren't very effective salespeople—no real surprise there.

But the strong extroverts weren't much better. The folks who fared the best—by a wide margin—were the "in the middle" group of ambiverts, and the odds are that if you are reading this book that's where you are too. So count yourself as having an unfair advantage and one you didn't expect, right?

Ambiverts are good at selling because they know how to find a good balance between asking questions and listening. They know when to talk and when to shut up. Extroverts tend to "pour it on a bit too thick" for their own good, which creates sales pressure that hurts their chances of closing the sale.

"The ambivert advantage stems from the tendency to be assertive and enthusiastic enough to persuade and close but, at the same time, listen carefully to customers and avoid the appearance of being overly confident or excited," Grant said. If you are wondering how many of these well-balanced ambiverts are out there, chances are you're one of them. Sixty-two percent of humans are thought to be ambiverts, which is ironic since sales jobs tend to hire extreme extroverts. This is why job ads often talk about "crushing your quota" and "10Xing" your commission. It pays to be an ambivert and, if that's you, congrats, you already have an edge.

I trust you're feeling relieved, hopeful, and excited with this new, fresh outlook on selling in a more dignified way. Most salespeople are ashamed to say they are salespeople. I say it with pride because I know that being a good salesman is one of the best skills a person can have and I have the power to help people solve their problems.

Upgrade your beliefs, upgrade your sales.

CHAPTER SUMMARY

At its most basic level, selling means *"making change happen."*

I started by telling you an uncomfortable truth: you sell almost every day of your life, but you don't think of it as selling because it doesn't feel like it. By the end of this book—and after you get some serious reps in—my goal is to make selling feel as casual and chilled as those everyday "mini-negotiations" in your life, like getting your way to watch your show on Netflix. Low pressure and easy.

And that's put an end to the first myth, which was that "you don't sell," because you now know that you *do* sell. *Every day.*

We then went on to bust three more myths:

- Selling is pushy, manipulative, and borderline evil.
- I'm not a "born" salesperson.
- You need to be a back-slapping extrovert.

As we flip the pages to the next chapter, we'll talk about the 9 biggest sales mistakes I see new and experienced sellers make over and over again.

EXERCISES

Exercise #1: What's your ambiversion? Take this 6-minute test

We've learned that ambiverts have an unfair advantage when it comes to selling. There's a good chance that you're an ambivert too, since 62% of people are. So where are you on the scale of being an introvert, ambivert, or extrovert?

Daniel Pink, one of my favorite sales authors, has made a simple test you can do in less than four minutes to see how ambiverted you are. Currently, you can find it here:

https://www.danpink.com/assessment

Take note of your result here _____.

Exercise #2: The 7-day sales test

I gave you a lot of examples of how you already sell every day—from talking the cop out of giving you a speeding ticket to getting your kids to do their homework, but you didn't realize you were selling because it seemed so natural. Selling is all about guiding a conversation in a way that leads to change.

Think about the last week. Write down three examples of "unconscious" selling activities in your life over the past seven days. You might be surprised at how easy it is to make this list, which shows you're already selling and just didn't know it.

CHAPTER 4

1. _____

2. _____

3. _____

5

Avoid These 9 Selling Mistakes Like the Next Plague

When my daughter was about six years old, she suddenly became very interested in just about everything in the world. Whenever I drove her to school, it felt like I was in a speed round on one of those game shows. She questioned everything. Nothing was too bland or boring:

Why is the sky blue? Why do some people get to use swear words but I can't? Are ghosts real? Why is the moon called "the moon?" Why don't crabs have eyebrows? Which superhero would you want to be?

One day, she asked me another question that seemed pretty harmless but one I continue to reflect upon today.

> Olivia began, "Why do you write with a pen and I have to write with a pencil?"

> "Ah, good question. With a pencil, if you make a mistake, it's easier to erase and then write again. You can't do that with a pen." I thought that answer made sense and that she would move on to another "why" question, but she wasn't done yet.

> "So, you don't make mistakes anymore?"

> "No, I make lots of mistakes."

> "But what happens when you write with a pen and make mistakes? What do you do then?"

Gosh, this was getting tougher. I was a little tongue-tied. But Olivia bailed me out with her own suggestion. She grabbed my pen and leaned over my notebook.

> "How about you just cross out the mistake with a small line like this, draw a little happy face near it, and then do it right?"

It was such a simple way to deal with a mistake—not just on paper, but in life. The lesson from my six-year-old: mistakes happen. Just own up to your mistakes and keep smiling, because that means you are moving forward and not going backwards.

It's only a mistake if you keep doing it

Did you know that Netflix started out as a service for renting DVDs by mail? But that small setback didn't last long, and while Blockbuster executives refused to see where the industry was going, Netflix changed its business model and bet everything on the future of video streaming.

This chapter talks about the nine biggest mistakes that will kill your sales effort—if you keep making them.

There are a lot of mistakes that both new sellers and sellers with a lot of experience keep making, but I want to focus on the top nine for this chapter:

1. Leading with products

2. Selling transactionally

3. Practicing sales incest

4. Scooping up more vanilla

5. Coming in too hot

6. Starting with the wrong intent

7. Not selling what you should be selling

8. Chasing

9. Behaving like an uninvited pest

Mistake #1: Leading with products (instead of problems)

What you sell is boring. Sorry, it had to be said. You know what's *not* boring? Your prospect's problems. So, what should you start the conversation with? Problems. This may seem obvious, but if you think about the last five times you were sold something, whether through email, direct messages in your social feed, or telemarketers calling you, I would bet that 95% of them started with what they sell instead of the problem they solve.

When I teach people to start their conversations with problems, they nod their heads in agreement. But when I listen to recordings of their phone calls or read their emails, they do the complete opposite. It happens all the time. I can only guess that it feels more comfortable starting with what they do and it's lazy to just list features and benefits in bullet points in brochures and God-awful value propositions.

But here's the rub: no one gives a crap about what you do or what you sell, and they certainly don't care if you cheer for the same NFL football team. One of the best ways to get people's attention is to start by talking about the problems you solve instead of the products or services you sell.

Not quite convinced yet? Let's take a quick look at a research study that proves this theory.

John T. Cacioppo's scientific research at the University of Ohio demonstrates how problems cause a spike in brain activity in people. People in the study were shown three sets of pictures.

The first set were images to generate positive feelings—a Ferrari, pizza, a beach.

The second set of images were meant to stir up problems—a dead cat, a disfigured face, a car accident.

The third set were neutral images—a plate, a blow-dryer, and a brush.

As you might expect, the brains weren't interested in the neutral objects at all. Plates are boring, right? The participant's heart rate went up when they saw the red Ferrari, but their *brain* activity went up a lot when they saw a dead cat or a car accident.

This study shines an important light on how you sell to others. Using neutral information to lead your sales efforts is boring and won't do much to get or keep the prospect's attention. It would be like showing them a plate, a blow-dryer, or a hairbrush. Instead, you have to get the prospect to feel their problems. As Robert Collier, one of the greatest copywriters, once said, "Always enter the conversation already taking place in the customer's mind."

If you're in sales, you hear these objections all the time:

"I'm not interested."

"We have someone already."

"We're happy with what we have."

The reason you get these objections early on is because you're pitching your product, not shedding light on the problems that person is having.

Here are two LinkedIn direct messages:

"I'd like to talk to you about an employee enrichment program for your company. I'd love to have a Zoom call with you next week and show you what we do at X. Can we set something up for Tuesday at 10:00 a.m.?"

Products have no value without problems. Here's what illuminating a problem sounds like:

"*The Harvard Business Review* says 30% of absenteeism is caused by employees who are not motivated and are not sick or on family leave. Instead, they are just protesting in a quiet way. We have a tool that can give you a score based on how you compare to other companies your size in less than 10 minutes and with only nine questions. I can send it to you, and you can do it on your own without me looking over your shoulder. Just send me an email with the words 'send over,' and I will do it right away. Then you can decide if we need to talk more about it."

Feel the difference? But how do you find problem language to use? Dig through case studies, look at testimonial videos for before-story quotes, and use the exact words your customers use to describe problems they bumped into before buying from you. Show your prospect you understand what they're going through and that you "get them." Then, use intrigue and curiosity to get them to raise their hands and ask how you've helped other people with the same problem. The eureka moment is when you can explain your prospect's problem better than they can. If you nail this moment, you'll feel the energy shift.

Nail the problem statement, agitate it, and show them you've seen it and solved it before. Because people buy solutions to problems, not your product or service.

We will talk more about this later, but science shows that people would rather avoid pain than gain the same amount of pleasure (look up "loss aversion theory" if you want to be a nerd). In other words: losing $10 is horrible. Winning $10 is cool, but not a big deal. As a general rule, people will jog toward pleasure but sprint from pain.

In other words, people are much more motivated to avoid pain than to get pleasure, and that is exactly what we need to tap into when we want to get someone's attention. Understanding and adapting to this fact will improve your sales skills and make things easier for you and the buyer, because it puts the focus on them, not you.

Mistake #2: Selling transactionally

Transactional selling is the way most sellers operate.

When you practice transactional selling, you behave like you're some kind of oracle and brazenly declare to any prospect that you can magically solve any problem they have without even qualifying them. If you look around on LinkedIn or other social media sites, you will find unethical sellers who are guilty of transactional selling.

How can you tell? They're the ones who try to sell you their services and slip into your DMs (direct messages) to tell you how great they are, without ever diagnosing the problem to see if it's something they can fix. This is unethical.

Why? Because how can anyone—even Socrates, if he came back from the dead—say they can solve a prospect's problem *without even asking what the problem is?* It's a lie. It's like a doctor diagnosing a patient without ever asking a question.

A more ethical way to sell is *transformational selling*. When you use transformational selling, you go into every sales opportunity with an open mind and no expectations about what will happen. Your only mission is to find the truth, not make a sale.

For example, if someone asks, "Why should I choose you over the other guys?" you can say, "I'm not sure yet if you should, because I'm not sure if I can help you yet."

You don't say this as a sales tactic, you say it because it's the truth. Transformational selling means that you tell the prospect right away that you have a very specific way of diagnosing them that will help you figure out whether the two of you are a good fit or not.

It also means you have the courage to be upfront with the prospect and tell them explicitly that if you don't think you're a good fit, which is a real possibility, you'll do your best to point them in a better direction.

Taking this open and honest approach from the start not only makes it easier to sell, but it also positions you as a trusted expert instead of a common salesperson, and it lowers sales resistance because prospects aren't used to hearing salespeople admit they "aren't for everyone."

When was the last time a salesperson you talked to admitted they might not be the best solution for you? When was the last time a salesperson told you it was fine to say no at any point in the conversation? Probably not too often.

When you practice transformational selling, you show up, sound, and behave differently than 95% of run-of-the-mill salespeople. If you break this rule of transformational selling and try to sell to **every**body, you risk letting every tire-kicker and information-hog into your world, which will not only drain your energy but also your dignity. Transformational selling is a very transparent way of selling when you openly give prospects off-ramps to leave the conversation—without feeling guilty or needing to tell little white lies.

The best part is that once you get the hang of it, selling won't feel like selling anymore.

Mistake #3: Practicing sales incest

I was guilty of sales incest for years.

In fact, I think it is why, at the start of my career, I joined a few small business groups and hung out over coffee with other salespeople who were struggling just like me. Sales anxiety is a lonely experience, and there's a false sense of security in seeking refuge with other people who might also be suffering from the same struggles around selling. Can you see how hanging out in these kinds of environments with the same people with the same problems could be harmful?

Picture this: a bunch of entrepreneurs, all suffering from sales anxiety, sit around sipping coffee, wine, or a round of beers, and comparing notes on what sucks so much about selling, with no solutions or remedies—just a bitching session. Like a bad Christmas gift exchange, a few people take some of your bad sales ideas, and you politely take some of their bad ideas, and you run back to your world and try each other's crappy ideas with the same crappy results.

This is sales incest.

Sales incest works the same way as real incest between generations: everyone gets uglier and dumber the more it happens. So, if you want to get rid of sales anxiety, you need to wave goodbye and escape the insanity of hanging around these unhealthy groups that will make your selling experiences even more miserable.

Mistake #4: Scooping up more vanilla

The average human being is 25 pounds overweight, apathetic, and moderately depressed. They also have low self-esteem, 0.75 best friends, and lead a boring life.

Inertia is the resistance for any human to change its motion unless acted upon by an external force. Inertia is very real, and to sell something to someone, you have to get them out of their comfortable, still state. To get someone's attention, you can't show up dull as dishwater. Showing up with another scoop of vanilla ice cream won't do it either.

So how can you bring a different flavor and be that interesting person who pulls them out of their apathetic, mildly depressed, boring lives and makes things interesting?

Remember this line: don't bore us, get to the chorus. *The Economist* did a piece showing that 40% of all the hit songs got to the chorus in the first 15 seconds.

When it comes to sales, it's not that different. Don't waste the precious seconds of your song on fake niceties like: "How are you doing today?" or, "I hope this email finds you well." It's wasted words and wasted time—the same vanilla every other salesperson is serving up.

Instead, quickly build tension by asking a question that makes the prospect curious about how they do things now and pointing out a problem they might not even know they have:

1. It can't be lazily answered with a yes or no.
2. It must create emotion and a "brain itch" that makes the prospect crave some kind of closure.

Land it. Lean back. And if the chorus doesn't stick, thank them and move on fast.

I think Aerosmith got the whole fast hook thing:

- *Janie's Got a Gun* — Huh? Who's Janie? Why does she have a gun?

- *Love in an Elevator* — OK, tell me more. Maybe I'm looking for love in the produce aisle of the supermarket.

Brains crave closure. Or do you just talk about vanilla things, like your company's history, awards, and high service standards? No. Hurry up and get to the chorus.

But what if what you're selling is boring? Ah, yes. This is a common objection I get from lots of business owners who believe their business is somehow unique and different and can't be made interesting. So, I usually ask them to think about the boring tag on the back of the shirt or blouse they're wearing right now. And I say, "Those little tags are pretty boring, right? I'm guessing this is probably the first conversation you've ever had about these tags because they're so unremarkable."

Everyone always agrees.

But then I say, "Tags do not have to be boring. Imagine if someone was clever enough to make a tag interesting and make someone 'feel' something. If *they* could do that, *you* could probably do it for your boring business, right?"

They always nod. And then I show them this, which I always have saved on my phone for such a situation (I use Apple Notes, in case you're curious).

Let's take what I sell as an example. Insurance can be as dull as dishwater, right? It doesn't have to be. In this case, reminding a client of an upcoming expiration date is boring because dealing with insurance is painful and not something any normal person looks forward to. So, instead of trying to hide from this universal truth, you "call it out" in a way that makes people laugh and makes them feel like they are talking to a real person and not a robot.

Here's a visual meme we sometimes use for the so-called "boring" renewal meeting:

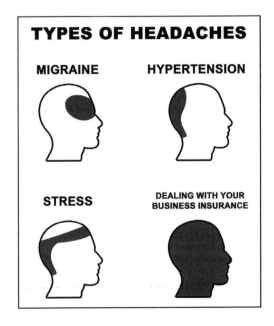

Now, here's another mistake that's no laughing matter.

I cannot tell you how many times snobs have told me in the last 20 years, "Kevin, do not try to be funny around really powerful people who work in high level positions. *It's just not professional.*"

Truthfully, that is some of the worst advice I have ever gotten from people who give sales advice but haven't sold anything in decades.

Here's my take on things: important people in business are still normal everyday people, so treat them like normal people. CEOs, CFOs, and office managers still laugh at the bad knock-knock jokes their kids tell and watch *Seinfeld* reruns when they are not at work. They probably even secretly enjoy *The Simpsons*.

Let's be real. Most "top brass" executives are wound up tighter than a golf ball with the stress of being leaders, and desperately need to laugh more to escape the chaos of their everyday world.

And no matter who you are talking to on the phone, from the receptionist to the CEO, you should start the conversation as an equal. You cannot act weak around these people, because they can smell weakness a mile away.

YOU   **PROSPECT**

YOU   **PROSPECT**

So, show up differently and rescue their miserable days with a dash of humor. Here's a real-life conversation exchange I've had with top brass:

Mr Big says, "We're happy with our current supplier."

"Oh, that's OK." Then I pause. "When you say happy, do you mean happy like 'newlyweds' or happy like 'roommates'?'"

Ninety percent of the time, that makes them laugh or chuckle, even though it wasn't what they were expecting me to say. In the seven years I have been using some version of that talk track, not a single Mr or Ms Big has ever taken that comment the wrong way. The risk is low, and the reward is high.

Let's play out that same conversation further, so you can see how I continue to keep it light and non-defensive. If Mr Big replies back and says, "Happily married and gushing with love," then my take on it is that's a perfectly acceptable answer, and I don't fight it.

As I will say many times in this book, our job is to find the truth, and in my world, a quick no is a mini-victory.

In a nurturing tone, I'd lean back and still gently challenge in a playful tone with something along the lines of, "It sounds like you are in a great place. I'm taking my sales hat off here and, selfishly, I'd love your advice so I can learn something from this. If you don't mind me asking, what does [Competitor] do so well that makes it feel like such a lovefest?"

Don't be surprised if the love story suddenly isn't such a love story.

I will leave you with this great exchange between me and someone who was "ghosting" me. Ghosting is another name for when someone seems interested but then disappears and stops answering your emails or phone calls. This happens a lot in the sales world. You can act like a lap dog and keep chasing, or try something radically fresh and different:

Step 1: Subject line: Just the prospect's first name and a question mark.

Step 2: Send a sad Muppet meme, like the one below.

Being ghosted? Lead or lie?

Just circling back to see if you received my last 69 emails. Still interested?

Subject: Calvin?

Your inner critic or maybe even someone you work with will beg and plead with you not to send this because it is "unprofessional," and sending a Muppet to a prospect could be disastrous.

But ask yourself: is it more professional to chase and beg like the email on the left? This is common in the sales world but makes you look desperate and needy.

Plus, who can get angry and offended at Kermit[1], right?

---

1 Hat tip to BowTiedSalesGuy, who I saw use Kermit for just this purpose. It might be a good idea to find your own "sad, lonely" Muppet or meme for your ghostbuster email.

Mistake #5: Coming in too hot

Reality check: 97% of your prospective buyers aren't in a position to buy the very moment you call. I know, I know—how can buyers be so rude and not buy when we're ready to sell? But that's the reality of how the buyer-seller world works.

First of all, you can't make people buy just because you're ready to sell. Lean back. Give them a reason to remember you when they are ready. Play the long game.

But how?

Here's an example. Have you ever heard of YETI? It's a ridiculously expensive travel mug for hot or cold drinks.

When YETI world crossed my world, I didn't have a mug problem. I wasn't ready to buy. YETI didn't panic or push the sale. They asked a few simple questions about summer life in Canada, and offered to send me some tips once a week on how to love the great outdoors.

The YETI people didn't come on too strong by peddling their products at me with flash sales and limited-time offers. Instead, YETI was smart and sent me short, useful tips once a week like how a normal, happy family can keep from killing each other after spending two nights together in a tent.

Simple tips, not pitch slaps.

It's as if YETI could read my mind, like they were listening in on a conversation I was having in my head about how to keep everyone happy in the middle of the woods, dodging mosquito bites where there is no Wi-Fi.

YETI just nudged me away with helpful content in my inbox.

Short and sweet.

Drip. Drip. Drip.

They didn't give me everything all at once but worked in a few provocative "Aha!" moments, hidden in their emails like Easter eggs. And at the end of each tip, they always told me about something new and interesting that made me curious, like the "MagSlider lid," which is a mechanism that keeps my hot coffee hot four times longer and my cold beer cold four times longer than other thermal mugs.

Hmm, cool.

Then, in the next email, another small reveal. The leak-resistant Stronghold Lid makes the travel mug spill-proof, which is great because I also spill coffee in the mug holders in my car, which is hard to clean.

Hmm, this is solving a problem I didn't even think of before. You know how this ends, don't you? I spent $52 on a damn mug—with zero buyer's remorse.

An AI bot can sell a new stove to a person on December 23rd, whose old stove just broke and whose family is showing up at their doorstep for Christmas dinner. That takes no skill, that's an order taker.

But the (un)selling experience is all about playing the long game and realizing people won't buy just because you're selling. It's about watering the seeds and adding something of value to the relationship over time, which will hopefully pay off when they're ready to buy.

Most sellers give up after the first exchange doesn't go their way, and that's a massive mistake because the research says that only 3% of people are in "buy mode" when you first make contact.

So take your foot off the gas and accept that this is how things are. You also need a plan for staying in touch and following up in a way that adds value (like tips, ideas, or inside information) and doesn't add stress (like meeting requests or 34-page whitepapers that no one reads).

Here's a quick image showing that most salespeople act like buying is a linear process.

The truth is the buying process has many stops, starts, stalls, and other problems. It is not a straight line. If you accept this fact, it will affect how you act and behave as a sales professional, and you will not come in too hot, expecting the one-call close.

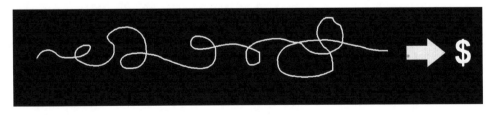

P.S. Don't let the one-call closers and sales savages in on our little secret.

Mistake #6: Starting with the wrong intent

Let's use an example that well-respected sales coach Josh Braun used to show what it looks like to start with the right intent and what it looks like to start with the wrong intent.

The wrong intent: Sale > Truth

Seller: I sell rib-eye steaks.

Prospect: I've been vegan for the past 10 years.

Seller: I talk to a lot of vegans like you, and many of them felt the same way you do. But did you know that beef has a number of nutrients that are important for adults and that vegans can't get anywhere else? Can I send you an email with a link to our "Carnivore Collection" and offer you 25% off your first order?

The right intent: Truth > Sale

Prospect: I've been a vegan for the past 10 years.

Seller: Nice. It looks like we are not a good match, which is fine. Do you mind if I ask one more question before we hang up? I've got some friends who also are vegans. Just curious, what got you started?

When you start a conversation with the goal of finding out the truth, getting a no is a normal part of the sales process and a perfectly fine answer. You don't ever want to be the rib-eye salesman trying to sell to a room full of vegans; it's just uncomfortable for both sides. Because the truth is, you're not for everyone. 70 to 80 per cent of the people you talk to will not fit into your world.

This could be because they don't feel enough pain to change; are afraid of change (fear of making a mistake); can't afford you; or don't have the power to make the decision.

So instead of "forcing the yes," I strongly suggest you "start with no" and let the prospect show you that they belong in your world. Going into a sales conversation knowing your only job is to find out the truth (even if it is no) makes selling less stressful.

When you seek the truth over the sale, some really cool things happen:

♦ You don't show up, look, or sound like a typical salesperson.

♦ You're no longer afraid to ask hard questions, because you know getting to the truth is more important than making a sale.

♦ You don't have to hide the elephant in the room, because you bring up objections and talk about why other people were not a good fit for you in the past.

♦ You talk about your competitors openly and name them. You do not act like they don't exist. Because you know 60% of the time there is "no decision" and things stay the same. So, as part of your questioning strategy, you stress-test the status quo by subtly telling them to keep doing what they're doing and asking them to explain why that's not OK. They need to convince you, not the other way around.

Seeking the truth will set you free and will also make selling more comfortable.

Mistake #7: Not selling what you should be selling

Consider a guy walking into the hardware store looking for a ¾ inch drill bit. You might make the mistake of thinking the customer wants a ¾ inch drill bit. Wrong. He wants the outcome: a ¾ inch hole. The ¾ inch drill is the what, the ¾ inch hole is the why. But the "why" goes even deeper. What is the guy *really* buying?

Is it avoiding a fight with his wife about a picture that has not been hung up in months, or is it a bigger deal? Putting up a picture of the whole family might be a way for this guy to surprise his family when they walk into their new house for the first time. In this last case, they are really selling self-worth and pride, not a ¾ inch hole.

The message is that you should always think about the outcome of what you are selling, and that is where you should build your story. Here are some other quick examples:

♦ Insurance isn't about selling policies; it's about peace of mind and keeping people from getting night sweats at 3:00 a.m. when bad things happen, wondering whether they're covered or not.

♦ A divorce lawyer isn't selling legal counsel; it's someone fighting in their corner for them.

♦ LEGO isn't selling blocks; it's selling imagination.

♦ The orthodontist isn't selling braces; they're selling a better smile, which leads to more confidence.

♦ The martial arts class for your kid isn't about self-defense; it's about building confidence and self-esteem.

The customer doesn't want products—they want an outcome.

Remember the iPod?

Steve Jobs first showed off this device in 2001, at a small press event at Apple's old headquarters on Infinite Loop. Jobs wasn't selling a more powerful MP3 player (that's what they were called back then). Instead, he was selling the freedom of getting rid of stacks of CD cases and being limited to putting 30 songs on the player.

He was selling freedom, and the way he put it is still one of the best ways to explain what the iPod was when it first came out.

He pulled the new gadget out of his pocket and used the famous slogan "1,000 songs in your pocket" to sell it. So, let me ask you: What are you really selling? And can you say it as simply as "1,000 songs in your pocket?"

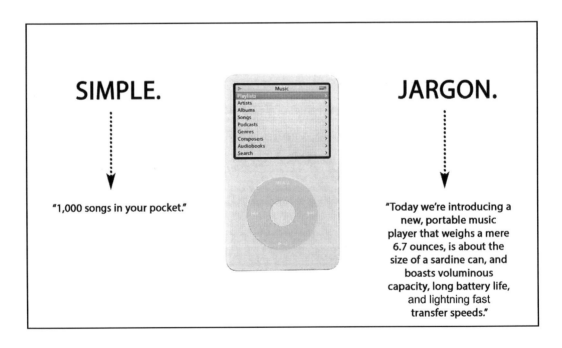

SIMPLE.

"1,000 songs in your pocket."

JARGON.

"Today we're introducing a new, portable music player that weighs a mere 6.7 ounces, is about the size of a sardine can, and boasts voluminous capacity, long battery life, and lightning fast transfer speeds."

Mistake #8: Chasing

Neediness is a big turnoff for prospects and creates reactance.

Reactance happens when prospects feel like they're losing their autonomy over their choices and run and hide to escape the situation. Because of this, "parental guidance" helped the music industry, and kids bought more music with warning labels because they didn't like being told what to do and what not to do. When people feel like they are being told to do something, they do the opposite and reactance kicks in.

Take these phrases and bury them at least 20 feet deep behind your house, so you can never use them again:

> "I hope you are doing well."

> "To be honest..."

> "In my humble opinion..."

> "Just checking in."

> "Just circling back."

> "Just following up."

> "Bumping this to the top of your inbox."

> "Did you get my email?"

All these phrases make you look needy and trigger reactance.

Think back to the YETI mug example and note how it's more give and less take.

"Kevin, I know you mentioned that you live on a pond and love camping. I've got a tip for this weekend that might make putting up the tent even easier, here it is."

Statements like that one from YETI subconsciously say, "There's no pressure, but here's something for you, no strings attached."

Here's a real example in my world:

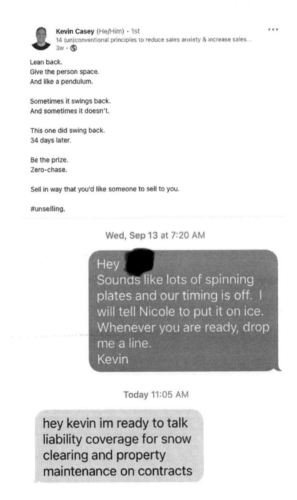

The fortune is found in the follow-up, but only if you don't come off too strong and pushy. Here's the ugly truth about chasing prospects:

The more you chase, the more they run. The more you chase, the more they hide. The more you chase, the more you crush your self-worth.

Stop chasing.

It's better to be the one being chased than to be the one doing the chasing.

Mistake #9: Behaving like an uninvited pest

Selling is a lot more fun when you're invited into their world like a welcome guest instead of being swatted off like a nasty pest.

If you call strangers out of the blue without warning, you're much more likely to end up in the "pest" pile.

Let me be clear: cold-calling works for a lot of people, and I have done my share of it—I have probably made 5,000 cold calls in my life.

But you're here because you feel anxiety around selling, and my mission is to show you ways to prospect and grow your business *without ever needing to make cold calls*.

In the upcoming chapters, I will talk about my top six "painless prospecting" ideas that do not involve making cold calls. In fact, "painless prospecting" will get them to raise their hand to you. People who are cold prospects need to be warmed up, not set on fire.

Let me leave you with the contrast between sellers and (un)sellers in how they operate:

Hard Sellers:[1]

♦   This is me.

♦   This is my company.

♦   This is my product.

♦   This is my price.

♦   This is the deal of the day.

♦   Buy now.

(Un)sellers:

♦   Does X feel like a struggle in your world?

♦   There might be a way to make X suck less.

♦   Or maybe "good enough is good enough for now."

♦   And that's OK too.

♦   Worth a convo?

♦   If not, no worries.

---

1 The hard sell pairs well with a 74-page PowerPoint deck and a "best of" company award that no one cares about and you probably paid for.

CHAPTER SUMMARY

This list of the nine most insidious ways you can sabotage your sales game is based on the biggest mistakes I made in my first 10 years of selling. Sad to say, not much has changed, and these are still the most common sales mistakes I see, even among experienced salespeople.

So, read these over again, print them out, and keep them close by.

1. Leading with products
2. Selling transactionally
3. Practicing sales incest
4. Scooping up more vanilla
5. Coming in too hot
6. Starting with the wrong intent
7. Not selling what you should be selling
8. Chasing
9. Behaving like the uninvited pest

EXERCISE

What are you really selling?

Expected effort: five minutes.

The scariest four-word question for most business owners to answer is:

"What do you do?"

I want you to do this in about five minutes and come up with an answer that doesn't sound like bullet points on a brochure. Let's use an example first. Here's how the late great chef, Anthony Bourdain, answered the "What do you do?" question in one amazing mic-drop sentence:

> "I would describe myself as a lucky cook who tells stories."

No jargon. Simple words. Emotionally charged. A third-grade class would hear this and say, "Hey, mister, cool job." A Harvard class would hear this and say the same. Just remove the "Hey, mister."

So, let me ask you:

How would you describe what you do for a living?

Keep it Bourdain short.

Not *War and Peace* long.

6

You've Been Framed

I am going to let you in on a little secret: I was addicted to something for about 15 years. An insidious drug that some say is more addictive than heroin.

I hope you won't judge me too harshly because it was a dark time and I have taken full responsible for everything I did over that period. Even though I have been clean since 2012, I am still ashamed to tell my closest friends and family about the things I did because of my addiction to this drug.

It hurt me, my family, and others around me. Since you made it this far into the book, it feels like this is the time to rip off the Band-Aid, and you can judge me accordingly. If I didn't tell you this, it would mean I was holding back, which wouldn't feel right to me.

The drug?

Side Effects
- Afraid to hear a "NO"
- Cross your fingers
- Needy
- Eager
- Chase. Stalk.
- Happy ears
- Excessive talking
- Subservient

Hopeium is just like any other drug in that it can lead to addiction. Some of the nasty side effects of this drug include endless bouts of neediness and weakness. This drug is especially useful when there isn't a formal sales system that can be counted on. It rears its ugly head when there is no clear definition of a qualified prospect, no agreed-upon way to qualify for pain or budget, or a shared understanding of the decision-making process.

How many times in my addiction years did I come back to the office and say the meeting went well, only on further examination to find that "went well" meant we had a good chat, I vomited a lot of valuable information for free, and left with no more than a half-baked "I'll think it over" from the prospect? I always thought I was getting closer to a sale, but the prospect was no closer to deciding to buy the product or service now than they were before the meeting.

In fact, I found out later that many of these prospects had already said no but just hadn't told me. I chased more lies than leads.

Who is the dealer behind this bad drug?

The prospect is the hopeium pusher.

The hopeium pushers are the prospects who have no intention of buying and are only there to kick some tires and steal some free advice so they can do it on their own.

Every prospect knows that most salespeople are locked in on their wallets, and that neediness and attachment are the rocket fuel that make them perfect candidates to become addicts. Thus, the main point of this chapter is this: *avoid coming off as needy.*

Take, for example, the typical freelancer or executive coach I've seen spin their wheels endlessly over the years. It goes like this:

♦ Jane becomes a freelancer.

♦ Jane gets waterboarded by bad sales training and starts selling like everyone else around her, which is "chasing instead of being chased."

♦ Jane gets frustrated because it isn't working.

♦ Jane behaves increasingly needy and desperate, thinking "more" will solve the misery.

♦ Jane gets ghosted more and blames everything bad on the economy or "stupid prospects," never admitting she is the cause of her own sales problems.

♦ Jane gives up, gets a "real" job, and settles back into being a cog in a wheel.

Here's the harsh truth about selling, which I know because I did it repeatedly for 15 years: If you come off as weak or needy, the prospect will pick up on that scent like a bloodhound and take control of the sales process. Before you know it, you'll be subservient and hooked on hopeium.

One of my sales mentors, who saw me endlessly chasing prospects and burning so many sales calories, smirked one day and said, "Kevin, even the blind squirrel eventually finds the nut."

In this chapter, I will explain a powerful idea called "framing," and show you how it can make you look like an expert right away and keep you from sounding like a desperate salesperson.

CHAPTER 6

The tale of two dogs

I grew up on a cul-de-sac near two dogs who couldn't be more different from each other. The first small dog was a terrier with a tail that wagged constantly. The dog was about the size of a football, never wore a leash, and he waited on a bended paw for anyone to make eye contact with him and give him some attention. This little guy just wanted to hang out with me and my friends, whether we were skating, playing street hockey, or playing spotlight.

For fun, we would throw a small red ball as far as we could, to see how many times he would be crazy enough to run after it without falling down and rolling over. We never did beat that little dog in that game of fetch. He never gave up. He kept chasing after the saliva-covered ball—just to get a pat on the head.

For the purposes of this story, I will call him "Chase" to protect his privacy, but mostly because it sounds way cooler than his real name.

During my first 12 years of selling, I was a lot like Chase. I wanted to be liked, so I chased every red ball that came my way, whether it was a lead or a lie.

Now, meet Case. Case was a different kind of dog. He was a mastiff, and he walked in a strong and regal way that made it hard to ignore him. But even though he was big, he was never mean or aggressive to the other kids or dogs on the street. Case didn't waste any of his energy on us kids like little Chase did. Case knew how to spend his time and hung out with the dads in the neighborhood a lot more.

Why? Because the dads were the "Kings of the Grill" during BBQ season, and Case was always there to clean up the rib bones and steaks

[116]

that didn't make the cut. Case knew his target audience, and it wasn't us kids!

Mike, who was the most athletic kid on the block and had an arm like Brett Favre, once stole some beef jerky from his house and brought it over. The handfuls of beef jerky instantly got Case's attention, and he trotted over to us. Case chowed down the first few strings of beef, like they were Tic Tacs. Feeling like he had a sudden connection to the dog, Mike picked up the street hockey ball, held it out in front of Case, and threw it as hard as he could. It seemed like the ball was in the air for a minute as it sailed across the street and over the roof of my house.

Case didn't flinch. He didn't even blink. He just glared at Mike, and if he could talk, I'm sure he would have said, "You've got the wrong dog. Get Chase to play your silly fetch games."

You see where this dog story is leading, don't you?

Chase isn't a dog; it's a needy mindset.

Case isn't a dog; it's an assertive mindset.

Me in 2012

Me after 2012

Chase: Low status	**Case: High status**
◆ Subservient	◆ Assertive
◆ Insatiable need to be liked	◆ Indifferent
◆ Needy	◆ Selective
◆ Constantly chasing	◆ Direct
◆ Happy ears	◆ Patient

This story brings me to what I think is one of the most powerful and liberating skills that helped me go from being a seller to an (un)seller. Even if you only learned this one skill and read nothing else in this book, you would be better off than 80% of the salespeople out there.

Welcome to framing

Framing is a powerful mental shift that will make you look, act, and talk like a professional and never like a hopeium-addicted, fast-talking salesperson. It's about showing up more like Case and less like Chase.

Frames are the mental structures that shape the way we see the world. They regulate how people interact with one another in any given moment:

- ◆ Are you the one in control, or is the prospect running the show?
- ◆ Are you wanting to be *liked* like Chase or *respected* like Case?
- ◆ Are you attached to the money (bad) or are you attached to your sales process (good)?
- ◆ Who's controlling the flow and sequence of the meeting?

Pitch Anything, by Oren Klaff, is a great book to read about the concept of framing, and I highly recommend picking it up and going deep into it. He discusses how very fundamental desires—like power, authority, strength, knowledge, and status—shape frames, which are under the control of the emotional portion of the brain (referred to as the "croc brain" or "limbic brain").

Whenever you have a sales conversation with someone, two frames will collide and fight to be the more important. The person with the winning frame will set the tone and agenda of the meeting.

Frames are not about being a bully, a know-it-all or flexing your ego to be dominant.

Rather, frames are more about planting your feet and positioning yourself as *the Sage*—the one "leading" the process, not supplicating in the moment and letting everyone yank on your chain.

If a third person were to parachute in and watch how two people talk to each other, it would be clear in a few seconds who is the leader and who is the follower.

Outside the world of sales, here are a few examples of frames that most people in the world accept:

♦ Doctor-patient: The doctor owns the frame, not the patient.
♦ Teacher-student: The teacher owns the frame, not the student.
♦ Policeman-speeding driver: The policeman owns the frame, not the speeding driver.

One person is leading and one is following. Buyers and sellers have a bad history together, because most salespeople feel so much pressure to make a sale and are so addicted to the result (money) that they will do anything to be liked and to get approval.

Since they don't have the confidence of a well-defined and repeatable sales process, they show up and do whatever the buyer says.

The result is that salespeople show up with a "weak frame" and spend most of their time being "chummy" with the prospect, giving away free advice, and chasing. This mindset shift and truth will help you control the frame:

♦ The prospect is the one with the problem, and you are the one who has the solution.

♦ They need your solution more than you need their money.

But it often doesn't go that way. Salespeople are focused on the result (the money), so they lose this leverage and become reactive to every prospect's request (like our little dog, Chase). They will do anything to keep the prospect happy because they are obsessed with building rapport and keeping the chemistry good.

When you lose at the frame game, bad things happen:

♦ Free consulting

♦ Time-consuming proposals

♦ Boring demos

♦ Being afraid to ask tough, truth-telling questions

♦ Not being up-front about dealing with common sales objections.

A weak frame game is a race to the bottom, and it's a race you just might win. You need to flip the script and own the frame.

And why wouldn't you? It's based on truth and facts. You have the solution, expertise, and know-how. The prospect is suffering in pain with a problem only you can solve. Doesn't that justify your ability to own the frame? Why would you surrender that leverage and allow the prospect to call the shots?

The battered Post-It note

Even though I have a lot of technology at my fingertips, it always surprises me how many different colored Post-It notes litter my desk and wall. A few years ago, I wrote five reminders on what is now a worn-out Post-It note to help me keep my emotions in check and keep my cool during sales conversations.

Even today, I always sneak a quick peek at my Post-It note to get myself in the right headspace before jumping on a call with the prospect.

It says:

1. They've got the problem, not me. Behave accordingly.
2. They need my solution more than I need their money.
3. Get to no fast, I'm not for everyone.
4. This is an audition. I'm Simon Cowell, but way nicer.
5. Be a little un-OK. Columbo.

If you don't learn frame control, you'll fall victim to the buyer's every wish and command, and you'll waste the one thing in life you can't get more of: time.

The 80/20 rule to the rescue

Have you ever heard the saying "80% of the results come from 20% of the effort?" Well, that's what the Pareto principle, also called the 80/20 rule, is all about.

The Pareto principle can be seen in many parts of life.

Think about the clothes in your closet. Most of the time, you might only wear 20% of your clothes, while the other 80% just sit there, waiting to be worn.

In the world of business, the Pareto principle can be seen too. For example, in a store, about 20% of the products might make up 80% of their sales. So, the Pareto principle teaches us that a small portion of something often has a big impact or makes a big difference. It reminds us to focus on the most important things that bring the most results, instead of getting overwhelmed by everything.

Over the past 10 years, I have studied and used at least 10 different frames. Luckily, the Pareto principle is going to make it easier for you. The good news is you only need to know about two of them.

And those two frames are:

1.   The prize frame
2.   The power frame

Let's dive into each of these simple but potent frames.

The prize frame

The prize frame states that you are the prize to be won. When you own the prize frame, you see your solution as the prize, and that commoditizes the money, which is the root of all neediness.

Here are some real-life examples to help illustrate the power of controlling the frame.

Prospect says:

I need to think it over (brush-off)

Of course, makes sense. Want me to call you next week?

Mind me asking a bit of a blunt question?
Most times, a 'think it over' is just someone being nice - a polite way to say, 'No'. I can handle a no, c'mon, I'm in sales. Whattya say?

How about this hilarious prize frame executed over a simple text exchange with someone buying a bike? And with just enough subtle humor not to be rude:

Let's look at even more examples.

Here's the key:

✘ = Weak/Frame lost

✔ = Strong/Frame kept

Lesson: Avoid supplicating language that weakens your status.

✘ "I know you're busy, but thanks for squeezing us in."

✔ "I'm glad I was able to fit you in. Let's get started."

Lesson: Stress-test the real urgency of a prospect's problem.

✘ "Oh yeah, we have the perfect solution for that."

✔ "Just curious… Up to now, what have you done to fix this problem?"

✔ "Why do you think it didn't work?"

✔ "What happens if you do nothing?"

✔ "How long has this problem been going on?"

See how the different approaches make one sound like a trusted advisor who is sure of himself, while the other sounds like a slave? When *you* control the frame, you stay patient and don't behave in needy ways. You behave and talk with the calm confidence of a respected doctor, teacher, or Michelin-starred chef.

The concept of the prize frame is simple, but it's not easy to put into practice. So many times, I had to keep my "prize frame intact" when I was stressed and worried about whether we would make the company payroll for the following week. As an entrepreneur, I have been in that cash-strapped situation more times than I care to remember.

But no matter how much pressure you feel, you need to plant your feet firmly on protecting that frame.

It takes a steel spine, and it feels uncomfortable—but if it were easy, every salesperson would be doing it, and they aren't. But you will.

Before we leave the prize frame I want to describe an ad I came across. It was an ad created by Young & Rubicam ad agency. The image was simply a backbone and the text below it read:

This is a backbone.

You can't become a good sales professional without it.

It often makes you say an honest "no" instead of an easy "yes."

It means giving service instead of servility.

Very often, the result is an outstanding sales professional.

Even though this print ad was created in 1966 the message still applies today in terms of how a salesperson thinks.

The main point of the ad is about having the "spine" to control the frame and not caring about things you can't control.

♦   Seek the truth, not the sale.

♦   Go for the fast no, disqualifying hard.

♦   If you feel it, say it.

♦   Be the first to blow up common sales objections.

♦   Lead, don't follow.

♦   Don't be subservient.

The power frame

I have had more than my fair share of prospects with big egos and puffy chests try to use the power frame against me and, for the first 10 years of my sales career, I folded like a cheap tent.

But if you can find the courage to break their power frame with a subtle refusal, defiance, or reluctance, you can break their hold on you. Think of what I am about to say as a series of small 2mm turns, not wide 18-wheeler-sized turns.

For example, I have been in a lot of situations where Mr Big or Ms Big puffed up their chests and barked at me with: "I don't have time to answer these questions; just send me the price and proposal!"

When I stopped rolling over and pretending to be dead, I learned to take a deep breath, pause for two seconds, and answer with the calm voice of a TED-talker.

> "I'm sorry, I can't do that. That's not the way we do things around here. We have a conversation first to see if there is a problem I can solve and to figure out if we are a good fit for each other. Then we talk about pricing. But it's your call and if you want to stop now, we can part ways. No hard feelings."

You've now broken their power frame and are back in control without being rude or behaving like a deer caught in headlights.

Here's another real-world example. Let's say Mr Big says something like:

> "We already have a company that does that for us, but we're willing to hear you out."

This is a red flag that you're about to play the starring role in a miserable shopping-around exercise just to keep the incumbent honest. You need to stir up the courage to break their frame and say something like:

> "John, I've been through this before, so I know it's hard to break up with someone. Even if you liked what you heard, it seems like it wouldn't matter because you're loyal to your vendor. Am I wrong?"

And yet another example: Ms Big flexes her dominance like a flamingo at Busch Gardens and challenges you in front of her team by saying:

> "Tell me why we should go with you."

You playfully break that power frame with something like this because it's the truth, not a tactic:

> "I'm not even sure you should go with us yet."

Then, just zip it, say nothing else. Don't break the silence first. This small act of indifference will shift the frame back in your favor.

Don't forget you get bonus points for using humor to break the power frame; it's a sales superpower.

If you do what 95% of salespeople do, and let your target keep their power frame dominant, Mr or Ms Big will quickly shut you out and treat you like the hired help and never see you as a trusted authority. Big shots aren't used to being challenged, so it's easy to break their power frames. They will automatically respect you for not being a coward and standing up for yourself.

Be careful: If you try to frame someone by acting hostile or aggressive, the prospect will see it as a sign of disrespect, and it is game over.

There is a big difference between being assertive and aggressive, and creating your own versions of these talk-tracks is something you need to role play with a safe partner. It will require paying more careful attention to your tonality compared to the words. Tonality and intentional silence are keys to executing power frames.

Mr and Ms Big like to test you and act in ways that make them look like they own the jungle. Here's a specific situation that's happened to me countless times. You bring a bunch of copies of your presentation as a leave-behind, and while the meeting is going on, you spot Mr Big in the corner of your eye picking it up and sneaking a peek at it. What would you do?

Pretend it's not happening, ignore it, or deal with it? Well, I deal with it, and so should you. Break the power frame move, and squash it with a smile and playful tonality: "Ah-ah-ah…not yet, Sam," while playfully pointing. A fun denial.

Or the one time I went to a kick-off meeting, Ms Big walked in out of breath with her assistant carrying her papers and said that the 45 minutes she had promised had been cut to 15 because her day had gone off the rails. A classic power move to remind everyone around them the world revolves around them.

What did I do? Well, in a playful way, I wanted to let them know my world doesn't revolve around them and I'm not one of their minions. One of my favorite ways to deal with this power timeframe is with a playful act of defiance that shows my status without pissing them off:

> "Oh, Lucy, that works for both of us. Because somehow I'm overbooked, and I only had 14 minutes."

Do it in jest, but really mean it, because remember the prize mindset:

They have the problem, and you have the solution.

One more example from my world of selling is business insurance. In this example, the prospect hits you with an objection designed to throw you off balance by saying, "Your price is higher than your competitor."

Chase: A weak frame

Ms Big: "Your price is higher than X."

Chase: "Well, if you let me try, ah, I can go back and find some more savings, please?"

✘ Game over, frame lost, and the commodity price race to the bottom begins.

Case: A strong frame

Ms Big: 'Your price is higher than X."

Case: "It depends, I guess."

Ms Big: "Huh? Depends on what?"

Case: "Well, I probably shouldn't have even said anything. Never mind."

Ms Big: "But you did. It depends on what?"

Case: "Well, all right. Like humans, no two insurance policies are the same. At first glance, you might think that our price is high. But if that bad thing happens and our policy covers it and you get the payout and the cheaper one doesn't, then all of a sudden, my policy seems like the deal of the day."

In this next example, a friend of mine is an executive coach who always got tongue-tied about dealing with her fee, and often spent two to three hours vetting a prospect without the fee being mentioned only to find out 60–70% were unable or unwilling to afford the investment. What a waste of time. Here's how I asked her to take control of the frame early in the first call and save both a lot of time.

The Coach now begins:

> "My fee is $250 per hour, or you can invest in a bank of 10 hours for $2,000. Knowing this, are you still comfortable to continue this call?"

> "Gosh, that is expensive."

> "I understand. I'll take that as a no?"

> "No, not necessarily. But why is your hourly rate so high?"

> "That's a fair question. Before I answer it, is it alright if I ask you what you think the difference is between a coach like me and another coach at $80 an hour?"

They'll answer the question for themselves, and you can fill in the gaps.

Isn't frame control manipulative?

No, it's about showing up and behaving like a professional. Prospects are hard-wired not to make decisions because they're afraid of salespeople.

Think about your own life, and you can see that we all have trouble making even simple decisions. I've had a conversation with my wife, Linda, at least 100 times about what to have for dinner.

We finally decide to eat out, and then it starts all over when trying to decide which restaurant to visit. A simple, low-risk buying decision between people who already know each other shows how hard it is for humans to make decisions.

You've probably had similar back-and-forth conversations when trying to decide on simple things, right? Seriously, if two smart adults who live together can't agree on what to have for dinner, how can we expect a stranger—who is dealing with a salesperson and scared of being persuaded into buying something—to make a confident decision?

Prospects are rarely going to act decisively, because decisive action is completely contrary to the behavioral system of the buyer. This is an uncomfortable truth to face, but it shows how important it is to show up and act like you have status; tell people what to do next; and ease their fears about making a change. This means you should act more like a doctor, French chef, or teacher than like a typical salesperson.

Prospects want to be led and guided on what to do next in a low-pressure way. Be the lighthouse that shows them the way, and don't be the tugboat that pushes them around with force. When you switch from a Chase to a Case mindset, good things happen and, over time, selling will not feel like selling at all.

Remember the Case mindset:

✔ Attached to a sales process, yet unattached to the outcome (the sale/ money)

✔ Not afraid to ask the hard questions because that's the only way to get to the truth

✔ Stingy with your time and totally OK with getting a no, as long as it's fast

✔ Being respected takes precedence over being liked

Will applying frames be hard for you to get right? Absolutely. It was the hardest thing I had to learn in sales, and I'm still working on it. But go for progress, not perfection.

The first step is to get some reps in and script out your own prize and power frame talk-tracks that you can test out and refine during your conversations with prospects.

CHAPTER SUMMARY

This chapter introduced you to one of the most powerful and confidence-building skills that will help you show up with a powerful calmness and quiet confidence.

Frames take time to get right, and if you want to show up strong in the frame game, you'll need to stop listening to your inner critic and find the courage to try it.

We met two very different dogs in this chapter, and I used them as a way to explain the theory behind the two types of frames.

Chase isn't a dog; it's a needy mindset.

Case isn't a dog; it's an assertive mindset.

If a prospect says, "Jump!"

Chase asks, "How high?"

Case asks, "Jump? Why?"

There is always someone in charge of the point of view. That person, by extension, owns the frames in a sales conversation. To sell in a more noble way, you only need to understand and master two frames:

1.   The Prize Frame
2.   The Power Frame

On the next page is a quick chart that captures the key mindset and principles of Chase vs Case.

Want me to throw you a bone? Check out my 'Fix in Six' video training where I delve deeper into the important concept of "Framing." You'll also find extra bonus examples comparing Chase and Case.

Watch it here: www.kevincasey.ca/twodogs or simply scan the QR code.

GOODBYE CHASE. HELLO CASE.

Subservient mindset	Top French Chef/Doctor mindset
Convince buyer (push)	Buyer convinces themselves (pull)
Seek interest	Challenge interest
Qualify gently	Disqualify assertively
Always be closing (ABC)	Always be disqualifying (ABD)
Give them the whole movie	Tease them with a movie trailer
Customer is prize	You are the prize
Seeks the sale	Seeks the truth
Appeal to logic	Create emotion, return to logic
Talks about products	Talks about problem
Finding clients	Attracting clients
Recruits one-time-customer	Recruits human lead magnet for life
Chase	Be chased

EXERCISES

Exercise #1: DIY frame scripting

I'll share some common brush-offs or objections you'll face during conversations with prospects. Create your own talk-tracks for each. Bonus points and a high five if you use subtle denial or humor.

Following the exercise, I've given some frame-control answers to each of the challenge questions to help you compare your work, but try it on your own first then look at these to improve what you've done.

1. **Situation: Pricing objection between you and the incumbent**

    Prospect: Acme came in 15% less.

    Write a talk-track frame here:

    _____

2. **You finally find the nerve to call a lead and within the first 10 seconds the prospect barks loudly:**

    Prospect: I hate sales calls!

    Write a talk-track frame here:

    _____

3. **Generic price objection**

Prospect: You're too expensive.

Write a talk-track frame here:

_____

4. **Write an email to a prospect who's ghosting you, ignoring you for weeks even though the initial meeting went well in your eyes.**

Write an email-track frame here:

_____

5. **Prospect is upset because you're asking too many questions.**

Prospect: This is a shit-ton of questions. Can you just give me your fee to fix it?

Write a talk-track frame here:

_____

Exercise #2: A simple trick to track frame control

It's important to be aware of who owns the frame as the conversation happens with prospects. This is a very cool method I saw used by someone called BowTiedSalesGuy:

◆ Get an index card.

◆ Mark in big letters: ME on one side and THEM on the other side of the card.

◆ As you move through the conversation on a phone call or Zoom call, keep track of the times you lose the frame and control the frame.

◆ Flip the sheet of paper: You/Them.

◆ Of course, you won't do this in a live meeting, but use it on Zoom or a phone call.

◆ Keep track of your ratio of frame control—it starts with awareness.

◆ We can't fix what we can't measure.

PART

2

the (un)tangling

7

Building Your Core Four

Gary Halbert, one of the best copywriters in the world, gave a room full of aspiring creatives a challenge about how to run a successful hamburger stand on the beach.

Halbert asked, "What's the most important thing you would do to ensure this hamburger stand is profitable?" The answers came fast and furious from the audience: "A secret sauce that makes the burger irresistible." "Make sure it's located near the busiest part of the beach." "Create a special blend of meats and spices."

Halbert grinned and declared them all wrong: "You missed the most important thing. For the hamburger stand—or any business for that matter—you need this one thing above all: *a starving crowd.*"

Your business is no different. Your job is to find the "starving crowd" and hand them the solution to the problem they are suffering from in a unique way that only you can.

Fair Warning: This chapter is tedious and, admittedly, the least fun, but it's one of the most powerful chapters in the book. What I'm teaching you here won't work if you cut corners, skip ahead, or try to be clever and put your own spin on it. Everything I have written down here is in a very specific order. The more work you put into this now, the easier everything else will be moving forward.

This chapter has four different exercises you can do in an hour if you stay off your phone and TikTok. OK, enough with the nagging. You get the point.

What's the Core Four all about?

Before you even try to sell anything to anyone, I need you to answer four important questions in a very specific way:

1. What type of client do you love?
2. What's the problem and pain you solve?
3. What are you really selling?
4. Why should someone buy from you instead of someone else?

Here's a quick overview of each piece of the puzzle before we go all in.

Let's begin from the top and go deep into each of the Core Four elements.

The Core Four

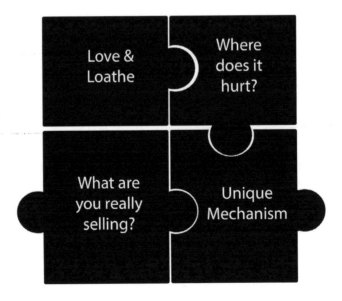

Core 1: What type of client do you love?

The biggest mistake you can make in business is to think that everybody is a good customer for you. If you don't choose a specific target audience, you will try to sell to anyone with a heartbeat and a wallet. And "spray and pray" is a surefire way to get tired, frustrated, and spend more time chasing prospects than closing them.

Here's a real-life story about Fiona to help illustrate this point.

Fiona the drifter

Fiona was a graphic designer who had just got out of school in 2006. She came to our ad agency for a job interview, but she wasn't there to get the job; she had other plans. Fiona was my ninth interview of the day, and she didn't waste any time telling me the truth: she wasn't there to get a job; she wanted to pick my brain.

She got lucky. After a long morning of meeting boring candidates, I was intrigued, and admired her guts for being so honest about her ulterior motive. So, the conversation began. She went on and on about how she wanted to be her own boss and use her skills to become a freelance designer. I asked one of those simple but not-so-simple questions:

"What kind of clients do you want?"

She didn't miss a beat and blurted out: "That's easy! Anyone with a credit card and a fat wallet."

There was awkward silence.

I wish the answer surprised me, but eight out of 10 times when I ask entrepreneurs who they serve, they tell me something as wishy-washy as that kind of answer. I wanted to challenge Fiona on the shallowness of that answer, so I turned up the heat a little to create some tension:

◆ What kind of companies? Butchers, candlemakers, lawyers, shoe shops, agencies, retailers, and SAAS companies?

◆ Not-for-profits that can't pay?

◆ For-profits that can pay?

◆ Companies that respect marketing, or those who will treat you like a drive-thru?

◆ People who open their wallets and pay right now? Or the ones you need to chase to get paid?

It didn't take Fiona more than a minute to realize she didn't know the answer to one of the most basic questions every business must answer. She didn't argue with me about it, though. She was like a sponge and wanted me to push her to get to a better place.

Who is your starving crowd?

We didn't figure things out that day, but we stayed in touch, and I had her do some "deep-dive exercises" to help her choose her ideal client and focus on a specific problem that would set her apart from the hordes of graphic designers who seemed to be everywhere.

Fiona was very easy to teach, and all her hard work paid off big time. In 2009, she was working on the design of complex software that the engineers and CEOs couldn't explain in simple terms to the venture capital community. She took a complicated 30-page document that even a NASA engineer would have trouble understanding and turned it into a one-page process map that left the CEO and engineers speechless. She took all the noise and complicated bits into a custom illustration that was so easy to understand that even a seventh grader would get it instantly.

This company used her visual creation in all its presentations, which helped them secure $120 million in funding. Fiona realized she had an uncanny ability to take really complicated theories and explanations of how things work and turn them into simple and stunning visuals.

Her "starving crowd" were tech startups that were so blinded by the "curse of knowledge" they couldn't explain to non-technical people what they were really selling.

As Fiona explained it, "All I do is create custom illustrations to explain complicated things that engineers who suffer from the curse of knowledge can't explain."

Fiona left Canada in 2010. Last time I checked, she was a solopreneur in California making over $400,000 a year by doing that one thing so well. She spends her days creating simple visuals to help explain very complicated theories and ideas that many Fortune 100 companies struggle to explain to the venture capital community.

And that's why you do the work on the problem you solve and the ideal client up front.

Talk about going narrow, right? Way to go, Fiona.

The problem is, you can't afford to market to everyone unless you have very deep pockets like Coca-Cola or Amazon, and you and I will never have pockets that deep.

Entrepreneurs usually fall into one of two groups:

1.   They can't describe their ideal customer, or
2.   They go on an endless rant with no commas or periods, which is really just a long confession that they don't have a clue what they do or who they serve.

When it comes to picking your "starving crowd," it's important to discriminate. In this context, discrimination is not a bad word; it's a safe passage to focus and prosperity.

Be a meaningful specific, not a wandering generality

Seth Godin provides some sage advice on this topic. He says, "There's nothing wrong with being a wandering generality instead of a meaningful specific, but don't expect to make the change you seek to make if that's what you do."

As Seth says, when you are a wandering generality, your mission is relegated to second place—and you might never move further up in the rankings.

Yes, I get it. It's scary to leave anyone out when you have bills to pay. When we opened our advertising agency, The IDEA Factory, in 2002, we took jobs from anyone with money or a heartbeat. We weren't sure what problem we were trying to solve or what kind of customers we even wanted. It felt like we were shooting arrows without a target; it was a game of blind archery.

Because we didn't go specific, we blended in with every other big agency. Blending in to look like everyone else is very dangerous. We were a black dot inside a sea of black dots.

We got off to a rough start, and I can tell you the sound of silence is deafening when you are a new business with no cash flow and no prospects. We were running out of time to stay in business. We hit "reset" and doubled down on focusing on a specific type of client with a specific problem.

We decided to stand out and be a red dot in a sea of black dots.

Here's how specific we got with our ideal client avatar: small business owners with annual sales of less than $5 million who feel taken advantage of and underserved by large advertising agencies that used "bait and switch" tactics to get the business with the A Team and then tossed them to the B Team.

The genesis of the gap we wanted to serve started with an impromptu conversation. We met a business owner who was angry that he had fallen for the trap of being courted by the A-players, but then being handed off to a bunch of junior staff so he never saw the top brass again. He thought he had been tricked and was ashamed that he had succumbed to their sweet talk.

We had a feeling this guy wasn't the only business owner who felt this way and we did some informal research and discovered many other small business owners were pissed off about the exact same thing.

This insight became our new calling card to stand out in the market. Now, all we had to do was call out the enemy (the big agency games) and stir up the pain so we could start a different conversation.

Our hook was simple, but it worked, and it was based on the story of David and Goliath. Our self-promotion didn't hold anything back, and we called out the villain:

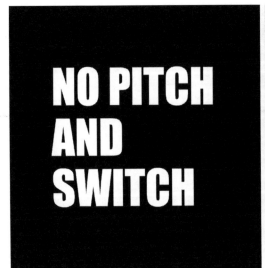 

The clarity about our "starving crowd" was a fundamental reason we were able to build a $6 million agency on an island with a population of only 500,000 people.

When you play small ball, your inner critic will scare you into thinking you are leaving money on the table. Casting a wider net might feel safe, but it's dangerous. If you cast your net too wide, you will also catch a lot of trash and bring a lot of the wrong people into your world. The graveyard of small businesses and freelancers is full of people who tried to be all things to all people.

Don't be a wandering generalist, be a meaningful specific.

But fair warning: going narrow will not feel safe because there will be that little voice in your head warning you that "going smaller" means you'll be leaving money on the table.

Ignore that voice.

Be a big fish in a small pond

Let's look at some examples to illustrate this idea of being a bigger fish in a smaller pond. We'll start with yoga. You want to open a yoga studio. That's too wide. Yoga studios are generic, and there's one around every corner. How can we make the yoga studio more of a meaningful specific? Just add imagination.

Off the top of my head, you could look at creating a studio focused on:

◆   Injury-free yoga for beginners
◆   Male-only yoga

Let's take the second one and stretch our thinking around male-only yoga. At the time of writing, I am a 55-year-old man with the flexibility of a titanium rod. Half my friends have the same trouble. I want to be more flexible, but the thought of walking into a yoga class full of women and men who can easily turn their bodies into pretzels is scary, and my inner ego would be screaming at me not to do it.

But what if a yoga studio did *not* focus on flexible yogis, but rather on people like me who are new to yoga and want to try it in a safe place with people like them? This is one way to look for "underserved" audiences you might be able to reach, but you have to be disciplined enough to narrow down.

And, just like with everything else, when you specialize, people pay more, so I would expect to pay more for a yoga class created for guys like me.

Got allergies?

Let's pretend you're opening an allergy clinic. You could say "all allergies," like everyone else and not stand out, or you could take a calculated risk and be more specific. For example, a clinic that only treats "cat allergies" could become the place to go for people who are allergic to their favorite house cat.

How would that one single decision make things easier on you? For starters, everything you say, every ad, every sales message, and your language all become centered around connecting to that one audience and that one tangly problem. If you had a cat allergy, you'd pay more to see a cat allergy specialist than a general naturopath, right?

While everyone is thinking ketchup, you think sriracha.

Caution: Demographics aren't enough

Just thinking about demographics when it comes to your ideal client isn't going deep enough.

There's something more powerful than demographics, and it's called psychographics. It focuses more on the kind of person they are—what makes them tick, their values, and how they want to live their lives.

And when you use psychographics to paint your ideal client profile, you begin thinking like the jolly guy in the funny red suit: Santa.

One of my great clients and dear friends, Dean, has this lifelong fascination with US presidential history. But one president stands above all others in his eyes: JFK. A number of years ago, I wanted to find a special gift for Dean as a thank you for letting my family stay in his Florida home. But what do you buy the person who seems to have everything?

One night, I was watching an old rerun of an episode of *The West Wing*. As the camera moved over Martin Sheen's shoulder, I saw a framed picture of the front page of a Dallas newspaper on the day JFK was assassinated. Boom! I just found the perfect gift for Dean by accident. I went to eBay and found it with two clicks. Soon, I would be holding a vacuum-sealed set of the actual newspapers from the tragic day JFK was shot on November 22, 1963.

I bought four different newspapers.

It was so good even Santa would be proud of how I used psychographics to my advantage. I remember having lunch with Dean and being so excited to put the gift on the table. It took his breath away. The same look I probably had when I was 10 years old and found a set-up Hot

Wheels racetrack under the tree on Christmas morning, ready to go. That's when you know you've got it right.

But what if I didn't narrow it down to JFK?

I could have chosen the day President Reagan was shot, the day President Nixon resigned, or the day President Obama became the first Black president. And all those options would have gotten a good reaction and a smile. But I would not have gotten the "10-year-old kid with the Hot Wheels racetrack" wide-eyed reaction.

That is the power of digging deeper and really getting to know what makes your clients tick, and that is where psychographics lives.

Target profile vs target audience

The Brain Audit by Sean D'Souza, which I highly recommend, taught me how to choose a target profile. This is very different from the more common advice about choosing your target audience.

The target audience approach is built around demographics—a segment of people based on age, occupation, where they live, and gender that makes them appear similar. On paper, they look alike, but they couldn't be more different.

Here's a Royal example.

Using only demographics, (the former) Prince Charles and the Prince of Darkness look like twins: both male, born in 1948, living in the UK, married twice, living in a castle, and filthy rich.

But these two polar opposites are nothing alike and operate in very different ways.

- Male
- Born 1948
- UK
- Married twice
- Hang out in a castle
- Filthy rich

- Male
- Born 1948
- UK
- Married twice
- Hang out in a castle
- Filthy rich

The case of Ozzy and Charles shows how dangerous it is to only use demographics to describe your audience. So what should you do? Go deeper than demographics and have the courage to pick *one real person* to build your business around.

Let's use an example that's even bigger: Google.

In 1998, Google was an unknown company, and there were a bunch of search engines around at the time, such as Altavista, Yahoo, Lycos, and Excite.

So how did Google stand out?

It solved a very specific issue that one real person was experiencing at the time: decluttering. The big idea was to get rid of all the visual clutter on the screen and make a search engine with nothing on the screen but one little box to type in. Your eye had nowhere else to go.

The founder of Google didn't like how cluttered other search engines were, and he figured he wasn't the only one who wanted a similar experience. He was right, and the rest is history.

Core 2: Where is the pain?

Back in the 1990s, when I was in high school and playing hockey, I broke my collarbone. I was in unbearable pain.

Do you think that when I went to the emergency room, I cared about where the doctor went to school, how many degrees they had, or whether they were keeping up with their credits? I only wanted someone—anyone—to fix my broken collar bone and give me some painkillers.

Pain is paramount when it comes to selling. Know this: No one cares about you; they only care about what you can do for them. That goes for your product, your mission statement, or even the new logo you just launched. No one cares about it—except maybe your mom.

People only buy stuff to solve problems. It's that simple. So, if you are a competitive runner, your 14-mile time not being fast enough is a big problem for you. But for me, it doesn't matter because I hate running, even if someone is chasing me.

Since running is not my thing, you couldn't even hypnotize me into buying a pair of $250 Asics running shoes. On the other hand, I love hiking. And getting a better grip on the trails in the unpredictable Canadian climate is a real problem for me. So, if you are talking about hiking and getting a grip, then you have my attention.

Not all problems are the same. Some problems, like a flat tire, need to be fixed right away, while other problems, like rotating the tires, can wait. Let's look at the issue of urgency around problems with a quick example.

The king of the grill

My Weber barbecue grill is 12 years old. The heat on the right side was getting more uneven, but I was used to it and could work around the problem. The problem wasn't big enough to buy a new grill. But that all changed last summer.

I had 20 people coming to my house and, like most guys who are proud to be king of the grill, I wanted to make a good impression. My right-side burners didn't heat up evenly, and this problem went from being a small annoyance to a big problem that needed to be fixed.

So, why the change?

I didn't want "that one friend" *(name withheld, yes, it might be you)* to tell me how much better his barbecue was and why some of the medium-rare steaks were still rare while others were done just right. Fixing the grill for me was about avoiding that sermon from that dear friend. Your prospect is no different.

Humans buy things to avoid pain, and pain is one of the most powerful motivators in sales. Pain comes in three flavors: emotional, financial, and physical. You might hear purists tell you not to use "pain language" because it's too negative. Instead, they will tell you to use "desire language," which is more positive. This is bullshit, and science proves it. Do not let the purists trick you into thinking it's easier to sell a vitamin than a painkiller, because that is not how people think and buy.

Sell a painkiller, not a vitamin. Because avoiding pain > seeking pleasure.

Remember the "Loss Aversion Theory" from Part 1? The theory won the Nobel Prize in Economic Sciences in 2002 and shows that people try harder to avoid pain than find pleasure.

People are naturally risk-averse.

When people find $10 on the ground, they feel pleasure. When people lose $10, they feel an emotion that is twice as strong as the joy they feel when they find the $10.

Finding your prospect's pain

What keeps your prospect up at 3:00 a.m., making them sweat and stare at the ceiling with their hearts beating fast and their mouths dry?

Let's use personal fitness trainers because it's an example we can all relate to. Does it make "logical" sense to pay $80–$100 an hour to do something you could do on your own for free?

If you asked someone who was paying a trainer why, they might say, "I want to take better care of myself and get in better shape." Yeah, right. This is a safe and acceptable answer, but it's not the whole truth.

My friend, who was 57 at the time, had been paying a "mobility specialist" $120 an hour for months to help him work out. When I first asked him about it, he gave me a typical answer: "I want to work on my flexibility and get in better shape."

By the end of lunch, he told me the real reason he spent $600 a month, which was a much deeper and more emotional pain. There was a very specific part of the first conversation with the trainer that stirred emotion and fear and made him go all in.

The trainer looked him in the eyes and said, "Steve, you're 57 now, and in 13 Christmases, you'll be 70 years old. Based on the assessment we just did, there is a real chance that at 70, you might need a handrail to help you get off the toilet if we do not fix some of these mobility issues."

The trigger moment was the thought of needing to use a handrail to get off the toilet. He couldn't unhear or unfeel the impact of that diagnosis. It hit him like ice water on his face in the middle of a heatwave.

That "cost of inaction" against the status quo is really what you are selling. Look beyond the obvious (logical) problem and attack the fears that come from not solving the problem, which is really the cost of inaction (needing a handrail to get off the toilet).

The trainer's vivid picture of the cost of inaction would make most 57-year-olds willing to do almost anything to prevent that loss of dignity. Notice it was about avoiding pain, not getting pleasure.

Think about your business and the problem it solves for your ideal client. What are the consequences for them now and in the future if they don't solve the problem? And what's the worst-case scenario?

The cost of inaction is what you are really selling. The clever folks at Durex condoms know they are selling more than condoms. They're selling the "cost of inaction."

Take for example two of their ads. One was a picture of a child car seat with a price tag of $217. Below the car seat was a picture of the Durex logo with a price tag of $2.50."

Another one simply said, "To all those who use our competitors' products: Happy Father's Day."

So, now you get it. You must sell against the status quo and not focus on your product. Prospects only care about what you can do for them, so everything you say must be about their problems. Then, you need to go one step further and show the prospect what it will cost to do nothing.

And one more thing to take note of:

Problems are less emotional and more logical. Pain is more emotional and personal.

Here's an example of the problem-pain in the world of business insurance. Let's say I am trying to sell to the CFO of a 120-person company who makes the decision. I need to go deeper than just problems and find a way for them to come to their own conclusions about the risks of not acting.

The problem: A coverage gap in your business insurance.

The pain: Shit, I'm the CFO in charge of signing off on this. If we have a loss and it's not covered because I signed off a crappy policy, I'll be fired, my reputation will be ruined, and no one will hire me again.

Think like a scientist, not a copywriter.

Let's pretend you're a website developer, and Jane calls because her website stinks and isn't drawing in new traffic for her business. You have coffee and, after asking the right questions, write down or record what she says word for word as she talks about how frustrated she is:

- "I feel trapped like a hostage to my agency every time I need to make a change to my website."

- "Every little change costs me money I can't afford to throw away."

- "The developer never gets back to me; I think he sleeps 12 hours a day."

- "I'm embarrassed in front of my team that I can't even change up a team member's photo."

- "This website makes me look like an idiot."

Feel the raw emotion in those statements? You can only get language like that from a real person, not from a persona.

So, you need to listen to your prospect's problems and start using their exact words, because that is the language they are thinking in. Do not try to interpret or fancy up the language. Imagine you are the court stenographer, and you are not allowed to translate.

And to make this happen, I have a little cheat sheet for you.

The "Coffee & Crispy Convo" cheat sheet

I'll make this super simple and practical. Here are five simple but powerful questions to ask your ideal client over a big cup of coffee (or wine, or beer). Here's your cheat sheet of questions over coffee or beer:

1. What are all the problems they are dealing with that might require help from someone like you?

2. What's their biggest problem? Why is that #1 and not #2? What's #2 and why isn't it #3?

3. What happens if that problem isn't solved? In other words, what happens if they just stick with the status quo?

4. For the second most serious problem, what happens if they do nothing?

5. Even if they knew they had to fix it, other than money, what do they think would be the biggest reason they might not pull the trigger on getting it solved?

That's it. Just five questions that get to the heart of the matter.

If you use the emotional language from the answers, something special will happen. Jane will be nodding and saying, "Yup, that's me!"

Warning:

Do not change their words or add your own meanings to make them sound better; use their exact words.

Take a look at the side of this truck for a moving company:

Sounds real, right? Can you "feel" the words? You can tell it came from a real customer, not a committee or copywriter.

So, stop here and buy a coffee or beer for some past clients you've helped or that "person" you think would be your ideal client. Use the five questions, then listen back to the conversation and write it down.

Core 3: What are you really selling?

Let's build your "Three-Story Message" that you can use in your messaging to attract your ideal client.

Stop reading for a moment and go get a pen, paper, or whatever you use to write down your thoughts. Ready?

I wasn't kidding, go get a pen and paper, please. Set the timer on your smartphone to five minutes and turn off all notifications. We are going to do three five-minute sprints.

The upside sprint (five minutes)

Just go ahead and make a list of all the benefits your clients will get from your product or service. Don't overthink it, just keep going. Write for the whole five minutes, and don't prejudge or edit the list until you're done. Think of it as a brainstorming exercise with full intensity, and don't let your pen stop.

The downside sprint (five minutes)

Start the timer again and give yourself five minutes to write down all the reasons why your ideal prospect would not work with you or buy from you. Again, write fearlessly for the whole five minutes, and don't prejudge or edit the list until you're done.

The excuses sprint (five minutes)

And finally, make a list of all the possible reasons you can think of why they haven't already solved the problem before crossing paths with you.

Go, go, go.

Let's look at how these three sprints looked for me—a sales coach for small businesses, freelancers, and coaches who have to sell, even when selling isn't their thing.

The upside list (all the key benefits):

♦ Sell without having to come off as pushy or manipulative.

♦ Sell with a sense of powerful calmness and confidence.

♦ Weed out the winners from the losers and don't get tricked by tire-kickers and cheapskates.

♦ Sell without having to pretend to be someone else.

The downside list (head trash keeping the prospect stuck):

♦ They curl up with anxiety at the thought of promoting or pitching to strangers—it feels like they're selling out who they are as a professional.

♦ Not a born seller—more of an introvert.

♦ Hate networking.

♦ The phone feels like a cactus. Cold-calling sounds like hell.

♦ Hate the idea of being rejected all the time.

Excuses (why they haven't solved the problem yet):

♦ My business is different than most; selling doesn't work.

♦ My clients are different; they don't like to be "sold to."

♦ I avoided selling my whole life, it's just not who I am.

♦ I don't have time for a month-long workshop to learn to sell.

Frankensteining the three 5-minute sprints

The answers you wrote down for the three 5-minute sprint exercises will now be the building blocks for your "three-story" message.

Take the three lists and then pick one entry to build your "three-story" message.

> How to [positive outcome]
>
> Without [negative reasons]
>
> Even if [excuses]

Again, using my example, here is how it might look:

> How to [sell calmly and confidently]
>
> Without [having to be pushy or pretending to be someone you're not]
>
> Even if [you avoided selling your whole life]

> How to [sell with confidence]
>
> Without [being sleazy or manipulative]
>
> Even if [you're not a back-slapping extrovert and hate talking to strangers]

The power of your "three-story" message

So, if someone asked me what I do professionally, I'd now be able to use this "three-story" framework to create a casual talk-track:

> "You know how some people get anxious about selling because it can come off as sleazy or manipulative? Well, I've come up with a fix for that and written a book about it. Ironically, it isn't about selling more. It's about selling less."

And then I'd just shut up and let that sit with them. I can tell right away if they are my audience by how interested they are. "Hmm, that sounds like me," or "What do you mean you are selling less?" Otherwise, I will know it didn't work because they will say something like "Nice" or "Cool," and I'll know right away they're not my audience.

Follow this simple framework to supercharge all your messaging, regardless of the platform—LinkedIn, Facebook, or even a cocktail party conversation. If I were writing a sales letter or ad, I could use this to follow the same flow:

1. Call out the audience you're talking to.

2. Highlight a dominant pain.

3. Twist the knife.

4. Tell them you have a solution (don't tell them what it is; the details are not relevant or appropriate at this point).

5. Invite them to respond if they want to know more about how you can help them.

It's that simple and easy.

Core 4: Creating your own unique mechanism

This is such a humdinger of a concept that once I saw it, I couldn't unsee it.

I first learned about a unique mechanism when I invested in the most expensive book in my library, *Breakthrough Advertising* by Eugene Schwarz, published in 1973, which I've seen on Amazon for over $800. Todd Brown should also be praised for keeping the Unique Mechanism concept going. Brown is a brilliant marketer, and his E5 Method has helped business owners all over the world grow their businesses in amazing ways. This idea is a big part of his method.

Creating a unique mechanism for whatever it is you sell is very powerful. Marketers often use something called "mechanisms" to make old products appear new and fresh. It's also a way to differentiate the product from competitors. For example, when it comes to mattresses, each one says that it has a special technology inside that makes it more comfortable than the others.

♦   TempurPedic has "SmartClimate" technology

♦   Serta has "Cool Twist" technology

♦   Purple has "Gel-Grid" technology

SmartClimate, Cool Twist, and Gel-Grid are all ways that mattress copywriters have come up with to make their product stand out from others. And, from a marketing point of view, being unique is clearly very valuable.

If you see words in "quotes" followed by the words technique, system, process, or technology, you are probably looking at a mechanism. You've seen lots of unique mechanisms around but probably didn't notice them:

♦   The P90X (muscle confusion technology)

♦   The Snuggie (a blanket with sleeves)

♦   George Foreman grill ("lean-mean-fat-reducing grilling machine")

Today's prospects are more skeptical than ever, and it's not enough to just promise the outcome or result you're selling. People are tired of overblown claims and "overnight miracles."

People want to know *how* that outcome is possible, and the Unique Mechanism answers that question in a way that makes you look very trustworthy and gives you ownership over the answer.

The unique mechanism cannot be a vague platitude like "we have better people" or "superior technology." Instead, it has to be a noun, or something you can name.

Let's go a little slower into this concept because it deserves it.

Unique mechanisms and commodity mechanisms

It's often easier to explain what a unique mechanism is by talking about its opposite, which is a commodity mechanism. In the real world, there are a lot of products and services that have what is called an "ordinary" or "commoditized" mechanism. It isn't unique to one brand or person, and it can be found in other products or services.

Calcium is a great example of an ordinary mechanism. Bottles of calcium are stacked on every shelf of every drugstore, under 20 different brands. With just one click on Amazon, you can find 300 options for calcium.

Let's imagine we got lazy and stuck a fancy pants name on this ordinary bottle and called it *Fortibone*. And your marketing said that if someone with osteoarthritis took two Fortibone pills every day, it would make their bones 30% stronger in less than 90 days. Then we told them the 500 mg of calcium in each pill is what makes Fortibone work like magic.

That's a commoditized mechanism that'll cost you a lot of money because any consumer can figure out it contains ordinary calcium—a dime-a-dozen commodity you can find in any drug store. The prospect then clicks over to Amazon and buys a bottle of 500 mg calcium for three dollars less than you can sell it as Fortibone. It's over, and you didn't even know you lost the sale. That's the danger of blending in with everyone else with a commoditized mechanism.

The challenge in this chapter is to come up with a unique way to make "all roads lead to you." This means you are the only one who can solve the big problem you solve because you know a secret way to do it.

There are thousands of sales books, but there is only one *(un)selling* book. And it is my one-of-a-kind technique, the Zero-Pressure Sales Sequence (ZPPS), which no one else on Earth can claim as their own.

So, all roads lead back to me. Salespeople can't get it from another sales trainer, or even from Elon Musk—unless he wants to make another ridiculous purchase and make me a *Godfather* offer I can't resist.

The "secret sauce" of your product or service is its unique mechanism. This is the system, process, framework, or method that makes your product or service truly unique. It's only available through you. Period.

The fitness industry is full of commodity mechanisms. For example, P90X was a very popular workout program in the 1990s, but it didn't work well until someone in the company came up with a unique method called "muscle confusion."

The muscle confusion theory says that you should train your body in different ways so that your muscles never get used to the training. This way, you would never "plateau" in your training, which can happen if you do the same workouts and weight training every day and week. That was their unique mechanism, and it exploded the dormant P90X to sell over five million units since its launch in 2004.

Another example of a unique mechanism is "Invisalign."

Once upon a time, people who wanted an orthodontist to straighten their teeth had no choice but to wear ugly metal braces. Metal braces do a good job of straightening teeth, but they're an ugly sight. Invisalign was the only way to get the same results as metal braces, without making it look like you had train tracks on your teeth.

Once you start looking, you begin to see unique mechanisms out in the wild.

Can you see how owning that process, steps, framework, or formula and giving it a name not only gives you more credibility, but if people search for it, all roads lead back to you?

A unique mechanism destroys the "apples to apple" comparison. We don't ever want them to say, "I can go and find this elsewhere."

A unique mechanism prevents the Google slap trigger. Because the reality is once you deploy your unique mechanism, if they go to Google, the only things they'll find are results that bring them back to you.

The power is not in the name. The power is in knowing how it works so we can explain why it can produce better results faster, easier, more consistently, or whatever is most important to your prospect. Don't get too caught up in the name's "spinning wheels." Spend more time being able to succinctly show why that thing you've named is able to deliver the results in a way that is superior.

Remember, we're naming the mechanism. If you are a chiropractor who helps people with back pain, "Lumbar Reactivation" would be a great name for what you do. Then you can educate and discuss why Lumbar Reactivation is a better alternative in a crowded market.

You see how powerful this could be?

First, you demonstrate understanding of their pain—You're suffering from low back pain and you've tried different methods—and then you educate:

"Did you know there is a new way to alleviate your lower back pain naturally without pain medication? It's very different from the common approach. This method uses what's called "Lumbar Reactivation.""

The name of the mechanism should be credible and not a gimmick. It should sound professional, and it could be read about in the *Harvard Business Review*. Someone credible could talk about it in a blog post or in a TED Talk.

Bad ones: Good ones:

♦   Income Explosion System   ♦   Cash Flow Compounding

♦   Big Potato Growth System   ♦   Lumbar Reactivation

♦   Back Pain Relief Protocol   ♦   Equity Reallocation

♦   Help. Heal. Happy Method   ♦   TripWire Activation

Here are the two steps to come up with a unique mechanism:

1.   Look at your competition.

♦   Do they have some kind of mechanism or way of doing things?

♦   What's good about it? What's bad? What's missing?

♦   What's negative about how they are delivering it?

♦   Does it solve just a symptom or a root cause?

2.   Interrogate your possible unique mechanism.

◆   What is my secret sauce, one-of-a kind process, or my intellectual property (IP)?

◆   Can you sketch it out in 20 seconds on a whiteboard?

◆   Can you give it a name?

◆   Why does it work?

◆   How does it work?

◆   Why is it different from others?

◆   What is faster, easier, safer, and more predictable?

◆   How did you come up with it?

◆   What changes for the customer when they use your unique mechanism?

◆   Why do you do it the way you do it?

◆   Is it in a certain order? Why?

◆   Why is not doing it in that order important?

◆   What happens if people skip steps or change the order?

◆   Why do you start with step one before step two?

This isn't pulling a rabbit and a fancy name out of the hat. I have a unique mechanism for (un)selling that I'll be explaining in the upcoming chapters. Here's a sneak peek.

The unique mechanism for (un)selling

The Product: (Un)selling

The Unique Mechanism: The Zero Pressure Sales Sequence

The Zero Pressure Sales Sequence

1 Illumination Hook
2 Painless Prospecting
3 Rapid Triage
4 Diagnosis
5 Follow-up

U.

CHAPTER SUMMARY

Congrats! You just finished the hardest chapter. Building your "Core Four" gives you noise-canceling clarity on four vital questions:

1.   What type of client do you love and loathe?

2.   Where does it hurt?

3.   What are you really selling?

4.   What makes you genuinely different beyond just claiming to be different?

We then went deep into each piece of the puzzle:

The Core Four

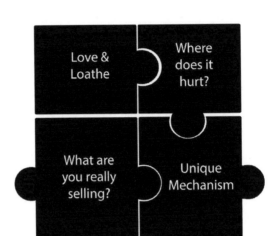

Core 1: Who do you love? Who do you loathe?

You love people who need your solution to solve a problem they may or may not be aware of. You loathe the types of people you want to avoid, ban, and never let into your life.

Core 2: What is the problem and pain you solve?

This is not about benefits or features, and it is not just about problems. You need to dig deeper and look for the pain that these problems cause and the cost of not doing anything about them. We also talked about why you shouldn't be tempted to choose four to five different problems because you think they are all important.

You should have one problem you lead with in your messaging. Just one. Not two, not three.

Core 3: What are you really selling?

People don't buy what you're selling; they buy how it makes them feel and the outcome. Once we could say what we were really selling in a compelling way, I showed you a simple framework called the "Three-Story Message" that you can use in all your sales and marketing efforts to keep things consistent.

Core 4: Why should someone buy from you instead of someone else?

The unique mechanism is a fancy name for "how" you solve the problem for your ideal client. It should feel like your secret sauce and your IP. Because you did the work, you probably already have a good idea of how to build a unique system that brings all roads back to you.

EXERCISES

You already did a lot of work within the chapter as we moved along, so you deserve a break and there aren't any end-of-chapter exercises.

PART

3

the (un)veiling

8

The Cure for Sales Anxiety

Fish don't know they're in water. If you tried to explain it to a fish, they'd say, "Water? What's water?" Fish don't know they're in water because it has always been around them. Fish don't know what they don't know.

Like fish, salespeople don't pay attention to what's really going on around them, and spend most of their days aimlessly swimming around and treading water in dangerous places.

I should know. I swam those cold waters for over a decade and let prospects yank my chain and throw me around like a human piñata. They pressed me for as much free information as they could get and, because I wanted to look "smart," I gave them all my advice without asking for anything in return.

I believed they could really "think it over" even though I knew deep down once they left the room, they wouldn't think of me again. Prospects purposely withheld information, and I was too chickenshit to challenge them because I was afraid to hear no. I would rather keep the mood light and friendly than ask a hard question. Prospects ignored and ghosted me, but I kept chasing them, and with every desperate "just circling back" email I sent, a little piece of me died inside.

I was no different than the poor fish. I was swimming in a red ocean, completely lost.

To change things, I developed the unique mechanism I debuted at the end of the last chapter: the Zero Pressure Sales Sequence (ZPSS), the repeatable sales process that took me eight years to perfect. ZPSS came about because I was shockingly unaware of the environment around me every day. I was just like the poor fish that doesn't even know it's in water every day of its life.

ZPSS is a five-step, low-pressure, low-commitment selling process where the only purpose of each stage is to "sell" the next stage and not your product or service. ZPSS will never come off like you're begging, pleading, or trying to get their money, because you are absolutely *not* doing that. In fact, you are doing the opposite of just about every salesperson they've interacted with in the past—you're (un)selling them at each and every step.

ZPSS lowers sales resistance, creates a safe space for the truth, and improves buyer receptivity to make selling more predictable and comfortable for everyone.

Modus operandi

Modus operandi (MO) is a person's usual way of doing things in a certain situation. You've likely heard the term used on TV crime shows, as it usually applies to the unsavory actions of the criminals. Here's how I see the sad state of MOs between the buyer and the seller.

The prospect's MO

I call the shots. I don't owe salespeople anything. I can't be upfront and honest with them because they'll use it against me. So it's OK to tell little white lies, mislead, and withhold information and my real intentions. They're just salespeople, right? Being lied to comes with the job; they'll get over it.

I have to call the shots because if I don't, they'll back me into a corner and take my money. I get to ask the questions. When I say, "Jump," I know the seller will ask, "How high?" because they want my money. And if they don't do what I ask or play by my rules, I'll go elsewhere. They're a dime a dozen.

The (un)seller's MO

The prospect is the one who has the problem. I'm the one holding the solution. They don't get to call the shots. They should feel lucky they even crossed paths with me today. The solution I have is the prize.

They want their problem fixed more than I want their money. I've seen and solved this problem hundreds of times before. Time is the one thing in life I can't get back, so I need to be stingy with it, because 80% of people I speak to won't fit my world, and that's OK. I'm not for everyone.

My job is to get to the truth. And if a prospect's answer is no, I want it as fast as humanly possible. I need to get rid of people quickly because I don't have time to help everyone, even if I wanted to. It's not my job to convince them; it's their job to convince me. The only way I can do that is by asking the right questions. I can only control my behaviors, not the outcomes.

Mise en place

One of my good friends is a brilliant chef. I was watching him cook along with 10 people who were watching his every move, and he felt no pressure. When I asked him how it all looked so calm and easy, he said three French words to me: *"mise en place."*

I looked back, perplexed, and said, "Huh?"

"Mise en place," he said. "It's the only French I know, but it means 'everything in its place.'" He went on to explain that it means all the preparation is done before he arrives at my house and long before any of the cooking begins.

Professional chefs use *mise en place* to organize and prepare the ingredients. Chefs do not start cooking until everything is in its place. This allows chefs to appear calm and in command—even when we're all watching their every move and the night brings unexpected issues.

Salespeople must exercise the same level of discipline and practice *mise en place* before they begin prospecting at random. It's all about planning ahead of time to avoid the chaos that can accompany a sales experience.

In the chapters ahead, we'll explore the five stages of the Zero Pressure Sales Sequence (ZPSS). It will be very well organized, free of coercion, and will not involve any trickery to force the prospect to buy against their will.

Just a few points from 30,000 feet before we zoom inside the Zero Pressure Sales Sequence.

Shift from a "qualifying" to a "disqualifying" mindset

A "qualifying" sales style, which is most often taught in sales training, is all about exaggerating fake rapport, asking a few weak questions, and having a "seeking the sale at all costs" mindset, which means doing whatever it takes to convince and persuade prospects and pull them into your side of the argument.

A "disqualifying" sales style is more sophisticated and subtly pushes the prospect away from your solution. By design, it also implies you stress-test the truth, have the courage to discuss why some people don't buy from you, and present alternatives to your solution to the prospect.

You are constantly testing the prospect's true interest and intent by doing this and, ironically, the more subtly you push them, the more they dig in and use their own words to defend their position, which is really your position.

Now, notice that I said "subtly"—it's not rudely rejecting or turning away prospects (unless they deserve it). The (un)selling is about challenging them and making them see things differently, so that the needle moves quickly in one of two directions: yes or no. Since you are detached from the outcome, either one is perfectly acceptable because with the (un)selling protocol, your number one job is to always get to the truth.

Consider how confident you will appear if you're the first to raise common objections and potential alternatives to your solution. It is known as "front-loading," and it gives you a lot of credibility and status.

In other words, you let the prospect sell themselves.

A sales strategy of "going for no" has two powerful benefits:

1. You get to the truth faster and don't waste time with people who were never interested in buying to begin with.
2. You close deals faster because you cut through the noise and had the guts to bring up all the big issues early on.

The Zero Pressure Sales Sequence (ZPSS) consists of only five stages, as opposed to 12 or 20 steps that will only add to the chaos and pressure.

Because the entire purpose of ZPSS is to make selling feel more comfortable and less complicated, it's a very simple step-by-step system.

In the following chapters, I will explain each of the five stages in detail, and provide you with numerous examples and frameworks to help you begin applying it in your own world.

Here's a reminder of what it looks like if you want to get it tattooed on the inside of your eyelids, like I did.

The Zero Pressure Sales Sequence

BONUS

Bonus time! I've made a video just for you that explains how to reduce sales pressure and dives into the destructive concept of "The Yes Mess."

You can watch it here:

www.kevincasey.ca/theyesmess or simply scan the QR code.

9

The Illumination Hook

As I mentioned in the foreword (you read my mom's blatant praise, right?), at the time of writing this book, my mom is 87 years old and lives in a wonderful retirement community, where she can play bridge and socialize with many friends without having to worry about housekeeping.

While visiting recently, I noticed an elderly gentleman in a car who was having difficulty getting out. I approached and extended my hand, and he immediately smiled, clearly embarrassed, and was able to rise and stand. He told me his knees were bad because he'd been a catcher in baseball for 30 years, and the arthritis in his wrist had gotten worse in the last few years, making it difficult to grip hard enough to pull himself out of the car. He loved the freedom of driving to meet his old pals for coffee and told me he feared his son would soon take away his car keys.

He thanked me, but I couldn't forget this moment. It could easily be my mom who could face the same challenge. Years ago, I saw an infomercial that reminded me of this exact situation and, after some Googling, I found it: a product called the "Car Cane." When considering the best way to present the product or service you're selling, infomercials are powerful models to emulate. Everything you sell starts with a big problem you can solve, and that will help someone do something better. As David Ogilvy says, "When you advertise fire extinguishers, open with the fire."

When I think about Mr Fox and the Car Cane, it looks like this:

Who: Senior citizens with physical restrictions who still drive.

The Job: Getting in and out of their car.

The Before: Struggling to pull themselves out and trying to stand. Hoping someone is around to give them help.

The Pain: Slip, fall, and get hurt (physical); loss of independence and dignity (emotional).

The After: Get out of the car safely and easily; reclaim your independence.

Selling is about creating a "before and after" picture for your prospect.

Note: In case you were curious, I happily bought the Car Cane for Mr Fox and, yes, it worked just fine. Unlike that damn Ab Roller I purchased from an infomercial that was a colossal flop.

The cure for a noisy world

Your prospect's world is noisy. Five Zoom calls, 321 unopened emails, 18 texts from the kids. Sneaking a peek at TikTok. Your prospects are being bombarded from every direction. Making more noise won't catch their attention, and talking about your product, your company, and your awards is like spraying a can of repellent.

The cure is the "Illumination Hook."

The Illumination Hook isn't a closing technique; it's an *opening* technique. A compact collection of words or a striking visual that grabs the prospect's attention in such a way they can't unsee or unhear it—creating an itch that must be scratched by the prospect. It can't sound like a sales pitch or a bunch of hype, because that stuff is ignored by our prospect's skeptical brain.

Illumination hooks are most effective when constructed in a "neutral" position, rather than leading the witness. You drop the hook, lean back, and let the chips fall where they may.

Most people are way too polite to let you know your hook was boring, and it's easier to just brush you off. It might sound like this:

- ◆   "Oh, that's nice."
- ◆   "Oh, cool."
- ◆   "Right."

And if you drop a powerful hook, don't be alarmed if the prospect's response sounds like one of these:

- ◆   "Huh?"
- ◆   "What do you mean by that?"
- ◆   "How do you do that?"
- ◆   "Seriously?"

Curiosity is one of the most important tools you will ever have, and it's what makes the most effective illumination hooks work so well.

The Netflix effect

Consider the "Netflix effect" to show how powerful intrigue and curiosity can be, when earning the attention of the prospect.

Think about the last 30 seconds of your favorite Netflix show. Your eyes are tired, and you're ready to go to sleep. But the show's creators have other plans for you. They drop the cliffhanger, which is Hollywood's version of the Illumination Hook.

Then, all of a sudden, you're wide awake, like you just chugged three cans of Red Bull.

You pick up the remote, hit "next episode" and you're back in the game, even though you were fighting sleep just a few minutes ago.

Illumination hooks are like cliffhangers—they create good tension, and tension creates attention. That's the one-two punch you're looking to replicate when building your hook.

To make that moment happen, you have to say something so compelling, surprising, unusual, or interesting that the prospect stops in their tracks and forgets everything they were doing in the moment.

People who are already nervous about selling frequently argue with me about the idea of intentionally creating tension, because they see tension as something to avoid. But this is a different kind of tension; this is "good tension."

Creating this kind of tension will set you apart from other salespeople who start off boring and long-winded and, because you sound different and start things off in such a captivating way, it will actually relieve your anxiety rather than make it worse.

Repeat after me: *good tension gets attention.*

The Illumination Hook has a rhythm and, when it's put together right, flows like this:

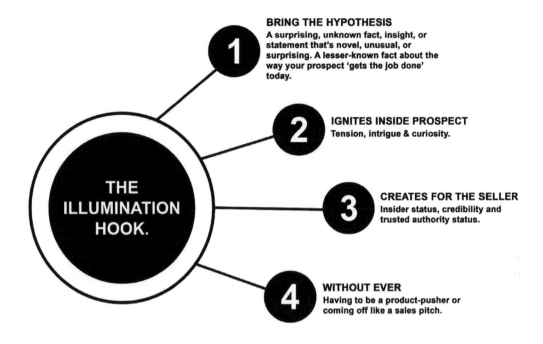

BRING THE HYPOTHESIS
A surprising, unknown fact, insight, or statement that's novel, unusual, or surprising. A lesser-known fact about the way your prospect 'gets the job done' today.

IGNITES INSIDE PROSPECT
Tension, intrigue & curiosity.

CREATES FOR THE SELLER
Insider status, credibility and trusted authority status.

WITHOUT EVER
Having to be a product-pusher or coming off like a sales pitch.

THE ILLUMINATION HOOK.

Curiosity: Your sales superpower

When you arrive at work on Monday, your coworker begins telling you about their weekend adventure. They mention swimming with dolphins, exploring hidden caves, and discovering this treasure map in an old chest.

But then they pause and say, "I'll tell you the rest later."

You're left with an unsatisfied curiosity because you want to know how their thrilling adventure ends. You cannot help but be curious, and you stop them from leaving because you need to hear the missing part of the story now, not later.

According to George Loewenstein, a professor at Carnegie Mellon University, "Curiosity is the gap between what your prospect currently knows and what they would love to know." This gap leaves prospects craving more. So the real challenge here is to come up with a hook that speaks to whatever problem in their world is causing them to stare at the ceiling in the middle of the night.

When done correctly, it joins the secret conversation going on in their mind, and they will feel compelled to let you into their world.

The origin of hooks

The best hooks often come from:

◆ A shocking statistic (e.g., a new regulatory change, a new piece of research)

◆ A contrarian claim (e.g., Buckley's: It Tastes Awful and It Works)

◆ An image, a meme, or a video that strikes at this "inner pain and secret"

Remember, the Illumination Hook has one job: To kick-start a conversation under imperfect conditions. Consider the hooks I've used throughout this book. It would be a lot duller if I just launched into the ideas without stories and anecdotes to pique your curiosity and inspire you to keep reading, right?

Those imperfect conditions could be a cold call, a cold email, a direct mail piece, or showing up in a boardroom to meet a prospect who just spilled coffee on their crotch 30 seconds before you showed up and is in a foul mood.

The Illumination Hook's job is to create tension, intrigue, and get them to question how they are getting the job done today without you.

Hooks are also great ways to disqualify prospects who aren't intellectually curious or maybe simply aren't ready to deal with the problem. If you land "the right hook" and the prospect doesn't show any emotion, that's a clear sign the problem you solve isn't itching their brain enough and you should move on.

Remember, time is the one thing in life you can't get back. Don't waste your time. Move on.

Curiosity and contrast: the Batman and Robin of the sales world

When these two superheroes, curiosity and contrast, are combined, it is like pouring gasoline on a smoldering fire.

Here's an example. If you walk for more than 15 minutes in any city, you'll come across an abandoned building or property. It hardly catches your attention. But one time I came across a picture of a particular abandoned building and etched on the side of the building like graffiti were the words:

> "Houses stand empty while homelessness grows. Who makes the profit? Somebody knows!"

You can't ignore it, so you read it, and then you feel it. The "good" tension.

Why is this building empty? (Contrast)

Why am I angry about it? (Contrast)

Someone knows why, but who? (Curiosity)

If they can make you feel that way in just 12 words, imagine how quickly you can make your prospect feel something about the problem you solve.

> Warning:
>
> PowerPoint decks, ROI statements, case studies, and company bios are not emotional; they are very logical.
>
> These types of "logic drops" won't make them feel anything but numb.
>
> They have no place in constructing your Illumination Hook.

Remember, you're sifting, not selling

I know I sound like a broken record, but I will say it again: it is always about seeking the truth rather than the sale.

This is such a fundamental principle of (un)selling that it will be mentioned several times again before you reach the end of this book.

The four-filter test

Like any good inspection process before it's certified, the Illumination Hook should pass a four-way test before it ever earns the right to be tested in the real world:

1. The hook makes the prospect the hero, with little or no mention of you.

2. It's emotional (makes them feel) not logical (makes them think).

3. It's positioned against the status quo; it addresses how they're getting the job done today.

4. It needs to be neutral and less like a product-pitch that is simply leading the witness.

Let's quickly cover each of these four filters:

Filter #1: Make the prospect the hero, not your product

Again, it may seem obvious, but many salespeople start off their conversation with a prospect by making it all about them and their company.

When people are nervous about selling, lack a plan, and are unsure what to say next, the easiest thing to do is read from a brochure with 30 bullet points or bring a PowerPoint slide deck.

It's not as simple as you might think to take a step back and say, "OK. Now, I am not going to talk about my product; instead, here's a hypothesis you have never heard before. Please let me know if you want to know more, or not."

Filter #2: Trigger emotionally, not intellectually

Imagine your brain is like a big playground, and the limbic brain is the super cool, emotion-driven section of that playground. When a salesperson wants to stimulate the limbic brain, it's like they're trying to get the fun and excitement going.

You know how sometimes you just feel super excited or really curious to know more? That's the limbic brain doing its thing. It's in charge of all those feelings and emotions that make you go, "Wow, I need that!" or "I need to know more!"

Remember the Loss Aversion theory from Part 1? The theory is a fancy way of saying that people dislike losing things more than they enjoy gaining them.

Have you ever seen a product with a "limited-time offer"? That loss aversion is at work because they inform the customer that a special price is only available for a limited time. This creates a fear of missing out on the lower price, and the customer may feel compelled to place a larger order to avoid losing the discounted rate.

Pain, anxiety, and the fear of missing out (FOMO) are all important ingredients to include in your Illumination Hook, whether you are selling the latest smartphone or something as mundane as insurance.

Filter #3: Attack the status quo, not your competitor

Brace yourself.

HubSpot, Salesforce, and many other independent research studies consistently show that in 60% of all sales situations, the prospect ends up "doing nothing" because it's safer to stick with the devil you know than to try something new.

Your biggest enemy isn't your competitor; it's getting people to go against the status quo.

I'll share a personal example of sticking with the status quo. I love my old sneakers. These sneakers have been with me through thick and thin and in seven different countries on vacations over the past six years. The soles are worn out, and there's more support in a beach sandal.

My wife cannot stand looking at these sneakers any longer, and she knows I'm not going to throw them away, so she takes charge and surprises me with a new pair out of the blue. When I opened the box, the new sneakers had innovative cushioning and superior arch support, and when I tried them on, it felt like I was walking on pillows compared to my old sneakers.

Despite the undeniable allure of the new sneakers, I had this pit in my stomach. I despise the idea of breaking in a new pair of sneakers because it's always been a painful process for me. The idea of enduring blisters and sore feet is daunting.

Plus, I've grown attached to my "old kicks," and parting ways with them felt like letting go of a faithful companion.

So, I kept wearing my old ones. The discomfort from the worn-out sneakers wasn't quite intolerable enough to warrant the switch.

I still wear those worn-out sneakers, occasionally reminiscing about the adventures we continue to enjoy together, just to irritate my wife. The new sneakers remain an unexplored possibility in the closet.

This story illustrates how, even when presented with a better option, people may choose to stick with what they know. The pain of staying with the old sneakers wasn't significant enough to drive me towards change. The fear of the unknown and the discomfort of breaking in new sneakers outweighed the potential benefits they offered.

It's a classic case of "good enoughs," which means things are not perfect, but they're also not so bad I need to change them. A lot of people have a case of the "good enoughs" and you can't pretend it doesn't exist.

Your Illumination Hook must address the cost of inaction because, if that doesn't happen, it's impossible to shake up the status quo.

Filter #4: It needs to be neutral and less like a product pitch that's leading the witness

Messages about saving time or money are everywhere.

It won't trigger an emotional bone in the prospect's brain because they've heard and seen it all before. Prospects are tone deaf to such common claims.

So, leave the "save time and money" claims to Warren Buffet's big fat wallet as he hammers away with GEICO's "Fifteen minutes could save you 15 percent or more."

You and I, as small businesses, can't afford to spend mountains of cash like GEICO, or show up as boring as the last 33 salespeople. Lazy "save time and money" hooks will make prospects treat you like that skip button that pops up when you're watching a YouTube video. But, unlike the skip button, you won't even get the full 15 seconds.

You need to find the hook; it won't find you. A great hook will hide from you. You've got to dig to find it. A great copywriter from the UK named Dave Harland made me laugh with this funny example of looking for something until you find it. It takes some effort, and chances are it took a while to find the right name for this band.

~~Ice Cold King Prawns~~

~~Fridge Cool Scotch Egg~~

~~Quite Warm Chicken Soup~~

~~Nuclear Lamb Vindaloo~~

Red Hot Chili Peppers

It's not brain surgery, but we do need to talk about the brain

Prospects are not buyers. Buyers are not prospects. You need to figure out which bucket people are in, so you know what to say and do next.

We won't go all deep like Einstein about sales psychology, but we do need to talk about the brain in the simplest terms when it comes to selling in a more comfortable way. People often call the limbic brain the "croc" or "old brain." This is where emotions live, like the "fight, flight, or freeze" response when you see a grizzly bear in your backyard or the mall kiosk savage waiting to sell you a miracle sea scrub to make you look young again.

The neocortex is at the front of the brain—think of this part as the "Spock" brain, which interprets everything in a logical way—very intellectual and non-emotional.

So you need to be clear in any selling situation: are you dealing with either a prospect or a buyer?

Prospects aren't buyers

You need to treat prospects and buyers very differently, which means right out of the gate you need to make a "best guess" on where the other person is on the buyer's journey.

Are they in the "prospect" bucket, which happens to be early in the buyer journey? If so, you need to tickle the limbic brain with curiosity, contrast, and intrigue. Are they a buyer in the latter stages of the buyer's journey? Now you can focus on the logical stuff that the neocortex craves through ROI, case studies, demos, and testimonials.

Most sales scripts and really bad illumination hooks focus on "logical" neocortex messaging when prospects are early in the buying process. This is the wrong time to use it, and it will flop. Logic-based messages, like dropping client names, testimonials, and case studies only speak to the neocortex of the brain.

If you start with logic with a prospect, you'll fail to get them to feel anything, and you won't get a second meeting. This explains why so many salespeople get ghosted or ignored: they think using logic will earn them an invite when it's more like a repellant.

Supercharging your message to appeal to the limbic brain is the only way to turn prospects into buyers.

Below is a little diagram of the "Buyer Journey." Keep this in mind at all times so you can figure out where the prospect is on the continuum and treat them accordingly.

The buyer journey

Where is your prospect when you enter their world?

Belal Batrawy deserves credit for introducing me to the Buyer's Journey in 2021. Knowing how this works has saved me a lot of time and energy, and I appreciate him sharing this information, which is why I consider him to be one of the top sales voices on LinkedIn.

> **Unaware → Aware → Consideration → Evaluation → Decision**

Unaware: No logic, no selling, 100% provocation

All you should do is share something new, unusual, unexpected, or even a hypothesis about how they're getting the job done today. For example, you could let them know about big changes in the industry their peers are facing and what the best companies are doing to deal with those changes. It's a give, give, give moment.

Aware: Still don't sell

Now you're attacking the status quo by telling them that these industry changes are so big that doing things the old way will become dangerous.

Consideration: Yep, still don't sell

You've shown them the world is changing, so now you need to figure out what those changes mean for their business. It's all about impact.

Evaluation: OK, OK, now you can sell

Unveil the new world view for the prospect. Tell them the Promised

Land is possible and show them how other customers got there and how they can, too.

Decision

We use the "old, limbic brain" to make emotional decisions first, and then the "new, neocortex brain" to make logical decisions to justify our purchases. This is where you use ROI and fancy spreadsheets to explain why they should buy from you.

That's how you match the sales process to the buyer's journey.

If I had known this in 2012, I would have saved a lot of time, money, and energy because, back then I treated everyone as if they were buyers, which you now know is not the case.

Fun ways to brainstorm your illumination hook

The Flip: Flipping a problem on its head. What is one thing that's been accepted in your industry as a best practice that you can prove to be wrong?

Fear of Loss: Lead with a threat, warning, or pain. We do all things to either avoid pain or gain pleasure, but it turns out humans will do a lot more to avoid pain than gain pleasure.

Shock and Awe: A shocking or surprising fact. A new statistic or trend that changes everything. A new rule or a way of doing things that not many people know about that you came up with to solve the problem.

FOMO: How did he get a better lawn than me? How did he get a better mortgage rate? Why did he get a grant from the government?

People—especially business owners—hate the idea of their competitors getting an unfair advantage or edge. FOMO is one of my favorite ways to get prospects interested, especially business owners who don't like the idea of someone in their space getting more than them.

Remember the feeling of being the last kid picked in gym class? Nobody wants to be last—it's a universal fear.

Great hooks in the wild

Enough with the theory, let's get into some real-world examples of great hooks.

Example 1: Atoms

Atoms is a new shoe brand that came out in a market that was already full of shoes. It would be easy to be just another vanilla scoop in a world full of vanilla scoops. But these folks created an illumination hook that appealed to a very specific target profile: creatives.

To come up with their hook, they took a mostly unknown fact and used it to build a spectacular brand.

Here it is:

The company bet everything on a scientific fact about everyone's feet that the other shoe companies didn't want to share with the rest of us.

And here's the zinger:

Seventy percent of people have *at least a quarter-size difference in their two feet*, and more than seven percent have a half-size discrepancy. This revelation creates an itch that must be scratched.

You look down at your feet and go:

◆ Huh?

◆ Are both my feet the same size?

◆ Is that why my left foot always cramps?

◆ I've got to know more

◆ I'm a size 10… hmm… or am I?

Now that's the making of a great hook, right?

I actually put Atoms to the test by ordering a pair. Atoms sent me three sizes: 10, 10.25, and 10.5, plus socks.

I tried them on.

Well, whaddya know, I'm one of the 70 percent of people with a quarter-size difference. My left foot was 10.25 and my right foot was a 10.

So, think about how hard the Atoms team had to work to find this truth and go against the industry norm to stand out from the crowd. What's the villain you're fighting against for your prospect that no one else is?

Hook angle: An ugly secret the big shoemakers are keeping from us

Example 2: Small business accountants

Business owners don't wake up with an accounting problem. Someone is looking after the books and the filing of taxes. But you know what business owners *do* care about? Other business owners like them, who are getting an unfair advantage or edge.

So when I got this email from a stranger, it tickled my limbic brain, and yes, it was worth the conversation.

Cold email example (using FOMO):

> Kevin,
>
> Tax season deadline is March 28th. How do you know your accountant is leveraging every opportunity in tax law to get you cash back in your pocket? Canadian small business owners are using a little-known tax method to get back $18-$25K on average. I don't charge a fee unless you make at least $10K.
>
> Worth a convo?

Example 3: HR recruitment

Hook origin: A unique, lesser-known process

A warm email example:

> Kevin,
>
> How are you standing out in a sea of résumés and cover letters?
>
> Sam used my method to land 11 interviews in two months and accepted an offer worth $27,837 more than his previous job. It involved a three-step process of creating a work sample that shows your expertise in a very unique way.
>
> You can take a peek here (link).
>
> Worth exploring?

Example 4: Plumber

Hook: Fear/pain plus a unique mechanism

Up-Sell Conversation:

> Plumber: Kim, have you heard of non-invasive leak detection? (Illumination question).
>
> Kim: What's that?
>
> Plumber: I don't know if this is the case for you, but a leaking faucet can sometimes cause more leaks, which can damage your walls, floors, cabinets, and other things. A non-invasive leak detection method finds the source of leaks so that you can limit the damage to your home.
>
> Kim: How do I get my leak tested?

Opening created.

Illumination questions make people scratch their heads and think, "Hmm, I'm not sure."

Example 5: Gas stations (a dime a dozen)

Hook: Fear of loss.

Texaco paid legendary copywriter Elmer Wheeler $5,000 in the 1930s for these seven simple words:

"Is your oil at the proper level?"

This Illumination Hook delivered over a million dollars in the first week to Texaco. You're probably thinking Elmer should have worked for a percentage of sales, right?

This is a great example of creating a problem that people didn't even know they had.

Here's where the tension is created in the prospect's head:

♦ Low oil = ruined engine + costly repair
♦ Low oil = my teen + stranded

Your job with the Illumination Hook is to shine a light on problems or missed opportunities.

Example 6: Sneakers

Hook: Unique method + FOMO

True story: A typical store probably has more than 125 different styles of shoes. Now, let's say you're a salesperson in that store, trying to sell sneakers. Where do you start?

Here's one way. My daughter was a competitive tennis player when she was in her early teens. She didn't have a sneaker problem, or so I thought. While Olivia and I were waiting between games in a mall, we entered a sports store and were astounded by the wall of sneakers that seemed to go on forever. If the salesperson had just walked up and asked, "Can I help you?" like 99% of salespeople do, I would have said, "No, thanks, I'm just looking."

This salesperson did something very different. She dropped a remarkable Illumination Hook. Here's how it unfolded:

First, the simple rapport part of the interaction. "Are you here competing at the National Tournament?"

Then she said something that was such a pattern interruption and so unexpected, I couldn't unhear it. "Have you ever had a gait test to measure the way your daughter moves?"

In a millisecond, my emotional brain reacts: Huh? What's a gait test? Why haven't I heard of it? Did the other kids in the tournament get the gait test? Am I a bad dad for not having a gait test done?

The next thing you know, Olivia is running on a treadmill in the back of the store while 11 cameras record the length of her stride from every angle and how her foot lands after each stride. Two minutes later, the salesperson plays back some of the video to show Olivia's landing position and pronation angle, as well as why a certain type of sneaker is best to prevent future injuries.

And, you guessed it, the sneaker she was wearing wasn't right for the way her body moved. The gait test was an all-in-one unique mechanism and illumination hook.

The salesperson knew something I didn't know, so she used FOMO as a way to get my attention, and painted a picture of what the cost of doing nothing would be without being forceful.

The saleswoman never had to make a pitch or try to convince me of anything. My inner voice and worries about Olivia getting hurt did all the selling for her.

She never once talked about deals, limited time price specials, or loyalty cards. She acted like a trusted advisor, not a salesperson. I left with $180 less in my bank account but felt like a good dad for taking action.

CHAPTER SUMMARY

♦ The illumination questions are a conversation-starter, not a sales-closer.

♦ Illumination questions are aimed at provoking, not closing.

♦ It's an incremental step—an opening move—not a sleazy closing trick.

♦ Coming up with the right Illumination Hook isn't easy; it's trial and error, but there are several areas to build one around: FOMO, Contrast, Novel Idea, and Unique Mechanisms.

♦ Always make the prospect the focus of the conversation, and use curiosity and contrast to elicit an emotional response.

♦ People buy emotionally and then justify their purchases with logic.

EXERCISE

Build your illumination hook

This is an exercise to help you start the process of finding your Illumination Hook, which can be difficult when you're staring at a blank screen.

The task: set the timer to 20 minutes.

1. What's tormenting your market?

2. What's the "villain" your product or service fights against?

CHAPTER 9

For the first 10 minutes:

Go to Amazon reviews, tech reviews, and private Facebook groups and write down *the exact language people are using around frustrations or pains.*

Don't interpret the language, use the actual words people use. "I feel like I'm locked in shackles" is not the same as "less contractual obligations." Think five-cent words, not fancy, forgettable $50 words that impress no one.

For the second 10 minutes:

How can you defend your prospects against these villains?

Stumped?

Here are a few kick-starters:

TESLA

Villain: Gas-guzzling, antiquated technology.

SLACK

Villain: Inbox chaos inside the company.

SOUTHWEST AIRLINES

Villain: Nickel-and-diming passengers.

This three-part template should help you with this challenge.

1. What's the villain you stand against?

2. What stinks about how your prospect is getting it done now?

3. What do they not know—that you know—that will make it less painful?

✘ No mention of your product or solution. ✘

Curiosity is your secret weapon in sales, and the "illumination hook" is your ticket to cutting through the clutter in your prospects' world.

If you're eager to dive deeper than this chapter, check out this video on crafting attention-grabbing hooks that halt people in their tracks.

Watch it here:

www.kevincasey.ca/thehook or simply scan the QR code.

10

Painless Prospecting

The Zero Pressure Sales Sequence

Imagine this scenario: you're on day one of your vacation, chilling poolside and finally getting a chance to crack open a book and sip on a mojito.

You open the book. Suddenly, a stranger taps you on the shoulder and says, "Hey, how's it going? How are you feeling? Is your day going OK?" Awkward, right? There's no context to the conversation, just a rude interruption. You secretly think, "What the fuck does this person want? I'm on vacation. Pick someone else."

Prospecting can feel awkward when done poorly, and for years I felt like the guy tapping on people's shoulders and getting met with resistance and blowback. I was prospecting like a pest, and when that happens, you hear a flurry of:

"Not interested."

"I'm all set."

"Call me later."

Prospecting like a pest is a waste of time and will deplete your dignity. Cringey activities, like cold calls and grip-and-grin networking, can be dirty, unpleasant work for most people.

As a business owner, there is no worse way to waste time than randomly "spraying and praying" for someone who has the problem you can help fix. It's a game of blind archery—shooting arrows at no target.

Coming up, I'll share my *six* favorite ways to find more qualified leads, and *none* of them involve cold-calling strangers. I thought you'd be happy to hear that last part. But first, there are some fundamental truths around prospecting that can't be ignored.

"Mr. Smith's office doesn't have a door. You have to batter your way through the wall."

CartoonStock.com

Prospecting: It's NOT an optional activity

Let's be honest about this. I have never met a successful business owner who enjoys prospecting. Those who do it anyway, despite their fears, do so because failing to do so could cost them their business. Desperation will cause you to engage in self-defeating behaviors if you don't have a pipeline of qualified sales opportunities. Having a full pipeline reduces your neediness and allows you to control the prize frame.

It gives you an "abundance edge," which is the belief that there are more than enough opportunities in the world for you to achieve your goals, and you enter every conversation detached from the outcome. You care and make every effort, but all you want is the truth, and if that is a quick no, that is an acceptable outcome.

This indifference of "whatever is meant to happen will happen" leads to contentment and better sales results because if you come off chilled, the prospect feels that same energy and resistance drops.

Prospecting for new clients can be the most terrifying experience a business owner can have and, if done incorrectly, can be equally terrifying for the prospect. Prospecting doesn't need to be drudgery.

The "industry average" success rate for cold-calling and cold-emailing is about two to three percent. Think about that for a second. How the heck can a method of prospecting that *fails 97% of the time* be considered a good standard? No other profession would accept that failure rate.

Engineers who design bridges that collapse 97% of the time? Doctors replace bad knees and hips that fail 97% of the time? Accountants get the year-end books wrong 97% of the time? Unacceptable.

Yet, the sales industry has been fine with a 97% failure rate for the past 40–50 years. I've never met a small business owner who has time or energy to waste on doing anything that fails 97% of the time. You're no different, right?

And I have some bad news for those who believe that pounding out daily blogs and posts on LinkedIn gives you a free pass to ignore prospecting. The last time I checked, Canadian, American, or UK banks still don't accept social media likes, reposts (formerly retweets), or the number of followers as a form of currency.

Without a healthy pipeline of qualified leads, you end up triggering the number one killer in sales: *neediness*.

Remember Mistake #8 (chasing) from chapter 5? Here are more words and phrases to avoid looking, feeling, smelling, and sounding needy. Destroy these words and phrases from your life:

♦ I hope you're doing well

♦ I know you're busy but…

♦ I'd love to…

♦ Just checking in…

♦ Just following up…

♦ Just circling back…

♦ Just bumping this email up to the top of your inbox…

♦ Did you get my last email?

♦ Pick your brain

♦ Quick call

♦ Just touching base…

♦ Fifteen-minute chat/coffee/Zoom

♦ Can I grab time on your calendar?

♦ Hope your kids and family are doing well

- ◆ Did you get my last 34 emails?
- ◆ I have a $25 gift card if you take my meeting
- ◆ I just wanted to talk about a potential collaboration

When you are desperate, you will do things like give discounts and let bad customers in, just to get the money you need to pay the payroll for the next week. Many entrepreneurs only decide to look for new business when they are on the verge of starvation or extinction.

If the thought of prospecting makes you nervous, I have good news for you. But there's a catch. The path to such a privilege requires a decision, which means if you haven't already, you need to dig in and invest the time and effort up front before ever making a sales call to work on the Core Four and the Illumination Hook in the earlier chapters.

And with that foundation complete, you'll be ready to prospect in a very different way that feels comfortable and allows you to stay true to who you are as a professional. Let's get after it.

Are you a pest or a welcome guest?

In the next six chapters, I will show you six of my favorite low-pressure ways to find new clients that won't scar your soul.

Before we begin, it is critical that we understand one of the most important truths that outdated sales training kept from us when they kept saying, "It's a numbers game," and "Always be closing."

This alpha-seller style of selling worked for Hollywood, but it destroyed the lives of millions of salespeople and led to the bad reputation for salespeople we see today.

The big lie is this: when you're ready to sell, the prospect is ready to buy.

"Always Be Closing" (ABC)

This ABC is an old way of prospecting that is still used a lot today, even though it has terrible results and leaves people emotionally exhausted and embarrassed to even tell their kids what they do for a living.

It's basically believing that selling is a numbers game. A set of beliefs that says if you just keep your head down, make more calls, interrupt more people, and chase more people, eventually you will make a sale.

It's wrong and degrading to any human to behave this way. In the words of the great Seth Godin, "It's tough to sell to someone driving past you with the windows rolled up."

My interview with Seth Godin in October 2021. Seth, thank you.

The Pain Triangle

Here's how most sellers behave. They show up, chests out like superheroes, ready to save the day: "I'm here. You have a problem; I have a solution. It's faster, cheaper, and better. Now hand over your wallet." It just doesn't work like that. Imagine how easy life in sales would be if prospects conveniently bought the moment you reached out. But you don't get to decide when others buy.

Let me share with you an important concept I learned many moons ago, which is why I decided to change the way I prospected. I call it the "Pain Triangle" and, once you see it, you will understand why 97% of cold outreach efforts fail.

The Pain Triangle applies whether your selling cars, software, mortgages, financial planning, or personal training.

Let's get into the nitty-gritty of the Pain Triangle:

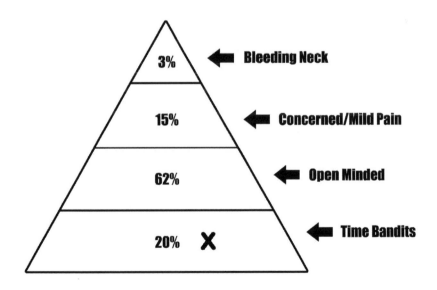

Level 1: Distressed/Bleeding Neck

The top of the triangle is made up of the 3% of people who are in serious trouble, and you just happen to magically appear like some kind of genie to save the day.

Let's say you have a dinner party for a large group, due to start in less than 24 hours. Your stove just broke down, and the guy selling stoves happens to call you in the middle of your panic attack. Unless you are a psychic, spotting people in distress and showing up is not something that happens in real life. This explains why cold-calling has an abysmal success rate and why you come off like a pest.

Remember the salesman trying to force-sell the rib-eye steaks to the vegan from earlier? Hoping to find the 3% is like trying to find a needle in a huge haystack. It's a fool's game and not a good way to prospect.

Level 2: Concerned/Mild Pain

"Concerned" describes the next 15% of prospects.

They are getting the job done without you. They have the "good enoughs" we discussed in previous chapters. People in this group may have minor issues and experience discomfort, but these issues are not severe enough to warrant switching.

Here's an example:

Remember my mom's Motorola flip phone? It's clunky. You can't share a video, and even sending a simple text message is cumbersome. To be the "hero son" I went out and bought her a brand-new Apple iPhone. The iPhone is sleek. And now the family and grandchildren can text my mom all the videos they want, and she can text them back.

When she opened it, she smiled and said, "Ah, Kevin, thanks, honey. But give this fancy phone to Olivia or one of the grandkids, I'm OK with the phone I have."

At that moment, I realized I had broken one of my own cardinal rules for selling, which is to be detached from the outcome ("the hero son") and just focus your efforts on shining a light on the prospect to improve their lives in some way. (Mom didn't have a "phone problem.")

I was selfish; the gift was about me and my goals. It isn't my responsibility to solve a problem that doesn't exist, nor is it my responsibility to decide what someone else considers to be a problem.

And my mom didn't want more texts and videos from her grandchildren; she wanted them to come see her more often and share the stories of the pictures with her *in person*. No pain, no problem, no sale.

Level 3: Open-Minded

Next on the triangle are the "neutrals," where 62% of prospects are at any given time in the buying journey. Prospects in this category may be unaware they have a problem unless you can find a way to alert them to it. This group contains a significant opportunity for us salespeople, but it must be handled with caution and patience.

Most people want to be better versions of themselves and are willing to listen if someone in a position of authority and trust can show them a better way to do something than they are currently doing. What do you know that they don't know? What bad things could happen to them if they stick with the status quo?

Here's an example of a neutral-state opportunity.

The taxi problem that wasn't a problem.

My friend Sam pressed a button on his iPhone. Three minutes later, a Lincoln Town Car showed up to take us to the airport.

It wasn't yellow. We didn't have to stand in the rain. We didn't have to hail one down like a game of Frogger in the middle of a busy intersection. The best part? At the end of the trip, there was no awkward exchange of money and tips. Suddenly, I had a problem with a taxi—yet, just minutes ago, I was neutral when it came to using taxis. Just like that, I went from being unaware I had a problem, to becoming a loyal user of Uber in every city in the world that offers it.

Level 4: The Time Bandits

At the bottom of the Pain Triangle are the 20% of prospects who are happy with how they're getting the job done, and are pain-free when it comes to the problem you solve. If you're selling ovens, the person you called just bought a new stove yesterday. If you're selling steaks, the person has been vegan for a decade. And, if you're not careful, these time thieves will drain your brain for free advice, quotes, and proposals, making your life a living hell.

Wasting time and energy with the 20% in this group is time you'll never get back. Your goal should be to get rid of them, congratulate them for figuring it all out, and move on as quickly as possible.

And those are the four stages of the Pain Triangle. It's an important model to keep in mind when planning where you want to spend your time and what kind of messages you need to make based on where they are inside the triangle.

OK, it's almost time to start prospecting in the most painless of ways.

Zero-pressure prospecting

Now that you understand the Pain Triangle, it's time to welcome you into the calm world of zero–pressure prospecting.

Here, you only invest time and energy with two groups:

The Concerned and Open-Minded.

Ready?

The ~~Richter~~ Ick-ter Scale

Prospecting can feel icky, but it doesn't have to. The "Ick-ter Scale" is an unofficial measuring tool I developed for this book that ranks the ickiness of the most popular prospecting methods.

PROSPECTING: THE ICK-TER SCALE

The good news is we will only be focusing on the less icky plays (levels 1-6), leaving the super-icky plays to the sales savages who prefer the agony of prospecting with a 2-5% success rate.

Clear your mind and take a deep breath. Here's a sneak peek at my six favorite painless ways to prospect, and we'll go over each one in depth.

1.   Lead Generation (Chapter 11)

2.   The Shock and Awe Experience (Chapter 12)

3.   The Simo Sequence (Chapter 13)

4.   (Un)Awkward Referrals (Chapter 14)

5.   (Un)Awkward Social Selling (Chapter 15)

6.   (Un)Thawing Cold Email (Chapter 16)

Let's begin.

11

Lead Generation

A car salesman will waste a lot of time trying to sell cars to people who already have good cars, cannot afford to buy one, or prefer to ride scooters.

People who visit car dealerships are much more likely to have a "car problem" which is why car dealerships exist. Allowing people who are in pain to come to you is more effective and profitable than attempting to persuade people who do not need or cannot afford a car to buy one. The same is true for just about anything we're trying to sell.

Wouldn't it be more comfortable if there was a way to get someone to raise their hand and come to you first? Traditional prospecting methods, such as cold-calling, can feel like you're a predator mindlessly hunting for prey. I've done my fair share of cold-calling, and it does work, but it's never been enjoyable, and it always leaves me exhausted.

And, for most cold-callers, it's built around some kind of selfish ask that fits your agenda:

♦   Asking for a meeting
♦   Asking for a free consultation or demo
♦   Asking for the sale

Stop trying to have sex on the first date.

The rules of communicating with others are the same whether you are on LinkedIn or Facebook, in the real world of selling, or even on the dating scene.

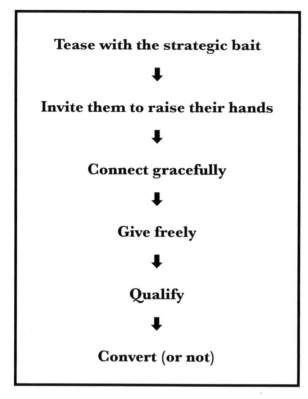

Pulling vs pushing

Traditional selling pushes.

1. I got this thing.
2. It's for everyone. You need it now.
3. Hope.
4. Pray.

(Un)Selling is all about pulling, not pushing.

1.   Drop some kind of irresistible bait.

2.   Get the prospect to raise their hand.

3.   Audition.

4.   Invite them in or out.

Your irresistible bait creates an open loop.

Something cool happens when you create "bait" for your ideal client and show the discipline to let them come to you on their terms.

The bait creates something called an *open loop*, shown in the graphic below.

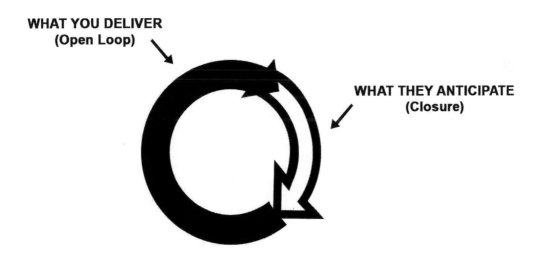

WHAT YOU DELIVER
(Open Loop)

WHAT THEY ANTICIPATE
(Closure)

Here are a few examples of intriguing open loops:

♦ Three secrets of Bruce Lee that you can use to make selling feel like you're not in a tug of war.

♦ Do you make any of these three mistakes when buying business insurance?

♦ Don't eat these two foods on an airplane.

♦ Can't do a push-up? This simple trick will get you to 30 push-ups in three days.

With the right open loop, you can turn even the most logical prospect into a toddler stamping their feet and flinging themselves to the floor, demanding to scratch the itch you just created.

But here's the really cool part: they don't get the itch scratched for nothing. To close the loop, you ask for a "quid pro quo" which could be as simple as the prospect's contact information. They give it to you so you can scratch their itch and give them the irresistible bait for free.

And the "thing" we put in front of them is called a "lead magnet." When that lead magnet is used, the prospect feels relieved because the loop is closed. Imagine how much less stressed you'll feel when your only job is to get someone to raise their hand to get access to your lead magnet, instead of calling strangers in the middle of their day.

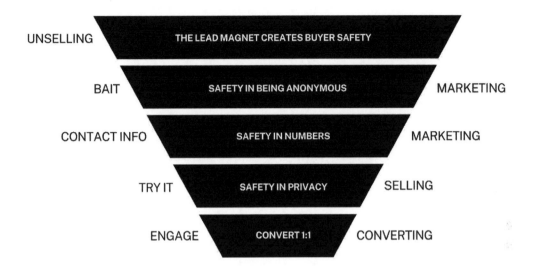

How your lead magnet creates buyer safety

The "bait" (your lead magnet) is a risk-free, low-pressure incentive for the prospect. It contains information that will greatly assist them with their problem, but it does not attempt to sell them on your product, service, or company. It's offered in a way that doesn't make the prospect feel intimidated or uncomfortable.

It isn't complicated. It normally involves a simple landing page where they can safely enter two to three pieces of contact information, which is a pretty safe step for most people. If the lead magnet piques their curiosity, they will gladly provide some of their contact information.

This is still a safe step because a lot of people have done it before, and it isn't like we're asking for their PIN number at their bank.

Creating the right lead magnet will elevate your status, and they will no longer see you as just a common salesperson. Rather, you will become more of an expert.

You see how this works so elegantly, right? The goal is to start slowly and make buyers feel safe by getting them to take small steps that might lead to bigger steps later.

What makes a good lead magnet?

There are six common elements that most good lead magnets have in common:

1. It solves a very narrow and specific problem.
2. It promises a quick win.
3. It is quick and easy to understand.
4. It has high value for your customers.
5. It's instantly accessible (no waiting).
6. It gives you instant insider-status and credibility.

You know you've come up with a good lead magnet if it makes you uncomfortable and a voice in your head tells you it's too valuable to give away for free.

> **Pro tip:**
>
> If you're not good with technology, can't build a landing page and connect emails to autoresponders, don't spend hours learning how to do it yourself. Instead, hire someone else to do it. Upwork or Fiverr have lots of experts doing this simple integration for a whole lot less than you'd expect. Use your time for high-value activities, like conversations with leads, working, and delivering the solution.

Lead magnet ideas to get you started

There are so many different types of lead magnets you could use as strategic bait. Here are some ideas to get your imagination flowing:

1. A test or quiz that gives them a grade or score

People like to see how they compare to other people who are like them, and Ryan Levesque's quiz funnels are the best I've seen around. I've personally invested thousands of dollars in Ryan's training around quizzes, and they're top notch.

2. Give away free short training videos

This could be on-demand webinars or even live group Zoom calls that solve a problem you think your ideal audience has. Jon McCulloch, the Evil Bald Genius, invites his email list to attend "Challenge Busters," 45-60 minute training sessions that deal with specific problems rather than generic ones.

Here's Jon's take on his lead magnet, which in this case is a simple email that doesn't even require a landing page.

Partial Excerpt:

> On Thursday, I will be delivering Yet Another Free Challenge Buster.
>
> This time, the topic is Email Marketing Mastery.
>
> And I'll share a couple of those weird little emails with you, so you can try them for yourself (and thank me later).
>
> Want to effortlessly win new business with short, simple, drop-dead, easy-to-write emails to prospects who WANT to hear from you? Even if you 'can't write well', 'have nothing to say', or have never sent marketing emails before?
>
> Then...
>
> Click here to reserve your seat
>
> Warmly, EBG

3.   **Live monthly Q&A sessions.**

4.   **A free guide to avoiding** *[whatever the deepest pain your prospect is struggling with]*.

5.   **A free instant download PDF report on** *[specific problems]*.

6.   **Access to an exclusive private Slack group.**

Creating your lead magnet

I won't tell you this is fast and easy to do, because it isn't.

Creating a great lead magnet will take some time, and how well you do this "small step" will affect everything else, so it's worth putting in the work up front.

Don't make the mistake of trying to make your lead magnets "high-level" and generic, or they won't work. Instead, think of one big tangly annoying problem, the kind of secret struggle that keeps your ideal clients up at 3:00 a.m., staring at the ceiling.

It's a simple flow:

1. Find a specific problem your audience wants to solve and test it with five or six people in your group to see if it interests them.
2. Tailor your lead magnet to address that problem specifically.
3. Create an enticing fulfillment offer (e.g., a free report, video, free workshop, quiz, etc.).
4. Use curiosity and intrigue to promote your lead magnet—with no mention of your product.
5. Leverage multiple marketing channels to advertise your lead magnet.

Ask yourself these questions to spark some ideas about the ideal client:

◆ What do they dream about?
◆ What do they desire?
◆ What do they love?

◆ What do they fear?

◆ What frustrates them?

◆ What angers them?

◆ What do they hate?

◆ What arouses their skepticism?

◆ What embarrasses them?

◆ What are they most thankful for?

◆ What are their sources of shame and guilt?

◆ What are their secret self-doubts?

◆ What are they proudest of?

◆ What makes them happy?

Break off a piece of one of the questions above and create and test two or three lead magnets that solve it.

The key elements of a lead magnet

The following are essential elements for making the lead magnet work:

Call to action (CTA): This is the button or link you share on social media. When people click on it, they see the "irresistible bait."

Landing page: This is where the visitor's information is collected from your lead magnet. Once the prospect sees the bait and it piques their interest, they can fill out the form with their name, email address, and any other information you think is important. Once they do that, they can access the lead magnet.

Thank-you page: The visitor-turned-lead now lands on a thank-you page with information on where to access their resource and is added to your mailing list.

Kickback email: This email is your follow-up message to the lead soon after the exchange. This email marketing campaign starts conversations with the leads to keep them interested in your business.

How do I get my lead magnet out there?

Paid ads are the fastest way to get your lead magnet offer in front of your ideal clients, but let's make things more challenging and pretend you have no budget for paid ads.

Here are several zero-cost ideas I've used to get my lead magnet into the hands of my ideal prospects:

◆ Are you a member of a business association or online group? Then send your lead magnet via email to prospects you can select from these affinity group lists or let the administrators do it on your behalf.

◆ Start swinging. Easy there Tiger, not that kind of swinging. List-swinging is a better word for it. That is, you use the valuable information in your lead magnet to form partnerships with companies that aren't in your category but have the same audience as you. You help them; they help you.

◆ Give your LinkedIn or Facebook network a new purpose beyond sharing random content or pictures of your cat. Simply drop your illumination question, dangle the bait, and ask someone to DM you to gain access to the lead magnet.

♦ Referral bait. When you ask a current client to put you in touch with someone you would like to do business with, the lead magnet becomes a convenient and less awkward way to make the introduction.

Final word on lead magnets

You don't have to leave the comfort of your home or office for this type of low-pressure prospecting, and you can even make a lead magnet in your pajamas if you want. Compare that to the embarrassment of wearing "Hello, my name is _____" plastic name tags, while approaching strangers at cringey network events.

It takes time and effort on your part to get the lead magnet just right, but the payoff of being treated as a welcome guest rather than an unwanted pest makes it all worthwhile.

Most lazy salespeople roll their eyes at this type of "gentle" prospecting because it requires so much work up front. Instead, they put their heads down and make cold calls or send emails to strangers with no thought.

To each their own, but I have a feeling you are still here because you don't want to go down the hard sell road. And it's worth repeating because lead magnets fit in so well with the (un)selling protocol: Lead generation is getting people to raise their hands, and it's not about selling them anything out of the gate.

When it comes to your lead generation program, curiosity and intrigue will be the stars of the show because they are the emotional triggers that will cause people to see you as a higher authority, raise their hands, and seek you out.

No chasing. No rejection.

12

The Shock and Awe Experience

The average businessperson receives 123 emails per day and picks up their phone 344 times per day to check them. Do the math, that's picking up their phone to look at it every four minutes.

In this second prospecting idea, I will share something 90% of people dismiss as being too old-fashioned because they believe everything outside of the internet and digital world is dead. They are dead wrong, and when they tried this idea for themselves, they were astounded by how well it worked. It has become a trusted go-to move in their prospecting plays for certain levels of higher-value prospects.

Get ready, because we are about to go "old school" with something called "The Shock and Awe Experience" and the forgotten art of sending lumpy mail.

I was in my final year of business school during the Gulf War in 1992, when the US forces overwhelmed Iraq with massive force. I couldn't tear myself away from CNN as the drama of trying to catch Saddam Hussein played out. I remember hearing the term "shock and awe" for the first time, and it's a phrase that has always stuck with me.

The next time I heard that catchphrase, was from one of the most brilliant direct response marketers of all time, Dan Kennedy.

I don't talk much about "old school mail" because I prefer to keep this aspect of my sales game under the radar. I have had a lot of big wins going back to "lumpy mail" in the last five years, especially as more people go "all in" on digital. It's so underused it's become new again.

What's a shock and awe experience?

A "shock and awe" (S&A) experience is a carefully curated collection of tangible items assembled in an impressive manner and sent to a client or high-potential prospect, who has already gone through the first stages of your lead generation or who came from a referral.

This kind of experience is not intended for random strangers or long-shot leads. To even be considered for an S&A experience, they should be prequalified and pass the early tests of being an ideal client. S&A could also be reserved for making a great first impression on referrals from respected clients who you know will never send you bad leads.

The goal of S&A is to live up to its name by introducing yourself in such an unforgettable and unexpected way that you gain instant status and credibility. When done correctly, it gives you the same feeling as when you first open an Apple product. Maya Angelou reminds us that "People may forget what you said, but they'll never forget how you made them feel."

The Amazon box effect

Every day, 300,000 Amazon boxes are delivered to people's homes. When they arrive, people experience a rush of dopamine, which reminds them of how they felt as children opening gifts on Christmas morning. Do you still feel like a kid on Christmas morning when your Amazon package arrives at your door?

Me too.

That's the feeling we want to replicate with your S&A package.

It should include a mix of logical (learning) and emotional (feeling) items, such as cookies, candy, swag, or other high-end props.

As an example, here's a flow of how S&A could fit into your prospecting sequence:

The lead magnet – small yes #1

They saw it, wanted it, and saw enough value in it to give you their contact information in exchange for the lead generation magnet as the first quid pro quo. This is a low-risk ask that feels safe to the buyer.

They "did something" – small yes #2

After receiving the lead magnet, the prospect took action, rather than simply leaving it in their inbox. Maybe they took the quiz, watched your free training video, or scheduled a 20-minute consultation.

S&A surprise delivery – small yes #3

The S&A box appears on their doorstep without warning about 10 to 14 days after they took the action. All these "small yes" moments compound, and you build likeability and trust.

By the time they finish unboxing it, you will no longer be a stranger, but a trusted authority, unlike anyone else who has tried to sell them something.

You can also include another low-friction call to action within the S&A box, such as another training or an invitation to an event.

Beware of the dull and thud

One of the most common mistakes I see people make when creating an S&A package is thinking you can just throw a bunch of office junk with your logo on it into a shoebox, such as a notepad and a crappy pen. That will not astound or amaze anyone, and it will end up in the trash, leaving them with a negative impression of your brand.

Everything inside the S&A box has to be there for a strategic reason:

♦ What is the purpose of each item?

♦ Is it something they can buy at Walmart or does it feel uncommon?

♦ How does the item fit into the "story" of your brand?

♦ Will the recipient know what to do once they open it?

♦ Is there a road map for what's inside?

♦ Is there a clear next step?

What should I budget for a S&A experience?

Wrong question. A *better* question is, "How much would you pay for a qualified lead?" Marketing should always be measured in terms of ROI rather than expense. Let's keep it simple.

If a new client is worth $5,000, wouldn't spending $50, $100, or even $200 be a sound investment? Be shrewd, but don't be cheap.

When do I send an S&A package?

Imagine you have a big meeting in 30 days with a high-potential lead. This might be the best time to send an S&A package to set the tone for your brand and status and get things moving. Wouldn't a $100–$200 investment up front—to establish your brand—be worth it for a high-value prospect?

Even if prospects are not ready to buy yet, S&A is a great way to stay on their "mental shortlist." This makes it more likely that they will remember you when they are ready to buy. Maybe your S&A box is the perfect "Welcome Package" for new employees, or maybe when you sign up new clients at a certain tier, this is their first impression, which will amaze them in its own way.

At our brokerage, we have also used S&A boxes as a way to thank clients who sent us good leads that turned into clients.

Alternatively, send an S&A to your client once the major project or work is completed. That will be your gift to celebrate, rather than a bottle of wine that no one will remember coming from you.

What's in a shock and awe package?

♦   A customized box. Putting your S&A items in a sleek, premium box will make it feel Apple-esque and special.
(Tip: packlane.com has some amazing options.)

♦   Crinkle paper or tissue paper. The sound of crinkling paper adds to the excitement of "unwrapping" or "revealing" something.

◆ Pens or white coffee mugs will kill the buzz. Consider a leather notebook, a favorite book related to your professional relationship with them, or a small electronic device, such as a Bluetooth® speaker, power bank, or other tech gadget. Again, this is a gift that requires more unwrapping and adds to the suspense!

Once you have your items, ensure they are nicely packaged and presented. Don't just throw them in an envelope or pile them haphazardly in a box. You have to control what they see first (the packaging), then second (the cover letter), then third, and so on.

Always FedEx your box or send priority mail—don't leave this to regular mail to mess up.

This is a cool example of a clever S&A:

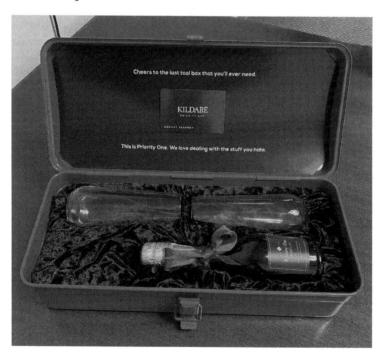

It's a welcome gift for enrolment into a special program. The Kildare crew takes all the stress and pain from members having to do the typical "duties and chores around the house" from plumbing to repairs.

The message reads, "Cheers to the last tool box that you'll ever need. This is Priority One. We love dealing with the stuff you hate." The "tool box" contains a membership card, two glasses, and Champagne to celebrate.[1]

And now you have lead generation figured out and you've learned the art of shock and awe, we move to one of the coolest prospecting methods you've never heard of.

Want more? Eavesdrop on this short Zoom conversation with one of the most remarkable marketing minds around, Mike Herberts. You'll never look at a rubber foot the same way after this.

Watch it here:

www.kevincasey.ca/rubberfoot or simply scan the QR code.

1 Image credit: www.thekildareway.ca

13

The Simo Sequence

Brace yourself, this prospecting idea isn't cheap, and you might want to consider a line of credit or refinance your home. Are you ready for the sticker-shock? It'll cost you a whopping investment of around $29.

Twenty-nine dollars? I'm not kidding. But don't let the ridiculously low ticket price deter you. This painless prospecting idea is one of my favorites, and I've only shared it with a small circle of people since I began using it in 2017.

You can find it on Amazon, Walmart, Staples, or any other office supply store in your area. What is it? It's a hanging wall file organizer.

The Simo Sequence

This prospecting strategy is a methodical approach to building trust and credibility gradually. It works well for high-ticket B2B sales because it has multiple touchpoints and mini events over an extended period.

What makes the "Simo" Sequence so powerful?

- It is highly targeted to a small list that's created up front.

- It requires some "intel" on the prospects, so you know what makes them tick. With this information, you can tailor each point of contact along the way.

- Each touchpoint is entirely focused on making the prospect feel special.

- It is not salesy or pushy. The goal isn't to make a sale. Instead, it is to build up enough trust and curiosity to move on to the next "small step," which is a conversation to see whether you are a good match.

What does Simo mean?

I spiced up this prospecting idea by giving it an unusual name. It exemplifies the concept of designing a unique mechanism. Simo is a tribute to the legendary Finnish Army Second Lieutenant Simo Häyhä, widely regarded as the most accomplished sniper in all war history. Nicknamed "White Death," Simo Hahyö tallied 505 kills, far and away the highest count from any major war.

Häyhä killed all the Red Army combatants in less than 100 days, an average of slightly more than five kills per day. Late in the war, a Soviet soldier fired an explosive bullet that blew off his lower left jaw and forced him to leave the battlefield. Simo lived a long life and passed away in a veterans' nursing home in 2002 at the age of 96.

Simo earned his title with meticulous preparation and precision.

The two most important things in your Simo Sequence are careful planning and accuracy:

1. **Your list is short and to the point.** Choose 10 to 20 high-value prospects who you believe would make excellent clients. Keep it around this size at first, because more than 20 prospects will make a careful prospecting sequence like this difficult. I know this firsthand because I once tried to juggle the Simo Sequence with 75 prospects and failed miserably.

2. **Problem-focused, not product-focused.** Your core message to the prospect, as well as how you can solve their problem in your own unique way, must be crystal clear. Don't try to sell pork sausages to a vegan.

Steps of the Simo Sequence

Step 1

Make a list of the 10 to 20 prospects you prequalified and would give your left kidney and half your liver to work with. Look at their website, social media, articles about them—even feedback from people you know who are connected to them—to learn more about how they live, work, and play. This is not to say you should hide in bushes and peer into people's windows; that would be creepy. Learn about their interests, awards they received, community work they've done, and anything else that distinguishes them and can be used to contact them.

Step 2

Break open the piggy bank and spend $29 on the wall-hanging unit I mentioned earlier. Make sure it can hold 20 files that are visible at a glance. This is intentionally old-fashioned and should be hung on your wall rather than being lost on the hard drive of your computer.

Nothing is hidden; everything is right in front of you. Make a file for each of your 20 prospects. Keep an eye out for anything that might interest them as you read and research. If you come across something relevant to their world, simply print it out and place it in their file.

Step 3

Put all the interesting articles, ads, research—or whatever you chose—in an envelope or small box and send them with a handwritten note every 30 days to explain why you thought they would be useful.

No selling. No call to action. This is important—don't ask for anything.

Step 4

Do step three for three consecutive months. Yes, 90 days. All you are doing is "watering the flowers"—patiently nurturing and asking nothing in return. And, by the way, if you think this is already a lot of work, you are correct.

However, you should be aware that lazy salespeople, who are only interested in making money on the first or second touchpoint, will never be patient enough to do this. That is why it works: you will be in your own league. There won't be any hard-selling, and you just stick to the plan.

On Day 120, when the fourth round starts, you do something different. At the fourth touchpoint, we discover an elegant way to make a safe call to action that asks the prospect to take a small step or do something in exchange. It could be something as simple as an invitation to a triage call, a free Blueprint Session, or access to a free service or gift. It could even be a free trial of some kind, if you have a subscription service.

Step 5

OK, so you have played the patient game, sent them valuable information, and now you are 120 days in and, worst case scenario, you hear nothing but crickets—the sound of silence.

What happens next? Don't panic.

Maintain your cool and send them another package of information 30 days later, on day 150, with the same "small step" offer. Do not make them feel bad or guilty for not taking you up on your offer at the 120-day mark; remember, we are looking for the truth, even if it's a no.

So, with the 150-day package, you add another twist that fits with the (un)selling method: a clear invitation to let the prospect know that it is OK to say no and end the relationship.

The power of this step is the gesture of returning the joystick to the prospect and giving them the option to "continue or exit." There is no in-between. You have been kind and helpful for almost six months now, which is more than any other salesperson or even their current partner has ever done. Prospects will find it difficult to ignore you because of your consistency in providing real value. You have earned the right to turn up the heat and give them the choice to decide what happens next.

Step 6

Approximately 70% of the time, by step 6, I have successfully connected with and had a next-step conversation with the prospect.

But what about the 30% of the time I still hear crickets? It's what I call "Truth Day" and it occurs around Day 180. This is when I send the "Farewell Package." It includes a hard copy of a book you discovered that you believe could be useful to their business, as well as your handwritten note and a version of the "Break-Up Magic Message."

This break-up message is important, and you need to be direct and not mince words while at the same time not being rude or aggressive. It is a fine line between "assertive" and "aggressive," so tread carefully.

You must be clear that you may have missed the mark, and since you were unable to connect in a two-way conversation, you must move on. This will be your final communication with them, and they will not hear from you again.

This is not intended to make them feel bad. Instead, it's a celebration of the fact that they no longer require you and that you are moving on, and you wish them the best of luck. And it's at this point that something magical happens about 70% of the time, even with high-value prospects who have been dead silent with me for nearly six months. It acts as a wake-up call, arousing something within them, and they finally make a connection.

You would be surprised at how many people who received these "final farewell" packages responded in some way, and many of them became long-term clients for me. In my business insurance industry, I only use the Simo Sequence with high-value prospects who pay at least $200,000 in annual premiums. You must decide what is appropriate for your business model and modify it accordingly.

14

The (Un)Awkward Referral

It still surprises me that more salespeople and business owners do not use the simplest and most effective way to find new clients, which is to have happy customers become sales ambassadors.

According to a 2019 Salesforce study, 83% of clients would be happy to introduce salespeople to someone else in their social circles, but only 17% of sellers ever request such an introduction.

Let me ask you an uncomfortable question: Last year, how many introductions did you request? What about the last three months? [Gulp.] In the last month? Any?

OK, maybe it isn't zero for you, but it's probably not as many referrals as you should be asking for, right? What if there was a ridiculously simple and low-pressure method that you could "plug and play" into your business to start asking for referrals in a way that your most time-pressed clients didn't have to lift a finger? And, after more than 30 years in sales, I can confidently state that 70% or more of my new business comes from referrals using the exact system I am about to demonstrate.

Are you ready for it?

I decided at the last minute not to include the (un)awkward referral method in this chapter. But don't worry, I'm not going to hold this one back; I just want you to have a slightly different experience with it.

Remember how we talked about the lead magnet in Chapter 11?

I thought it would be cool for you to see and feel the elegance of the lead magnet experience from beginning to end, which is how you will get instant access to *The (Un)Awkward Referral Playbook*.

Cool, right?

Just go to this link: www.kevincasey.ca/referrals and seconds later, it will be in your inbox. Or scan this QR Code if you hate typing.

15

(Un)Awkward Selling Over Social Media

Yikes, selling over social media. No wonder I left this one for last, right? You cringe just thinking about selling on Facebook or LinkedIn because you've been burned by so many hard-sellers and pitch-slappers who do it wrong.

Fear not, and cringe not. When it comes to selling on social media, I see three kinds of sellers:

1. **Pitch-slappers:** Relentless pests, carbon-copy messages, and a severe case of commission breath.

2. **Hamster-wheelers:** Show up, post some stuff without any intention, and are professional visitors to social media without any business objectives.

3. **Invited guests:** People who give more than they take, share thought-provoking insights, and generously follow and comment on other's work. By design, these professionals invite a specific type of person into their world with some kind of irresistible bait and only connect with those who raise their hands in response to such offerings, never bombarding strangers.

You should have figured out by now that the only way to be seen is as an invited guest.

How do "invited guests" show up?

♦   Lead with curiosity

♦   Trigger a hand-raise

♦   Start a conversation

♦   Seek the truth (fit or no fit, both are acceptable)

How do you get people to raise their hands?

When you compare the social world to the real world, nothing really changes. Boring in the real world is boring in the social world. Selfishness in the real world is selfishness in the social world.

The same foundational principles of (un)selling apply to both worlds. It is still about deciding who your ideal prospect is, and then using the power of curiosity to attract the right people into your world with small-step bait rather than heartless pitch-slaps.

Preheat the oven, we're about to create some pre-baked cookies together. You don't bake? No worries, it's just a chewy metaphor.

The pre-baked cookie is similar to a lead magnet, but is better suited to digital communities, like LinkedIn and Facebook. It's about welcoming people into your world as if they had just walked into your home and you had offered them a hot, fresh, delicious cookie they couldn't refuse. If someone you know took the time and effort to bake you a cookie, it would almost be impolite *not* to accept one, right?

Whatever kind of pre-baked cookie idea you decide to make, the goal remains the same:

1. Get someone to raise their hand ("I want that cookie.")
2. Start a conversation exchange over DM/text ("I want to take a bite of the cookie.")

That's it. The purpose of the first cookie is to start a conversation, not to sell.

The cookie jar

Let's reach into the cookie jar and see which cookie comes out first.

1. The "one-bite" cookie

Framework:

I just created *[what]* with *[result]* as a *[call out your ideal client]*.

Kevin Casey
🌐 Public ▾

I just shot a 6-minute video with the 3 steps to get your next 10 clients in under 30 days as a coach.

Type "Game On" in the comments section, and I'll DM the video to you.

2.   The "5130" cookie

It isn't called "5130" because it's made up of random numbers. Each number has a purpose in the framework:

5 – the number of people you're looking for (you can change this number, of course).

1 – the single biggest outcome they are searching for is this.

30 – a specific length of time to achieve the result.

Then, to avoid attracting the wrong prospects, include a "crisp qualifier," which means calling out a specific audience and possibly even calling out and being up front about who should not apply.

Here's how a 5130 post might look for a sales coaching business:

> "I am looking for 5 business owners who feel anxious about selling but are ready to conquer this anxiety and prove it to themselves by making their 1st sale in the next 30 days.
>
> You must own a business that is already up and running—and can't be a start-up or one that's pre-revenue.
>
> If that's you, reply with "Let's go," and I'll fire you off the details.

3.   A "green-red" cookie

This cookie is ideal if you have an idea that's been circling in your head and want to get a quick read on whether demand exists for it, without spending a fortune on market research.

This is a simple invitation post that serves as a mini-feasibility study with your target audience to determine whether there's sufficient demand. When compared to building it first and hoping it works, this saves you a lot of time and money.

The framework:

I'm thinking about putting a small group together to help *[Call Out Who You Help]* with *[Achieving Desired Outcome]*.

In X *[period of time]* we will *[what you'll get done together]* without *[the things they hate or fear that made them fail before]*.

So far, I've helped:

[Social proof #1]

[Social proof #2]

[Social proof #3]

[Paint picture of upside and reduce risk promise.]

If I did this, would you be interested?

If I get enough yeses, I'll put together a simple Google doc with the details for those who raised their hands.

---

4.   The "list-builder" cookie

Use these cookies to initiate private conversations via DM or after you've been following their work and commenting freely on their posts for at least 60 days, so you're no longer a stranger. It would then become an invitation to join your email list, giving them access to valuable content from you.

#1

ChatGPT is going to revolutionize online business in 2023. But most people aren't taking full advantage of it. So I recorded a full video explaining three ways I'm using ChatGPT to help me grow my online business in 2023.

Comment "AI" and I'll DM you the video.

#2

My businesses generated $2,232,557 in revenue in 2022 thanks to cold email. I just recorded a 28-minute video showing you exactly how to get clients from cold email in 2023.

Comment "Video" and I'll send it to you.

#3

I studied guys like Seth Godin, Warren Buffett, and Jeff Bezos to grow two of my businesses to seven figures in 2023. I made a video that shows you exactly how they teach you to make successful business offers.

Comment "Video" and I'll DM it to you.

So there you have it, that's four kinds of cookies you could bake for your social media audience. To recap:

1.   "One-bite" cookie
2.   5130 cookie
3.   Green-red cookie
4.   List-builder cookie

Don't let your cookie crumble

Think of these three things as the "three eggs" that will keep your cookie from falling apart as soon as the prospect picks it up.

Be specific

Instead of:

"Looking for struggling realtors," be specific:

> "Looking for ambitious women real estate agents looking to double their listings and increase listing value by 30% or more."

Disqualify with radical transparency

You want to get people talking so be clear, and call out the wrong prospects in a direct but nice way. Example:

> "I'll be direct. Working with me is not cheap, easy, or free, but if you're serious about [xxx] results and ready to invest in the fast track to [xxx] growth, let me know."

Use their currency, not yours

Real estate agents' currency is "listings."

Musicians' currency is "booked gigs."

Restaurants' currency is "reservations."

Weight loss clinics' currency is "pounds lost."

Make sure your qualifying questions use their currency:

> "Which of the following best describes your current situation:
>
> 0-5 deals per quarter? 6-14 deals? 15+?"

The answer to this question is a strong sign they have enough money and experience to buy what you're selling, even if they don't say so outright.

The non-sleazy way to ask for a LinkedIn connection

If your direct message feed is anything like mine, you are getting "pitch-slapped" with the same boring, long, and annoying people asking to be connected.

I met Jon McCulloch, who goes by the name Evil Bald Genius and is a brilliant business coach from Ireland (I mentioned him earlier). I really like how Jon asks to be connected in a way that doesn't make him seem like a desperate salesperson.

Here are two examples of how it might look, again using my business as a model for you to follow.

Example 1:

> Greetings [Name]
>
> I'm just connecting to grow my network before we all die of the next plague.
>
> Kevin
>
> PS: A lot of business owners love what they do, but selling is hard for them because it feels awkward and salesy. I've spent three years writing a book for people who aren't good at selling but need to start.
>
> Here it is:
>
> [Link to book]
>
> No pitch. No opt-in required. No games.

Example 2:

> "I saw we have X in common, and you mentioned that you did X, so I thought you might enjoy Y."
>
> Here's Y:
>
> [Link to Y]
>
> No conditions. No opt-in. No pitch.

So, with all factors in mind, one thing is for certain: mileage will vary. It's up to you if the cookie crumbles—or not.

16

(Un)Thawing Cold Email

What's the objective of a cold email? This should be easy to answer by now. It's not a meeting, coffee, or begging for time. A cold email has one job: to provoke curiosity and start a conversation. Curiosity pulls. Persuasion pushes. Your job is to pull, not push.

In this chapter, I'll share the psychology around building cold emails that won't show up dead on arrival in your prospect's mailbox.

The anatomy of a killer cold email

As a sales leader, I use an exercise I call the "Teardown" to teach salespeople how to write better emails. During a teardown, everyone works together to take an email that didn't do well and rebuild it bit by bit until it performs.

I'm pretty sure the email on the next page is not getting many responses. Still, it's funny that it was so bad it got my attention enough to be in this book.

There are five key elements of any good sales email:

1.   The from line
2.   The subject line
3.   The hook
4.   The corkscrew
5.   The call to action (CTA)

From: Frank Zappa

Subject: 15-minute chat

I'd love 15 minutes for a complimentary audit with respect to your tax-saving strategy for your small business and how you could be paying less and getting possible rebates.

We specialize in small business tax strategy and understand the specific laws most accountants miss, so you can pay less in and get more back.

This is my Calendly link and you can pick the time that best fits you.

Sincerely,

Frank Zappa

888-398-6969

All five elements must work together to drive the reader to do three things:

✔ Open it.

✔ Read it.

✔ Respond to it.

And that's why I want you to think about "assembling" the email, instead of just trying to "wing it." Every part must work together to accomplish the mission, which is a response.

Here's how it's all interconnected:

♦ If the "from" and "subject" lines fail, the email won't be opened.

♦ If the "hook" and the "corkscrew" flop, the email won't get read.

♦ If the CTA is too "aggressive" then you'll never get a response.

As you can see, every building block of a sales email has an important job to do.

The Teardown

Element #1: The from line

The purpose of the "from" line is to gain trust and credibility in a millisecond. It must be from a person, not a company. People connect with Alan, not Acme. I changed it from "Frank Zappa" (don't know him) to "Frank from Taxback Inc." because it's less formal. I want the email to feel like a conversation.

Whenever I meet someone new in person, I won't say my whole name. It sounds and feels more natural, and it gives just enough background information not to set off alarm bells.

Before:

From: Frank Zappa

After:

Frank from Taxback

Element #2: The subject line

How many cold emails do you delete without opening them? Subject lines for emails that don't get noticed are linear and boring, like these:

♦   Re: "New Cyber Insurance Policy"
♦   Re: "End of Year Sale"

Boring. Delete. Keep Scrolling.

You could send the most interesting cold email anyone has ever written, but if the subject line is boring, no one will ever open it, and it will remain the best kept secret. One way to write interesting subject lines is to leverage the power of curiosity, like Netflix with a cliffhanger.

Here's a simple framework for the cliffhanger subject line:

> [first name] [cliffhanger]

Like this:

> Kevin, unusual idea for you

Mailchimp's subject-line analysis (2021) found that using someone's first name had the highest open rates. People respond positively to their name because people's brains react in a special way when they see or hear their own name. It makes someone feel special. And being curious is a superpower in sales that should always be part of your sales DNA.

The cure for boredom is curiosity. There is no cure for curiosity. Use it generously. Except with your cat.

Here are some more ideas for subject lines that use the power of curiosity.

♦ [Referral source name] said we should connect.

♦ [Competitor name]

♦ Per [referral source name]

♦ Quick question, Kevin

♦ Idea for Kevin

♦ Kevin, unusual idea for you

♦ Your post on LinkedIn yesterday

♦ Your interview on [show/podcast]

♦ [Their name] and [competitor name]

Subject lines needn't be 100% clear. It's fine for them to be a little vague or confusing. Try out different subject lines, but don't make them any longer than five words.

Use the following qualities:

♦ Intriguing—pique curiosity without giving away too much information.

♦ Validation—few subject lines are more effective than referencing someone's name.

♦ Relatable—speak to a benefit your potential client will realize.

♦ Provocative—challenge the current way of thinking.

♦ Personalized—use the prospect's first name.

OK, let's change the subject line on this email. I could have used any of those, but I like to use their first name and a hint of mystery to make them want to open it.

Before:

> Re: 15-minute chat

After:

> Re: Kevin, an unusual idea for you

That's all there is to the subject line, but it's important because, when done right, it will stop the prospect from mindlessly scrolling.

Element #3: The illumination hook

We're 75 percent of the way through the book, and I'm sure you're tired of hearing me talk about how important it is to create an "Illumination Hook" that makes the prospect feel tension and curiosity—to create an itch, that needs to be scratched.

Well, repetition is a great teacher. This quote from David Hoffeld captures the essence of the hook: "Questions hijack the mind. When you hear a great hook that starts with a question, you can't think of anything else."

Here's what good illumination questions, when used in a cold email, might look like:

♦ "Are you aware that 89% of 'wired' home alarm systems can be cut and disabled with a pocketknife in less than 28 seconds?"

♦ "Are you aware that your sales reps are spending 83% of their time on non revenue-generating tasks?"

Illumination questions make people think differently about how they are getting the job done today but do so in a neutral way that doesn't feel like leading the prospect into a yes trap.

Let's revisit the original email:

> I'd love 15 minutes for a complimentary audit with respect to your tax-saving strategy for your small business and how you could be paying less and getting possible rebates.

Meh. It's boring and needy.

It starts by asking for time, which is the one thing that people with busy lives don't want to give away—not to mention, who wants an "audit?" It sounds sneaky, and most business owners hate the word.

Tension is our friend. No tension, no attention. Here's the hook, rewritten in the form of a provocative question:

> Tax deadline is 67 days away. How do you know if your accountant is using every opportunity in tax law to get you cash back this year?

Element #4: The corkscrew

This is where you take the hook question and gently turn the knife a little more to make the person feel something, like hope, anger, relief, or desire. The best way to do this is make them feel like they're missing out by using the bandwagon effect or some other third-party validation.

Fear of Missing Out (FOMO) is a powerful motivator, especially in B2B sales. When we look at the original email, it twists more like a butter knife:

> We specialize in small business tax strategy and understand the specific laws most accountants miss, so you can pay less in and get more back.

No one cares about what you do, they only care about what you can do for them.

Here's the rewrite:

> Small businesses in Canada use a tax loophole that isn't as well known to get tax rebates worth an average of $13,482. No fee unless you collect at least $7K in your pocket.

There are so many little (un)selling tweaks at play within this 33-word corkscrew paragraph:

✔ Lesser-known tax loophole

People worry that their current accountant may not be "in the know" and that they may be missing out on something.

✔ $13,482

Whenever you can, use exact numbers instead of round ones. Numbers make a story more believable and break up a pattern. For example, "lose weight" is not as convincing as "lose weight in 30 days."

✔ "No fee unless you collect $7K"

This makes the decision less risky and remember that the invisible enemy you face is always the possibility of doing nothing and keeping things as they are.

This part of the corkscrew is meant to make you want to do something and learn more.

Human psychology principles support the elements of the corkscrew:

◆ People want what other people have (Bandwagon Effect), especially in business, where owners do not want another owner to have an unfair advantage or be able to say they found a loophole.

◆ People want to avoid pain (loss aversion theory). Business owners don't want to be outsmarted by other business owners and they don't want to give away more money to the taxman.

◆ By reminding the prospect that "the tax deadline is 67 days away" we elevate the urgency of this from a later problem to a now problem.

Element #5: The call to action (CTA)

The call to action (CTA) invites the prospect to do "something" without creating pressure. This last part is where most sellers go wrong because they make an "ask" that is too aggressive and threatens buyer safety.

The CTA should be easy and painless, and should feel like you're giving them the power to make the call. You can even give off a hint of indifference or pull back a little and let them "feel" that you're OK with them saying no.

In the original, it read:

This is my Calendly link, and you can pick the time that best fits you.

That CTA is terrible.

Basically, it's "You want me to stop what I'm doing right now, click on your Calendly link, and schedule a meeting with someone I'm not sure I want to spend even two minutes of my life with?"

No way, see you later. This CTA is asking way too much, way too soon.

Remember, all we are trying to do is start a conversation, not get married!

It's also important to include only one call to action and not confuse the buyer with multiple options.

1.   Click this link.
2.   Watch this video.
3.   Jump on a call.

Pick one.

Go for no

Remember the idea of reactance? When making decisions, people like to feel in control. You can give people the feeling of being in control by passing the baton back to them and giving them permission to say no.

Simply end your cold email with a phrase like this:

> "Is this worth a quick email exchange or not really?

If someone ghosts you, you can also give them permission to say no:

> "Hey John, want to put this project on ice?"

Here are some lower-friction calls to action you can use:

◆ "Don't want to talk to a salesperson? I get it. Here's a two-minute video so you can determine if a conversation makes sense."

◆ "Would it be OK if I sent you a three-minute video on how this works?"

◆ Would you be open to getting a free guide called 'The four things buried in small print the Tax Man hopes you never discover'? By free guide, I mean a thinly veiled sales pitch, but still, you'll get some new ideas.

◆ "I'm not sure if this is of interest. But if it is, would an email exchange make sense to determine if this is worthy of a conversation?"

◆ "Are you open to a brief email exchange so you can determine if this is worthy of a conversation?"

In the rewrite below, I decided to take my foot off the gas and create a low-pressure CTA:

Worth a quick email exchange to see if a conversation is even warranted? If not, no worries.

Let's zoom out and look at the full Before-and-After revision in all its glory:

The before blah—71 words

From: Frank Zappa

Subject: 15-minute chat

I'd love 15 minutes for a complimentary audit with respect to your tax-saving strategy for your small business and how you could be paying less and getting possible rebates.

We specialize in small business tax strategy and understand the specific laws most accountants miss, so you can pay less in and get more back.

This is my Calendly link and you can pick the time that best fits you.

Sincerely,

Frank Zappa

888-398-6969

The after ah!—65 words

From: Frank from Taxback

Re: Kevin, an unusual idea for you

The tax deadline is 67 days away. How do you know if your accountant is using every opportunity in tax law to get you cash back this year?

Small businesses in Canada are using a lesser-known tax loophole to get tax rebates on average of $13,482. There is no fee unless you get $7K in your pocket.

Worth a conversation?

If not, no worries.

Frank

888-393-6969

And there you have it. We just rebuilt, line by line, an email that will be hard to ignore. Again, I hope you understood more than just the words in the email. You should also know how each part fits into the sales psychology.

CHAPTER 16

Lethal cold email mistakes

Now, let's move on to seven of the most lethal mistakes I continue to see when it comes to cold email.

Mistake #1: Jargonese

You have heard this countless times so far in this book: stop using marketing language and start using your customer's own words.

Imagine your ideal prospect sitting down after a long day of work, pouring a stiff drink with you, taking a deep breath, and saying:

> "God, I am sick and tired of X. There's gotta be a better way to do Y."

Those are the words you need to use in all your outreach (phone calls, emails, LinkedIn messages, direct mail, etc.) because that's how your prospects talk about their problems.

So, let's say you sell "insurance" and have this cool risk-mapping tool that can spot invisible risks that could wreck a business. No business owner survives a long day, cracks open a cold beer, and says:

> "I wish I had a risk-mapping tool, that would have made this day better."

Don't laugh. That's exactly how smart people get all weird and use those fake words to sell every day through email. Then they blame the lack of responses on something else, when, really, it's their core message that stinks.

Kill the jargon. Use real words.

Mistake #2: Thinking your email is a novel

In 1992, on my first day at a job that didn't require a hairnet, the owner threw me a worn copy of *Ogilvy on Advertising* to pass the time, because everyone forgot I was starting that day.

Since those mullet-wearing days (hey, Gary!), I must have read that book at least 32 times. I have only seen *The Godfather* four times. Ogilvy is that damn good and his 1982 words still apply today

> *"One should use short words, short sentences, and short paragraphs."*

Nobody wants to look at a giant text blob. Contrary to what your eighth grade English teacher told you, the old rules for paragraphs and sentences no longer apply.

Think smartphone short: 65 words or less.

You send short and sweet emails, and when you think you have written something short and sweet, you make it even shorter and sweeter.

Eighty-five words is good. Seventy-five words is better. Sixty-five words is great. If you're too damn busy to even call your mom back or find an hour to finish watching your favorite Netflix crush, what makes you think the busy CEO or time-starved business owner has time to respond to you?

They don't. Be short, sweet, and to the point.

Mistake #3: Dressing up your email like it's going to a gala

Formal writing feels almost too perfect. Casual writing feels more relatable and inviting.

Imagine you're hooked up to an EKG. Which sales message below would make your heart rate spike more?

Version A: "We help protect businesses with the right insurance coverage."

Version B: "Dealing with insurance sucks. You have a business to run!"

Can you "feel" the difference? Remember, selling is emotional—you need to make them "feel" something—angst, curiosity, joy, sadness.

Casual looks like this:

> Ever feel like trying to understand your insurance policy is like learning a foreign language?
>
> Words like subrogation, coinsurance, blanket insurance, and aggregated limits make it seem like a daunting task. It's all gobbledygook.
>
> Then they hover over your shoulder and expect you to sign it in 23 seconds?

A few other quickies when it comes to formality:

- **Don't** open the email with "Greetings."
- **Don't** open with "Dear" – you're not sending a holiday wish.
- **Don't** open with "Yo," "Hey," "Bro," or "Sis" – you're not 17 anymore. Hang on, are you still wearing skinny jeans?

- **"Hi," "Hello,"** or just simply [their name] accompanied by a comma will do just fine.

- **Don't** write that you hope the email you're sending finds them well. It's not arriving by pony.

- **Don't** fork over the fake formalities. Both the recipient and you know you don't truly give a damn about how their day is going.

Think of your email as being written like a text message. When you text somebody, it's casual, right?

I mean, you wouldn't type this into a text message:

"Hey Kev, I have the latest and most groundbreaking innovative product that I think will revolutionize your life and 10X your sales in the next 29 days."

Instead, it would be more real and casual, like this:

"Hey Kev, I remember you telling me that you were having trouble with clients disappearing on you. Lots of people tell me the same thing. I actually might have a way to help with that. Wanna chat?"

Mistake #4: Being too vague

The vast majority of emails I get are way too generic and full of clichés. You have to be crisp and specific if you want to get someone to read it.

Two hundred percent faster is BS, but 203% sounds more believable.

Getting more meetings from your cold emails is boring; booking nine meetings from 30 cold emails is intriguing.

Mistake #5: Way too needy

Avoid coming across as needy and desperate. Remember that you are trying to demonstrate that you are indifferent and detached from the outcome.

Attached and needy looks like:

◆   20-minute meeting?

◆   Grab a coffee?

Detached sounds like:

◆   Think this might help?

◆   Worth exploring?

◆   Worth a convo?

◆   Open for a look or not really?

I keep this cheat sheet on my desk at work, and I still use it every time I send a cold email. I rewrote it so it wouldn't hurt your eyes as much because, to be honest, my handwriting is terrible.

1. Uncomfortably short: 65-75 words.
2. If you can avoid even one mention of your product, bravo.
3. Can it be read without scrolling on a smartphone? Bravo.
4. Jam 1-3 of these: intrigue, curiosity, FOMO, competitor name drop, a result that isn't a rounded-up number (e.g. 13.8%).
5. Status: no ask for time.
6. Casual CTA: Worth a convo?
7. Status: Invite a "no" (e.g. "If not, no worries").
8. Light takeaway: "Might not qualify," "might not fit."
9. Sign off with your first name. No titles. No logos. No "follow me on" nonsense.

Mistake #6: Product over problem

I have probably said this to you so many times that it's starting to annoy you, but it's worth saying again because it's easy to get stuck in loving your own product or service. Your product is boring to them. Their problems aren't boring.

Lead with problems, not products.

Mistake #7: Don't be creepy

Personalization is overrated. If you play it too much, you can get into the "creepy zone" which can be a big turnoff and shows you don't have much going for you and are desperate. Just because you both love the Green Bay Packers doesn't mean they'll give you a $60,000 contract.

Personalization is a great stalling tactic, can be a huge time-suck, and you end up doing more research than prospecting.

Put your entire effort into creating an illuminating hook that can be scaled up and directly addresses problems that people in certain positions frequently face. Bring something new or novel about how they currently do their job, and use intrigue to suggest a better way.

This is far more potent than the fact that you both have two kids and live in a suburb.

Get visual: beyond just words

Only 10 to 20 percent of people in a 2020 study at The Wharton School of Business could remember what was said or written in an email, but more than half could remember what they saw.

This matters, because when a prospect sees your visual image, they'll be more likely to remember you.

1.   Visuals provide insight where words cannot.

Most cold emails have the same look and are text heavy. By using pictures, you stand out from the sea of sameness.

2.   Images tell a story and convey emotion.

Remember the golden rule: people buy emotionally then justify logically. Get them emotionally curious first, then follow with logic.

People forget what they hear or read quickly, but they remember pictures for a long time. Images are stored in long-term memory, while words and texts are kept in short-term memory.

Here's a good example of a visual email (see next page):

Boring old T-shirts

T-shirts. Whoop-de-do. But Neil didn't treat the T-shirts like commodities, as you can see on the next page.

Fifty thousand cold emails later, the results speak for themselves:

✔ Open rate: consistently above 50%

✔ Click-through: some campaigns/sectors got a huge 25%+ CTA

✔ Total revenue: client might reveal full details at a later date. But its CEO did say: "Tens of thousands of pounds, dollars, and euros."

✔ Massive PR around the campaign by bloggers, copywriters, and social influencers.

Hey!

Nobody likes cold emails, do they?

So to make this a little less awkward, here's a photo of me in your company t-shirt..."

Friendly opener.
Acknowledge that
cold emails suck.

Whoa! He's
wearing my
company t-shirt!
I'll keep reading...

To make it even less awkward, I'm putting the unsubscribe link here instead of hiding it away at the bottom of the email.

Flag unsubscribe
link in easy to find
spot = trustworthy

Anyway, this is what we do - we print fantastic quality t-shirts at a great price for people like you. Our website (RampTshirts.com) makes it **ridiculously** easy to get these t-shirts for events and teams. Saving you time and money. Click the link to get an instant price, upload your artwork, then checkout. Simple.

The pitch

Flossie Hunt
@flossiexrose

Just ordered @igniteaccel tshirts from @RampTshirts - 2mins 17s from start to finish, couldn't have been easier 🎽🏃

Stopwatch

02:17.34

02:17.34

5:00 PM - 13 Sep 2018 from Camden Town, London

5 Retweets   9 Likes

Screengrab of
tweet backing up
exactly what we
said we do.

If you need something other than t-shirts, just hit reply and I'll help you out. And if you'd like to find out how startup mammoths like Uber use merch at Christmas to raise awareness, click here.

Something useful

Thanks for listening!

Neil (co-founder and CEO)

*For the technically minded who are asking questions right now - Hunter.io's API, plus Clearbit's API, plus some smart image-processing work from our team allows us to automate this whole process.

Tech info about
how we did it.

The Trojan Horse email

This email will not work for every category, but it has a response rate of 65-75% whenever I use this structure. A common mistake people make in email is coming off like Captain Obvious and telling people what they already know. That's boring.

When you tell them something they don't know that can help them do their jobs better today, the magic happens.

The Trojan Horse email requires you to spend some time up front to demonstrate "proof of concept," similar to how Houdini did with magic and illusions. You give them something for free, which demonstrates your effort and makes it difficult for the prospect to ignore you.

The Trojan Horse could come in many forms:

♦ It could be a three-minute video teardown of someone's landing page, where you tear it down and then make the effort to create a mock-up of a new landing page, illustrating how they could convert more sales.

♦ If you were a talent recruiter, create a critique of a company's existing job ad that is running, and show them what a more powerful ad could look like with their name on it, using concepts that are proven to attract better talent.

Investing some time to "show" (not just tell or make claims) around new ideas that solve expensive problems and customizing your emails for each person will get you double-digit response rates.

Here's an example of a Trojan Horse email:

Re: Idea for the Talent Agency

For the past week, my team has been working on a bit of a secret project, and you've been the star of the show.

We grabbed the latest round of job ads you've been using to search for a Chief Financial Officer for Acme Inc. (Yes, I study these kinds of things for a living.)

We think we've come up with some creative tweaks for the campaign, using some lesser-known copywriting techniques designed to increase the quality of applicants and filter out the type of talent you don't want to attract.

You can take a sneak peek at some of the rework we did on your ads here, and they are yours to keep:

[insert video link]

Every ad is different, but you might have spotted some of our work in the past for clients like X, Y, and Z.

Worthy of a conversation?

Regardless, it's great to see you folks expanding outside the Boston area and growing in such a tough economy. Well done.

A breakdown of brilliant emails from one-person businesses

Lawn care service

This gem came from a landscaper in my neighborhood who works alone. It wasn't a flashy, well-designed brochure, but it was so good it deserves to be included.

When I got home on a cold April day, there was a handwritten note with his company's logo on it, waiting for me:

> Kevin, I know some days still feel winterish, but summer really is just around the corner.
>
> How are you getting ready to make your lawn lush this summer?
>
> We just limed and aerated a few of your neighbors' houses earlier this week. Nick up the street mentioned you were a Habs fan—good to see not everyone has jumped on the Leafs bandwagon.
>
> Open to me swinging by and taking a five-minute walk around your property and leaving an estimate behind?
>
> Whatever you decide, at least I know there are more Habs fans than just me in the neighborhood.

The deconstruction

Trigger: The event that's coming and creates urgency.

> Kevin, I know some days still feel winterish, but summer really is just around the corner.

Illuminate: Create some tension, done elegantly with a question.

> How are you getting ready to make your lawn lush this summer?

Bandwagon: Shit, others are ahead of me = FOMO.

> We just limed and aerated a few of your neighbors' houses earlier this week. Nick up the street mentioned you were a Habs fan— good to see not everyone has jumped on the Leafs bandwagon.

Low Friction CTA: No pressure. No effort on my part.

> Open to me swinging by and taking a five-minute walk around your property and leaving an estimate behind?

Humor: Personalizes/shows empathy.

> Whatever you decide, at least I know there are more Habs fans than just me in the neighborhood.

How many replies can you expect from cold emails?

The industry will probably tell you that a 20% response rate is adequate, but we don't want to be average, do we? I consistently get 40-50% response rates to my first cold email, and if it's less, I tweak and change parts of it until it works.

If your response rates are below 40%, there may be several factors you need to diagnose and modify, such as:

♦   You may be contacting the wrong person. (This may seem trivial, but it's a serious issue that must be confirmed before sending the email.)

♦   Perhaps the pain points aren't resonating sufficiently, and you should split-test a few options.

♦   You might be using jargon and not speaking your customer's language.

♦   Is your CTA focused, simple, or confusing? Are you coming in too strong at the end with an aggressive ask?

CHAPTER SUMMARY

Cold email isn't Shakespearean. It's the kindling needed to kick-start a conversation. Nothing else.

Here's a quick recap of the hot points we just covered:

♦   Write the way your customer talks. Don't use marketing jargon or $50 words when five cent words carry more punch.

♦   Good copy is found, not written.

♦   Kill jargon, like: cutting-edge, streamlined, scalable, synergy.

♦   Don't exceed 65 words.

♦   It's OK if it feels uncomfortably short.

♦   Be specific, not vague, when using numbers. Round numbers don't feel as credible.

- Never send the exact same email to everyone. Tweak a little.

- Focus on their problem, not your product. Their problems are interesting, your product is boring.

- One idea. One call to action per email. Don't confuse. Never more than one.

- Social proof adds trust. Name-drop casually, pick someone who will give them FOMO.

- Never ask for time or beg for a meeting. Low friction includes: Worth a chat? Worthy of a convo? Worth an email exchange to see if conversation is warranted?

EXERCISE: DO THE WORK

Referrals are the best way I've found to get more clients and to let other people open doors for me. Write your "one-two punch" emails using the (un)awkward referral playbook you should now have in your hands.

It's time to bake. I'd like you to bake two different kinds of cookies to get your ideal prospects to raise their hands. Interrogate the specificity and intrigue of your pre-baked cookie and test it in your social channel. Review all the different types of hand-raisers we covered in this chapter and pick a couple to try in the next seven days:

- Lead magnet (e.g., PDF, webinar, consultation, audit, quiz, etc.)

- "I made this for you" post

- Validation post

- 5130 post

- Connection request post

Now that good prospects are putting up their hands to start a conversation, you might suddenly realize you have a new source of stress. Assume you complete the work and implement some of the prospecting strategies, and OMG...

Someone raised their hand and wants to talk to you. Oh no, a real-life human wants a conversation. Don't run. You want to know exactly what to say next to this hand-raiser, don't you? Well, fear not. The next step in the Zero Pressure Sales Sequence, called Rapid Triage, is designed to do just that.

Want to learn more about crafting psychology-driven cold emails that won't end up ignored? In this quick "Fix in Six" lesson, I uncover four major mistakes and teach you how to get a response rate of over 40%.

Check it out here: www.kevincasey.ca/coldemail or simply scan the QR code.

CHAPTER

17

Rapid Triage

The Zero Pressure Sales Sequence

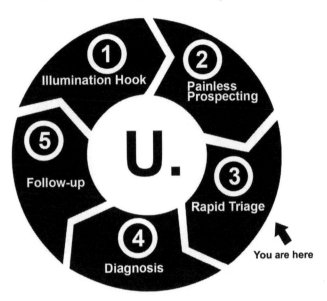

It's natural to get excited and see these prospects responding to your lead magnet or pre-cooked cookie as signs of good fortune. But beware; they might be throwing banana peels at your feet.

Do any of these phrases from prospects sound familiar?

♦   Can I just pick your brain?

♦   Up for a chat?

♦   How much do you charge for X?

♦   We're just curious.

♦   I heard great things about you. Can we meet for coffee?

Even people who raise their hands could be time-wasters, people who are addicted to free information, or cheapskates who will never pay you to solve their problems. Now is the time to look at the people who raise their hands and figure out who is a pretender and who deserves to be invited in as a prospect.

As entrepreneurs, it's so easy for us to jump into "action mode," put on our superhero capes, and rescue people in trouble by:

- Jumping on a phone call
- Scheduling a Zoom meeting
- Agreeing to have a coffee or, worse, lunch
- Being "nice" and getting sucked into giving free advice and consulting

For any of the above banana peels being thrown your way, I offer two words of caution:

PLEASE STOP

Well, that was kind of dramatic, wasn't it? Big, bold font and all.

But it's easy to get excited when someone raises their hand and fall into the trap of letting the person decide what to do next.

Time to talk about my favorite part of the Zero Pressure Sales Sequence, the one step that has saved me thousands of hours and, more importantly, my sanity.

Welcome to Rapid Triage.

"Triage?" A bit dramatic, don't you think?

In December 2019, we said goodbye to our sweet dad.

When I went to the emergency room in December, I saw how the nurses and doctors were able to assess and give a level of urgency to what seemed like hundreds of people over the course of an evening. As soon as a patient comes in, the medical staff asks a few key questions to quickly assess the situation and decide how urgent it is. The nurses in triage were very skilled and knew just what questions to ask to figure out how urgent each patient's condition was. I couldn't believe how calm and confident they were, even though people's lives were in danger.

I know sales is not about saving lives, but I liked the idea of triage and wondered if it could be used in the sales process. Triage is about diagnosing problems and pains. Here's an uncomfortable truth about problems that most people choose to ignore:

Even if a prospect has a problem you can solve, that doesn't mean they have the desire to fix it.

Many people with real problems either do not care about fixing them or think that "good enough" is good enough. If they do nothing, the status quo wins. You need to deal with this in Rapid Triage.

The only goal of Rapid Triage is to find out whether the person's problem is something that can be fixed, and if so, how bad the pain is and whether the person wants the problem fixed now or later.

Rapid Triage is an important first step that allows you to spend more time with clients you want to help, and less time with people you cannot or do not want to help.

Triage is the ethical thing to do

Remember seeking the truth is always more important than trying to make a sale. This "detached from the outcome" intention changes how we think, and how we think changes how and what we do.

There is zero selling when it comes to Rapid Triage. It's all about getting to the truth, the whole truth, and nothing but the truth. And like every single stage of the Zero Pressure Sales Sequence (ZPSS), the goal of each stage is to sell the next step, not the outcome of whatever it is you are selling.

The magic of Rapid Triage

Imagine if there were a simple way to tell the real prospects from the fake ones without ever having to get a phone call, drink another bad cup of coffee, or join a time-wasting Zoom call.

That's what you'll love so much about Rapid Triage: you don't have to do any of those energy-zapping activities. Now, there is one big rule when it comes to Rapid Triage, and I want you to follow it to the letter:

Pro tip

I strongly advise you not to do triage over the phone or on Zoom calls until you've done at least 20 to 30 sessions over email, text, or DM. When you're just starting out, it's much easier to stay in charge and on track if you don't have to deal with the stress of a real conversation.

You see, it's much easier to fall into a prospect's traps during a phone call or Zoom call and let them take over the call and throw you off your game. It has happened to me and so many other people, and I cannot stress enough how important it is to only triage through emails, texts, or direct messages for the first 20 times.

Now we know the one golden rule, let me explain why triage will become your new best friend. It all comes down to the simplicity of focusing on only three questions.

Triage Trinity of Three

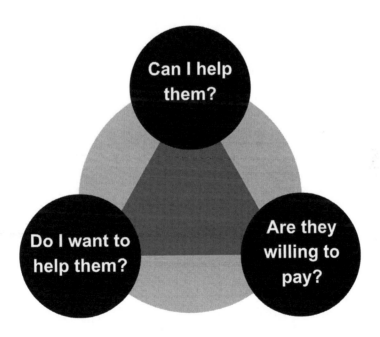

Rapid Triage's only job is to get clarity on three vital questions:

1. Can I help them?
2. Do I want to help them?
3. Are they willing to pay for my help?

That's it. Nothing more.

And it doesn't matter if the answer to any of those questions is no, because what matters to you is the truth, not the outcome. "No" is fine, especially if it is a quick no, which Rapid Triage makes possible.

Let's get into the three vital questions. If the answer to any of these is no, it is over. The prospect is no longer a good fit. If that happens, you should do the right thing, be kind, and try to point them in a different direction. Rapid Triage is about being stingy with your time and not wasting it on the wrong people.

Question #1: Can I help them?

It does take some direct, blunt questions to get to the truth. The following truth-telling questions will shed light on the type of problem and its urgency:

◆ What's giving you the biggest headaches right now?
◆ Can you give me an example?
◆ How long has it been going on?
◆ What have you done to try to solve it?
◆ Why do you think that didn't work?
◆ Have you tried [share some alternatives to your solution]?

♦ It sounds like you have a lot of spinning plates in the air, what happens if you do nothing?

Pick a few of these questions to help you figure out whether you can solve the problem and how important it is to them. Is it big enough to change the status quo? Challenge it with some of the nurturing yet assertive questions above. It's important to keep the tone casual and conversational, not like you're questioning someone in a back room.

Depending on how you answer, you will know if this is a real problem they want to solve or if they're stuck and willing to live with the problem. It won't be hard to tell if the prospect is more curious than committed, so you need to figure out which camp they're in. If they try to hide the truth or only give one-word answers, that's a red flag that they might not be serious about solving the problem and are just looking around.

Question #2: Do I want to help them?

In this part of triage, gut feelings and personal judgment are even more important. This part is more like choosing which friends we want to hang out with and which ones we want to avoid.

This is more of a feeling than a direct question, and it has to do with whether you'd like to work with this person.

If you know what to look for, you can still see the warning signs.

♦ Does it feel like they are being honest and open with you?

♦ Do you feel like they're withholding information?

♦ Are you getting too many vague or one-word answers?

♦ Are they asking about the price too early?

Even though it's done through email, direct messages, or texting, you can still feel the person's energy. Red flags include using vague or dishonest language and giving short answers of one or two words.

Throw them out quickly if you sense danger or bad chemistry. One bad apple can ruin your business, your day, and maybe even your life.

Question #3: Are they willing to pay for help?

This is where the rubber hits the road.

Now you can see if they really want to solve their problems and whether they are willing to put some money on the line.

With this third question, it is a red flag if a prospect keeps asking about price so early on. This is a sign you're dealing with a price-hunter, and you need to call it out.

Pick two or three questions from below to get a better read on the urgency of the problem:

◆ Is this more of a "now" or "later" kind of problem?

◆ What kind of budget do you have in mind to solve this?

◆ Who else needs to be involved in making the decision to fix this?

◆ Usually when someone brings up price this early, it's because that's what they are using to make their decision. Is that what's going on here?

Frameworks to keep you calm and in control

As I got better at selling, I started writing and recording a lot of "talk tracks" that I could use to keep my emotions in check and make sure I stayed on top of my game.

I'll show you some frameworks to help you stay in charge and feel more confident when you're in an uncomfortable situation. These frameworks are not meant to be copied word for word but showing them this way lets you see how they work for me.

Follow the structure, but add your own personality and style, just like everything else in this book.

Frameworks are all about making quick decisions, remaining calm and in control, and staying in charge of the process.

For the Magic Message on the next page, there are only three possible outcomes:

1.   They ghost you. (Perfect, bullet dodged).

2.   They fire back with a nasty or ignorant reply about having to pay for diagnosis. (Perfect, bullet dodged, it's a sure sign of a cheapskate.)

3.   You get paid up front (a promising early sign they're serious about solving an urgent problem).

The "invite message" always works because you always get the right answer, even if it is not the one you want.

Magic Message: The Invite In

When to use it: When you get three yeses.

OK, from what you've just shared with me, you have a problem I've seen and solved many times before. I recommend the best thing to do is to jump on Zoom for a [Blueprint Session] but I don't do that for free.

It's a [$X] investment, and it will take about 45 minutes. We'll use that time to learn more about your specific situation and figure out what's really going on and what the root causes of the problems are, not just the symptoms. You'll get a recording of the call, and within 24 hours, I'll send you a one-page plan for how to approach solving the problem, even if you do it on your own.

Also, if I decide on this [Blueprint Session] I can't help you, I'll refund your investment, and if possible, I'll point you to someone who might be a better fit.

If we end up working together, we'll use the $X as a credit against the future work we do together. What would you like to happen next?

Asking for the money up front

Gulp! When I tell people about this part of the sales process, they usually look at me like a "deer in the headlights" and think of all the reasons why they can't do it for their business.

You might not be able to legally ask for money up front in some situations. If this is the case, you'll need to come up with another way to test their intentions. But most of the time, people don't want to ask to get paid up front because they are afraid of being rejected or looking selfish. Asking for money up front goes against everything you think you know about selling, and many others will tell you that you cannot dare ask for money up front or you will be stoned in the town square.

However, if you look closely at how I've set this up, it doesn't cost the prospect much money because you can use it as a credit for future work, or give it back if you decide it isn't a problem you want to solve or they aren't the kind of person you want to work with. If they won't pay you $150 to $250 for a proper diagnosis, you can be sure they won't pay you for anything else. This is a sign that they will not be a good customer, so stop right away.

But the main reason I want you to agree to the rule—that you get paid up front—is I want you to start acting and positioning yourself as a real professional and trusted expert. This means doing the opposite of what the average salesperson does, who will do anything for free to get approval and look smart.

If your family pet got sick and you took it to the vet, would you expect it to be free? Not a chance. So, why would *you* settle for anything less?

The go-away message

This message is sent when the prospect doesn't answer yes to all three questions, and it's time to wish them well and say goodbye nicely.

This template is polite but gets right to the point, so you can end the conversation without being vague and making the prospect think you might change your mind.

Magic Message: The Go-Away

When to use it: When the prospect fails to get three yeses.

Thanks for sharing your situation, Sam.

It's clear that this project doesn't fit my world, so I'm going to stop things right here so we don't waste each other's time.

I do appreciate you being so open in our short exchange, and I wish you the best in finding someone who is better able to solve these kinds of problems. It's just not my thing.

(Note: If you have a recommendation or can point the person in the right direction of someone who might be a better fit, be a nice person and do that.)

Banana peels: Watch your step

A "banana peel" is an objection or challenge thrown at your feet by the prospect during triage.

Remember, if you don't control the process, the prospect's buying process will take over and mess up your world. Prospects will try to get you to break your own rules, boundaries, and values by being nice, making you feel guilty, and morally blackmailing you. Once you trip on a peel thrown at your feet, you can't stop yourself from going down.

Here's what a banana peel might sound like:

> "We need this done right, but we're early in the game and we don't have the budget to pay full fees yet. But I can assure you there's a ton more work down the line we can do together at full price if you can cut us some slack now."

One of the most common banana peels I've slipped on in my sales career seems to be the false promise of more work in the future. I'll explain precisely how to deal with that specific situation in a bit.

Banana peels get easier to spot when you're on the lookout for these kinds of wishy-washy phrases:

◆ "We're looking at…"

◆ "We might be…"

◆ "We're thinking about…"

◆ "We're possibly…"

◆ "Would you just look at…"

◆ "Would you mind just telling me what you think of X?"

I've put together some "Anti-Slip Frameworks" to help you avoid slipping on such peels. It's made up of three parts:

1.   Acknowledge what they said (empathy).

2.   Assert your position with direct language (frame control).

3.   Repeat as needed (consistency).

It's important to keep in mind that none of these templates are meant to sound aggressive. Instead, they're about being *nurturing* and *assertive*.

Banana peel:

"Can't you just give me an estimate of what you would charge?"

Magic Message: The Price Hunter

It's hard to say because I don't know what you need at the moment.

It's a bit like going to the doctor. They cannot tell you what is wrong and what to do about it until they look at you and ask, "Where does it hurt?" That's why I always start with a Blueprint Session so I can figure out what to do next and give you a plan that's just for you.

It's possible I'll decide I'm not the best one for you and if that happens, you'll get your money back.

Does that make sense?

Kevin

If they still argue about the $150-$250 cost of the Blueprint Session, it's time to tell them to "Go away" and end the conversation.

> **Magic Message: The Go Away Now**
>
> On reflection, we're not a good fit for each other, so I'm going to stop right here. Nonetheless, I do appreciate you taking the time to inquire about my services. I wish you all the best in finding someone better able to serve your needs for this project.

Banana peel:

"Can we stop this DM thread and talk for five minutes on the phone?"

> **Magic Message: The Chatty-Chatter**
>
> Sure, we can jump on a call.
>
> As you can imagine, I get a lot of people asking me to do just that, so I can't do it for free. It's $150 for a Blueprint Session; it'll take about 45 minutes so we can go deeper to understand your situation, and within 24 hours I'll give you a one-page road map showing the recommended course of action to take you from where you are now to where you want to be when you solve the problem.
>
> If I feel I can't help you, I'll refund your money, and if we end up working together, I'll apply the $150 as a credit for future work.
>
> How would you like to proceed?

[315]

Banana peel:

"I've never had to pay up front before."

Magic Message: The Tight-Wad

Fred, I understand there are some business owners out there that do this for free, but that's not the way I do things.

I don't discount my rates, because it prevents me from giving my paying clients the best support they deserve. Before I can give you a proper diagnosis, I do need to ask you some questions. But if that's something you don't want to pay for, that's your call to make, and there's no hard feelings here.

What would you like to happen next?

Banana peel:

"There's a lot more work down the road, if you can just give me a break on this first project?"

Magic Message: The Future Freeloader

Fred, I appreciate that. But, keeping it real here, I don't even know if I can help you yet, and the next step in my process is the Blueprint Session.

It's $150 and it'll take about 45 minutes, and we'll use that time to go deeper to understand your situation, and within 24 hours I'll give you a one-page road map showing the recommended course of action to take you from where you are now to where you want to be when you solve the problem.

If I decide I can't help you, I'll refund your money, and if we end up working together, I'll apply the $150 as a credit toward future work.

What would you like to happen next?

Banana peel:

"We need someone with your type of experience but isn't going to charge us an arm and a leg."

Magic Message: The Go-Away

I agree that finding the right person for the job is critical.

I don't negotiate my fees because it prevents me from giving my paying clients, who deserve my time and best work, the support they deserve.

I'll be up front, I'm certainly not known as the cheapest option, and if you want someone who runs their business that way, I might be able to point you in a different direction.

What would you like to happen next?

Banana peel:

Getting ghosted or not returning calls.

Getting ghosted by prospects is an epidemic, and it's something I get asked about all the time. But your concern with it is simply a sign of a much bigger problem, which is being too attached to money and not having a clear and transparent sales process for the prospect.

Sending "following up" or "just circling back" emails reeks of neediness and repels prospects even more because they can smell your desperation.

You will be shocked at how many people suddenly respond when you use the template below. It makes it clear that you don't need the work and are willing to let them off the hook. I call it "The Ghostbuster."

---

*Magic Message: **The Ghostbuster***

Fred,

Enjoyed our exchange last week.

It looks like you solved the problem on your own, which is great. Congrats on that.

I'm going to close this file for now, and if you need me, you know where to find me. Best of luck.

Kevin

With the above message, one of three things will happen:

1.   The prospect continues to ignore you. (That's OK, stop chasing, move on.)

2.   They come back to you with an explanation or reason for why they've been quiet. (Perfect, you now have control of the frame again and you continue.)

3.   The "Aw shucks" tone of the email shows you're not desperate, so the prospect feels free to tell you the truth or say no or not now.

Will you lose a good prospect by charging for the Blueprint Session? Yes, you might lose a good prospect who flat out refuses to pay a small fee up front, but that's a small price to pay compared to all the bad things that will happen when the nightmare client gets into your world.

If you charge a small fee up front, you won't have to deal with cheapskates who can ruin your business and your sanity. Believe me, I've had to learn this one the hard way.

CHAPTER SUMMARY

- Rapid Triage is a powerful method to weed out the prospects from pretenders.

- Rapid Triage is the first micro step to disqualify the time-wasters, tire-kickers and window-shoppers in minutes.

- The Golden Rule: don't perform triage over the phone or Zoom until you get confident with staying neutral and on message. I'd suggest at least 20 to 30 sessions under your belt.

- Conduct the Rapid Triage over text, email, or DM. It can usually be done in four to five minutes, which is why it's called "rapid."

- Having multiple "Grab & Go" magic messages at your fingertips for every kind of situation allows you to remain detached and control the frame. Rapid Triage also eliminates the curse of most salespeople, which is not getting paid for your time. This is about ending the practice of giving away your expertise and advice for nothing. Doctors, vets, and engineers don't work for free, so why should you?

- Ghosting is a topic I see so many salespeople gnash and grind their teeth about all the time. Now you have a powerful framework to neutralize ghosting once and for all.

- Prospects will throw banana peels at your feet as a test to see if they can take charge. Now you have a bunch of anti-slip magic templates, you can work with even the slickest peels.

EXERCISE

Who ya gonna call? Ghostbusters.

Step 1: I want you to think about the last 10 people who seemed interested in working with you but then stopped talking to you and left you in the dark over the past few months.

Step 2: Now send your own version of the Ghostbuster email to them and see what happens.

Don't be surprised if two or three prospects respond to your email to get back in touch after seeing you be open and honest in a way they don't usually see from salespeople.

Create your go-to templates

The magic templates were never meant to be stolen. Stealing is for people who can't think for themselves, not for smart people like you. So now is as good a time as any to make your own "Grab & Go" collection that shows off your own style. Avoid diluting any of the templates by using wishy-washy words like: "I feel" or "not quite right" as they dilute their potency. Be crisp and clear.

No matter what you do, never apologize for how you run your business or process. You are not responsible for their problems, and saying you're sorry for disqualifying them lowers your status and opens the door to more unnecessary exchanges, and you don't have time to waste.

So, for those prospects who answered yes to all three questions and paid you up front, they are now in for the next stage, which is called Diagnosis or the Blueprint Session.

Pro tip on getting paid up front

Your "lizard brain" will give you a million reasons not to charge up front, but that's exactly why you should, so you have to fight it.

Seriously, you're not asking someone to pay a king's ransom and remortgage their home. We're just asking for a small fee to see how serious they are.

If you want to be treated like a professional, you need to act like one, and that means getting paid. If you don't like the idea, think about getting a vet for your pet or a lawyer to help you buy a house.

Why are you of any lesser value?

If prospects refuse to pay you a small sum of money now, it's a sure sign that getting money from them later will be difficult.

CHAPTER

18

Diagnosis

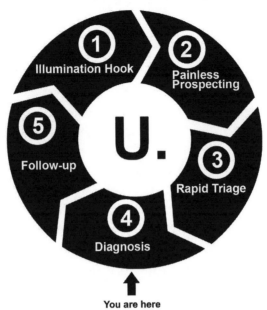

The Zero Pressure Sales Sequence

1. Illumination Hook
2. Painless Prospecting
3. Rapid Triage
4. Diagnosis
5. Follow-up

U.

You are here

At this point in the selling process, you have just finished the Rapid Triage, and the prospect has answered the three core questions in a way that moves them on to the next step in the (un)selling sequence, the Diagnosis or Blueprint Session.

The purpose of the Blueprint Session

This meeting can be called anything you want. I call it "Blueprint" but you could also call it "Road Map Session," "360 Session," or "Pathfinding Session."

Just do me a favor and never call it a "Discovery Session." Even the word "discovery" sounds sneaky, so most prospects will be suspicious when they hear it. Who wants to be "discovered" by a stranger at a session? Let's leave the ugly word "discovery" to the lawyers.

The Blueprint Session is not a sales pitch

By now, it should come as no surprise that this isn't about making a sales pitch. Instead, you have to decide if the prospect is someone you want to let into your world.

Just like the steps that came before it, this step's focus is on moving on to the next step or getting a no, and either choice is fine.

No winging it

This is not a random conversation; it is very orchestrated. Let's go through what I call the "Seven Boxes" of the Blueprint Session, one by one. Like everything else in this book, use the model as a guide but make changes to make it work for your business.

Each of the seven boxes is designed to make you look like the expert, give you control, and keep your time safe. In my case, the guide is meant to be used for a 30- to 45-minute session.

The "seven box" blueprint script

- ◆ Box 1: Control the Frame
- ◆ Box 2: Zoom Out
- ◆ Box 3: Gentle Knife Twist
- ◆ Box 4: Reality Check
- ◆ Box 5: Sooner or Later
- ◆ Box 6: Label the Problems
- ◆ Box 7: The Two Doors

Box 1: Control the Frame

Me: Hey ____, so we have 45 minutes together, and I do have another call straight after you, so I'll keep this to the time we agreed upon. OK?

Prospect: Sounds good.

Me: OK, thanks for that. I have a process I stick to that's really simple. It may seem like a lot of questions, but they will help me figure out if or how I can help you.

If I feel like I can't help you, I'll let you know and do my best to point you in a better direction so you're not left stranded, and I'll refund your investment for the call.

If I can help you and you feel the same way, we'll credit the $150 you paid for this call towards our future work together.

If you decide to do it on your own, that's OK, too, and I'll give you the recording of this call and a one-page blueprint for handling the problems with some key steps you can tackle yourself.

How does that sound to you?

Prospect: Yes, great.

Me: OK, let's get started.

Box 2: Zoom Out

I'd like to get a very brief snapshot of your business. And to keep things neat and tidy, I'd like you to answer, as best you can, three quick questions right off the top of your head:

♦ Who do you help?

♦ What problem do you solve?

♦ How does it work?

Box 3: Gentle Knife Twist

When people take time to hop on these calls with me, it's almost always because they have a problem they're trying to solve.

♦ What's the biggest struggle you feel is holding you back at this very moment?

♦ How long have you been dealing with X?

♦ I'm guessing you have lots of balls in the air, like every [similar titles] I speak to, why is now the right time to deal with X?

♦ What have you already tried in the past to solve this problem?

♦ Why do you think it didn't work?

♦ There's [alternative solution] out there that might be able to solve this, have you considered that option?

♦ Let's pretend you don't fix the problem, what's the worst thing that can happen?

Box 4: Reality Check

Where are you at right now in your business, and where do you want it to be?

Establish metrics: Where are you now, where do you want to get to? (Probe for numbers, not platitudes.)

Establish gap: "If you keep doing what you are doing and nothing changes, can you make up that gap?"

Box 5: Sooner or Later

Just keeping it real here, with everything on your plate, is fixing X more of a "later" thing or a "sooner" thing?

In the grand scheme of things, on a scale of 1-10, where 1 is "This would be nice to fix" and 10 is "This feels like an emergency room situation," where do you see things now?

Box 6: Label the Problems

I've been taking a lot of notes, and I want to make sure I'm on the right track. It sounds like your top [two or three] problems are:

◆ [Problem 1] > What sucks about it/impact
◆ [Problem 2] > What sucks about it/impact
◆ [Problem 3] > What sucks about it/impact

Did I get that right?

Did I miss anything?

Box 7: Decision Time—The Two Doors

1.   Show them the door

OK, I understand.

So… I said at the start that my job today was to ask you a bunch of questions to see if or how I could help. I promised that if I couldn't, I'd let you know politely and try to point you in the right direction.

Now I know more about your situation and what you need, I don't think I'm the right person for you. You'd be better served with someone who specializes in [more of that thing] and that's just not me.

If I were you, I'd check out [recommendation] because [reason why]. I wish I could do more. But [repeat name] could be a really good fit for you. Thanks for your time. It's been great getting to know you, and I wish you the very best for the future.

2.   Invite them inside the door

OK, I understand.

So, at the start of the call, I said I'd ask you a bunch of questions to work out if or how I could help you. Based on what you shared, the good news is you have problems I see all the time with people like you, and I solve these on a regular basis.

There's some work to do, but it's 100% fixable. There are a few options for what happens next, and it's totally your call:

Option #1:

I'll send you an email with a full recording of this call as well as a one-page blueprint with five to six key action steps you can take on your own or with the help of someone else.

Option #2:

If you want to keep working with me, we can set up an "Action Session" where I'll walk you through a custom plan for how to solve your specific problems, what the steps in the plan look like, and how much time and money you'll need to get there as quickly as possible.

This won't be one of those long, boring proposals with 60 pages of boilerplate information no-one reads and destroys acres of forest. Instead, it will be a short, two- to three-page document called an "Action Plan" that is tailored to your situation and lists the key steps, costs, and time estimates.

This session will be more intense than the one we had today because it will focus on all the problems and challenges we talked about on this call, and you'll have some homework to do before the session. By the end of that meeting, we'll know exactly what needs to be done to get the [summarize the biggest positive result they want to achieve].

This Action Plan session usually takes about 90 minutes, and the investment is $X. If you decide to work with me to carry out the steps in the action plan, I'll automatically use the $X towards future work together. You can also just take the Action Plan as more of a Do-It-Yourself option.

But this is about what feels right to you, and there's no right or wrong answer. So, let me ask you, what would you like to happen next?

CHAPTER SUMMARY

- The Blueprint Session is a paid consultation call where you go deeper than you could with the Rapid Triage call.

- The Blueprint Session is made up of "Seven Boxes" to keep it as tight as possible. This is important because prospects can easily take over and lead conversations down random paths, which can lead to trouble.

The seven boxes that make up the framework are:

- Box 1: Control the Frame
- Box 2: Zoom Out
- Box 3: Gentle Knife Twist
- Box 4: Reality Check
- Box 5: Sooner or Later
- Box 6: Label the Problems
- Box 7: The Two Doors

This is the opposite of "winging it" which is dangerous and puts you at risk of getting into a long conversation the prospect controls.

I made this cheat sheet I use all the time. It makes it easy to write down key points of a conversation on the spot, so you can stay in charge and know what's coming next.

Here's what it looks like:

The Perfect Prospect Triage Call - Cheat Sheet/Capture Sheet

① The Strong Start	② Toe-Dip: Business	③ Why Now?/Knife Twist
④ Now --> Future	⑤ Later Or Sooner? (Scale 1-10)	⑥ Label & Pinpoint Problems

⑦ Which Door?

☐ IN ☐ OUT

Pre-Research Notes:

_____

_____

_____

_____

_____

_____

_____

Key Content:

Name: _____

Email: _____

Date: _____

BONUS

11 powerful truth-telling questions

I often need to use some more truth-telling questions if I'm getting too many vague answers or if I think the prospect is holding back.

Again, I don't want to tell you which questions to ask because each sales situation and prospect has its own challenges. But here are my 11 favorites, which I keep on a sheet and look at when I want to learn more:

1. Help me understand how you are getting the job done around X today.

2. What does your current process look like for X?

3. Why are you focused on this problem now?

4. How big of a problem is this?

5. What is this costing the company?

6. What is it costing you personally?

7. What can't you do because of your current situation?

8. What happens if you don't solve this problem?

9. What's stopped you from solving this problem in the past?

10. When would you like to have a solution in place?

11. What does success look like?

Impact questions—peeling the onion

These questions allow you to dig deeper and get a sense of the impact of the problems on them personally, professionally, or financially.

- Why do you think that is?
- Tell me more, what is that causing?
- What do you mean by [vague statement]?
- What good things happen if you do that?
- So why is that a problem for you?
- Is that stopping you from…?
- How long has this been going on?
- What made it hard to fix in the past?
- Why do you think it's not working?
- What happens if you just keep kicking it up the road?

No matter what you sell, it's important to remember that everyone is "getting the job done" before you show up. Even though these prospects aren't ready to buy right now, that doesn't mean you should forget about them and move on. That would be a big mistake, and this group of "not ready" people has a lot of potential.

The "not ready" group is ignored by hard sellers and one-call closers as they swing their 50-pound sledgehammer around the sales world. There are small fortunes to be made inside the "not ready" group.

Let's take a look.

19

The Fortune is in the Follow-Up

The Zero Pressure Sales Sequence

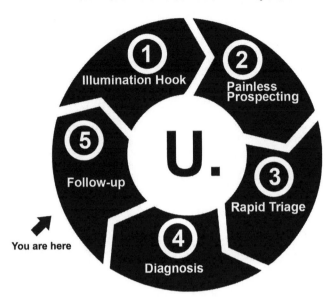

I don't like math, so I promise to keep this super simple. Let's say you invest $1,000 in advertising and it delivers 50 leads, which means each lead costs you $20. And out of those 50 leads, 10 people actually bought, while the other 40 leads didn't buy yet. You still paid $20 for those 40 leads, and you can't get your money back just because the timing wasn't perfect or they didn't qualify.

Now stop reading for a moment and grab a $20 bill. Got it? Now, tear the $20 bill into little pieces, find the nearest restroom, and flush it down the toilet.

It sounds crazy, and no sane person would do something like that, right?

But salespeople do just that, every single day.

Ready for a shocker? You might have to touch a prospect 15 times before you can get them to the finish line and make them buy. Yes, you read that right. There can be up to 15 touchpoints, and if you don't do it right, it will seem like harassment.

In this chapter, we'll talk about the good, the bad, and the ugly of following up with ideal prospects. I'll also give you a bunch of ideas and examples that you can use right away in your follow-up sequence.

Following-up without coming off like a pest

The dating scene is a good analogy to sales. Let's say you're single and want to dip your toe into the dating scene. Your best friend suggests you join an online dating site because it worked for him. You cringe, but it beats hanging around nightclubs, so you reluctantly sign up.

You look around the site and find someone who seems like a perfect match. But we all know dating sites are full of lies, so your outer shield is up and resistance is at its strongest. Your outer shield is at full power.

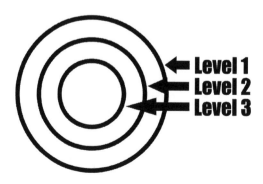

You land on someone's profile and like what you see. After hovering your finger over the button, you reluctantly decide to connect with them. You introduce yourself, and they accept, but you play it safe by using the chat feature on the dating platform.

Over the next few days, you found out you both worked in the same field for 10 years, you both laughed at the same funny stories, and you both had the same ideas about what was most important in life. When the middle shield knocks down the outer shield, you both become more open. You move beyond talking on the dating site and exchange phone numbers. Now you're texting.

A week later, you decide to meet at the local coffee shop. The middle shield is still up because you've been burned before and don't want to be hurt again. You go out on dates and have an unplanned sleepover. Then you bring some clothes and a toothbrush over to their apartment. Now you're at ease and in the inner shield of trust.

You decide to go to Italy together, and it turns out to be the best trip you ever had. They seem like "the one," and the "thumbs up" from your friends makes you even more sure of your choice. Lastly, you meet each other's parents. Then someone gets down on one knee, and everyone has a happy ending.

To follow up with a prospect, you need to take a series of small, safe steps, just like in this love story. But studies show most salespeople do not follow up or play the long game. Instead, they start too strong, which is like asking to meet someone's parents on the first date.

So, send your follow-up messages with the same care and patience you would if you were dating. Make the person you like the hero of your love story and remember to "give" more than you "take."

Dirty laundry

I once met an entrepreneur who was locked into the dry cleaning world and made quite a fortune from it. He had a model he followed and a recipe for success.

He would go around cities looking for dry cleaning businesses that weren't doing well and offer to buy them. In many cases, he saved the owner who was in trouble.

His formula for nurturing and following up, which he used over and over for 20 years, went like this:

♦   Buy the laundry shop at a discount.

♦   Clean up the place a bit and put up a new sign.

♦   Send out postcards to a targeted community around the store.

♦   Make a "Godfather offer" that's too good to refuse.

♦   His offer was always unexpected and bold: "Free dry cleaning for whatever a person could carry in their arms." He said it became a circus where people showed off how much they could carry in their arms.

♦   When they picked up their "free load," they'd get a second offer. A 10-day coupon for 75% off a long list of things that could be dry cleaned, like drapes, slipcovers, and winter coats—again, with an outrageous offer: "Everything they could carry in."

♦   Each time they came back, they got a compelling offer until they made five visits.

Now, because of these offers, people have new habits and muscle memory, and the five visits have made them more loyal to the brand. He made millions by just replicating this follow-up strategy over and over again.

When I went to see a friend who owned a flower shop, I asked her what the hardest part of her job was.

"The one-time customer who doesn't come back," she said.

"What do you do to get them to come back?" I asked.

"Well, we don't do anything right away. We send them emails around holidays like Mother's Day, Christmas, and Easter."

Ouch. That's the lethal mistake. That's too late. No muscle memory or brand affinity.

Once I've sent flowers to my wife or mother, you need a way to get me to come back and send flowers to someone else within the next two weeks. If you can get me to do that three times in a short amount of time, you'll be the first person I think of everywhere I go.

That's following up with purpose.

The 7 biggest mistakes in follow-up

Now, I see a lot of mistakes when people try to keep in touch with prospects, and here are some of the most common ones I continue to see, even today:

Mistake #1: Relying on memory

You're running a business. You can barely deal with the stuff that needs to be done right in front of you. How the heck can you even bother with opportunities that are "not yet ready" and won't be ready for three, six, or nine months? You can't.

What they need isn't a harder pitch or harder push. They need an orchestrated way for you to keep in touch that is automated and doesn't need to rely on your memory.

Mistake #2: Being a one-hit wonder

You now know the hard truth is that people buy when they want to buy, not when you want to sell. You have to keep showing up in front of these people so when they're ready to buy, they already have you in mind. And if you do not have a system in place to nurture good leads who are not ready to buy yet, you are missing out on huge opportunities for your business.

Mistake #3: Following up like a pest

You already know the sales industry has a reputation for being pushy or aggressive. And you're here because you don't want to be "that person."

But most follow-up messages look like needy phrases that create even more resistance like: "Any thoughts?" "Just following up." "I'm just bumping this to the top of your inbox."

Floating and bumping emails to the top of inboxes is what irritating salespeople do, and it creates a "red zone of resistance" for the prospect.

The problem with "following up" is you send the same needy message over and over again, which makes things worse. Instead, think of your follow-up sequence like dating. Don't make seven moves at once. Make a bunch of small, safe moves.

Mistake #4: Treating all your follow-up leads as equal

Not every lead is the same, and you need to make some decisions here and discriminate with purpose. I don't have the time or patience to listen to those experts who say you need 73 different lists of segments, which would confuse even the smartest NASA scientist. Instead, keep it brain-dead simple and organize leads into three groups:

1.   Hot (ready now)
2.   Warm (interested but not quite ready)
3.   Cold (long shots)

Mistake #5: Thinking there's a secret to creating urgency

There is no secret. Focus on planting lots of seeds with the prospect. You can't make flowers grow faster because you need to meet payroll next Friday. But you need the right amount of water and just the right amount of sunlight to help prospects grow.

Think of making deposits (advice, ideas, and tips) and not making withdrawals (meetings, chances to meet, 15-minute chats).

1.   Produce follow-up emails that make your prospects smarter about a topic they're interested in.
2.   Send the emails once a month.
3.   Automate it and keep it in the message track. Give them an easy way to unsubscribe that is not buried in tiny type.

Here are some examples:

Email 1: "John, 83% of clients said they would be happy to give referrals, but only 17% of salespeople ask for them. It's crazy because it's better than calling strangers out of the blue. Anyway, I have a three-minute slideshow where I share my three-step plan for asking for referrals without seeming pushy or awkward. Is this something you'd like me to fire over?"

Email 2: "John, I liked your take on [something you read on his LinkedIn/In/news article]. It was interesting to hear your thoughts on [key point of the message]. Just wanted to say thanks as I was able to use it today in a conversation with a client and [how it helped]."

Email 3: "John, I thought you'd enjoy this HBR article on [whatever topic he'd be interested in]. In particular, the bit about [X, Y and Z]. Enjoy the read."

That's watering the seeds. And with each thoughtful deposit, some of your prospects will decide it's time to connect with you, and some will just need more water and sunlight because they're not ready to buy.

Others will take the water and sunlight for granted, do nothing, and make progress without you. But you don't get all worked up because you know you can't control what happens. You can only control what you do. That's the liberating mindset when you practice (un)selling.

Mistake #6: Scoops of vanilla every single time

You need to throw in some mint scoops every now and then, or the prospect will get bored. I try to use a bunch of different flavors, so I don't get trapped in "Vanillaville."

You have to think beyond email. Now technology is around, things like handwritten notes and lumpy direct mail seem out of date. Each year, I get maybe one handwritten note and one or two unique pieces of direct mail. It's almost extinct, and that's where the opportunity is.

People get an average of 126 emails a day, so their inboxes are full and they skim rather than read.

But, I could count on one hand how many handwritten cards I get, yet it makes me feel special, like someone made some real effort.

Send them a book, with a note on the inside. If they like salmon fishing, send them a couple of handmade flies. This strange idea has helped one of my sales reps make almost a million dollars. Yes, fishing flies!

Use your imagination and try different ways to keep in touch. I'm almost 100% sure that your competition isn't.

Mistake #7: Afraid of rejection

Many salespeople are afraid to follow up because they don't want to bother the prospect, look like spammers, or lose a possible sale because they followed up too much.

So they do something even worse—nothing. But keep in mind our goal is to find the truth, not to make a sale, and if someone unsubscribes or tells us to go away, it is a gift because you now know the clear truth and will not waste any more sales energy chasing after the fake yes.

The building blocks for your follow-up campaign

There are three main parts to the follow-up:

1.   Education

If you show up with nothing to give, you won't be invited back for long.

Every time you connect with someone, you need to bring something to the table—something that shows you understand their world and deserve to be trusted.

2.   Repetition

Since we were kids, we've known that we need to hear the same thing over and over again before it sticks. The same is true for follow-up.

Don't think a prospect knows what you're saying just because they heard it once.

3.   Variety

This has nothing to do with changing what you want to say; it has to do with how you say it. Do not put all your faith in an email. Use direct mail, handwritten letters, flowers, chocolate or even a rubber foot.

Change things up. Don't wear the same clothes all the time.

18 ideas to help you create your follow-up program

1.   Send them a book with a handwritten note inside.

2.   Send them a short screen recording video you did for them, covering something that's a pain point in their business.

3.   Send them a handwritten card out of the blue.

4.   Invite them to an event where you are a sponsor or speaker.

5.   Send them a cool article you found that would help them solve a pain you know they are struggling with.

6.   Follow them on social media, set an alert, and start leaving thoughtful comments.

7.   Call them out publicly on social media for something they've recently done.

8.   Send them an unexpected act of kindness—a bottle of wine, chocolate or book.

9.   The Good Old Birthday Card.

10.   Text them a funny meme or cartoon about their industry.

11.   Tell them about a special offer available if they act now.

12.   Offer them a free sample of what you can do for them.

13.   Send an announcement about a new development in your business.

14.   Give a free teleclass or webinar and invite all your prospects.

15.   Invite them to an open house, reception, demonstration, or free workshop.

16.   Offer to give a talk or brown-bag lunch for their organization—at no charge.

17.   Refer them to a prospect for their own business.

18.   Volunteer for an organization where they also serve.

CHAPTER SUMMARY

A great follow-up strategy is like a secret weapon for success in the crazy world of sales. But research shows many salespeople don't do a good job of following up.

A study by Brevet found that in 80% of sales, it takes an average of five follow-ups to close the deal. However, 44% of sales reps only follow up with a prospect once before giving up. To make matters even worse, 94% of salespeople give up after just four follow-ups.

That's a lot of sales and money being left on the table because of a weak follow-up system.

Some of the biggest mistakes when salespeople follow up are:

◆   Mistake #1: Relying on memory.

◆   Mistake #2: Being a one-hit wonder.

◆   Mistake #3: Following up like a pest.

◆   Mistake #4: Treating all your follow-up leads as being equal.

◆   Mistake #5: Thinking there's some secret to creating urgency.

◆   Mistake #6: Scoops of vanilla every single time.

◆   Mistake #7: Being afraid of rejection.

Sales and dating have more in common than you might think. If you approach your prospects like you're playing the dating game, you'll avoid some hilarious blunders.

(Except that one time I told a prospect I loved him…)

Remember, it's all about making a killer first impression, playing it cool, and respecting boundaries. So, slow your roll, be an attentive listener, personalize your approach, and avoid going full throttle from the get-go.

When you play the game right, you'll build trust, make real connections, and be in a better position to compete for business when your competitors drop the ball or circumstances change.

Embrace follow-up as a vital tool in your sales arsenal and watch your results soar.

PART

4

(un)tapping

20

~~Floss~~ Voss Daily—5 Simple Techniques for More Comfortable Conversations

Ronald Reagan once said, "If you're explaining, you're losing." Most sellers go into "pitch" mode when they're desperate to make the sale. Prospects are very turned off when you try to explain, teach, convince, or persuade them about something.

There's a much better way to sell, and you're about to learn five simple but powerful techniques you can start using immediately—not just in sales but in life.

It's called tactical empathy.

Tactical empathy is being able to understand how the other person is feeling and what they're thinking in the moment. To show tactical empathy, you need to interpret in real time how the other person feels, and be able to say it back to them in a short, concise way that lets the prospect know you're listening and you understand.

Empathy is not the same as sympathy. Sympathy is feeling sorry for someone. To have empathy, you have to look at the world through their eyes. It has nothing to do with being nice or even feeling bad for them. It's just a matter of showing you listened to them and understood their point of view. Empathy accelerates collaboration, so what we're really talking about here is better communication.

Chris Voss knows empathy. He worked as a hostage negotiator for the FBI for more than 20 years, negotiating with the most brutal hostage-takers in places like New York, the Philippines, and the Middle East. I've read this book, *Never Split the Difference*, at least 19 times, and most of the pages are beaten and battered.

Yes, it is that good.

Now, I know you're just trying to get more comfortable with selling, and you've got no dreams of becoming a hostage negotiator. But there are some big lessons to be learned from Chris Voss that you can apply to make selling feel more natural and less confrontational, which is why it deserves its own chapter.

This chapter touches on a few of his book's most important lessons as they relate to (un)selling.

> **Author note:**
>
> You should really go out and buy that book right now. It's a bargain and I can't do it justice inside this chapter. Think of this chapter as the trailer. Get the movie, it's better. Goes well with popcorn.

Five effective techniques for reducing tension and improving listening

Here are the five techniques that create tactical empathy between you and the prospect:

1. Labeling
2. Calibrated questions
3. The accusation audit
4. Mirroring
5. No-oriented questions

#1: Labeling

I will start with a simple but powerful tactic I've been using for over six years with prospects, employees, and even my irritating neighbor (it's not you) to create tactical empathy.

For a label, you must name the feeling behind what you are hearing, and then tell the prospect about it in a very casual and curious way.

Labels are about being genuinely curious and should not be confused with agreeing with the position of the prospect; it's about letting them know you get them and understand what they're facing. Labels may appear to be so simple it's difficult to believe they can be such a game changer, but you must test them for yourself.

Labels are not just word-for-word repetitions of what you hear. That is called being a parrot. Rather, it means you rephrase what you heard in a way that shows the other person you listened and tried to understand. Labeling is similar to slapping a Post-It note on someone's forehead.

A ridiculously simple trick to using labels

There are three-word combinations that make labels so easy to use. Labels always begin with:

- ♦   It sounds like
- ♦   It seems like
- ♦   It looks like
- ♦   It feels like

With just three simple words, you can let the other person know right away that you heard, acknowledged, and understood them. After you say the label, you stay quiet and resist the urge to talk. Ninety nine out of 100 times, the prospect will keep talking and go deeper into their answer because they know you are interested, curious, and listening.

Labels cut to the truth.

A go-to list of labels

Keep this with you the first few times you want to use a label until you get those reps, and remember that after you use the label, you should shut up, enjoy the silence, and let them keep talking—but now at a deeper level.

"It sounds like this is important to you."

"It looks like you've given this a lot of thought."

"It sounds like you might have given up on finding a solution."

"It seems like you have a reason for [saying, thinking, feeling, doing]."

If you get a question that baffles or confuses you, it's a great time to label it:

"It seems like you have a reason you're asking this?"

I even use labels when someone is meandering, wishy-washy, or contradicting themselves. Just label it:

"It seems like there's something here I'm just not getting."

There is one major caveat: be quiet after you've presented the label. Count to three and wait for them to speak, because it won't be long. You'll get the desired reaction once you add the label.

It's almost one of "Thank goodness, you know how I'm feeling right now." Both parties are rowing in the same direction now and you haven't lost control. The other side now sees you as a partner.

#2: Calibrated questions

Who is in control of the sales conversation: the person talking or the person listening?

According to Sales Hacker, the "highest yielding" B2B sales conversations hovered around a 43%–57% talk-to-listen ratio (seller/prospect), and the worst sales performers have ratios where the seller talks 65–75% of the time.

The person in control is not the one talking, but the one who asks questions and listens. Most sellers do a terrible job here and think they're winning by hogging the conversation. The opposite is true; they're losing.

Pro tip

Spend a few bucks and download an app to record all your sales conversations. You can use the voice recorder on your smartphone. Or, I use Otter.ai which automatically records and transcribes the conversation. Highlight your talk track in green and the prospect's in yellow. You'll probably be surprised at how much you talk versus how much you listen.

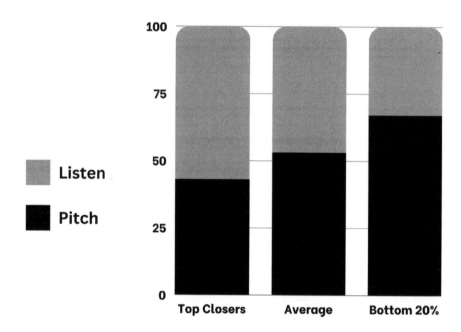

However, asking questions is risky because some of them are landmines that will make people upset or resistant. If you ask too many questions, it can feel like an interrogation to the prospect. The right questions are calibrated questions.

Calibrated questions are a fancy way to say "what and how" questions. Questions that begin with "what" and "how" sound curious, which can lower resistance, lower people's guards, and get them to open up more.

Calibrated questions force the prospect to think about the issue and focus on problem-solving. It gives them a little freedom—they can answer however they want—but you frame the scope of the conversation. Calibrated questions have the power to educate your prospect on what the problem is, rather than causing conflict by *telling* them what the problem is.

Use calibrated questions early and often. There are a few you'll use at the beginning of nearly every conversation.

Depending on the situation, here are some great "what" and "how" questions to get to the truth and keep them talking openly:

- What about this (issue) is important to you?
- How can I help to make this better for us?
- What happens if we fail?
- What happens if you do nothing?
- How do you make sure you're not overpaying for insurance?
- How are you making sure your BBQ doesn't have a "slow-leak" in the propane line?
- How would you like me to proceed?
- What is it that brought us into this situation?
- How can we solve this problem?
- What are we trying to accomplish here?
- How am I supposed to do that?
- How do you want me to move forward?
- What happened to put us in this situation?
- How can we get out of this mess?
- How can I help to make this better for you?
- How would you like me to proceed?
- How can we look at this in a completely different light? What if we could put in an "x" instead of "y"?

Calibrated questions make your counterpart feel like *they're* in charge, but *you* are framing the conversation.

Avoid WHY

Why looks harmless, but using it is like throwing a grenade into a conversation. "Why" questions are very confrontational. It's like being scolded by your parents or teacher as a teenager—it triggers defensiveness.

Remember when you were a kid and did something in the house that you shouldn't have? When you spilled Kool-Aid all over the white couch, these big, scary creatures called "adults" swooped in and always asked, "Why?" As in, "Why did you do that?"

That negative feeling is permanently burned into our brains, and ever since, "Why" questions trigger our fight-or-flight responses. Imagine an interview with someone who regularly pays more for rice, in which I ask three "Why?" questions in a row:

♦ "Why do you buy this brand of rice?"

♦ "Why is this brand of rice worth paying more for?"

♦ "Why don't you buy a more affordable rice?"

You can see how people would get defensive after just three questions. Instead, calibrated questions are more curious and less abrasive:

♦ "How would you describe the rice you use?"

♦ "What do you love about this rice?"

♦ "What does this rice do really well?"

♦ "If this rice were to go away, what would you miss?"

Asking "Why?" is counterproductive because it puts people on the defensive and presumes there is a rational explanation. By forcing people to take a position they are unlikely to change, it shuts the door on untold other explanations that "Why?" questions just don't allow.

The 7-38-55 percent rule

Albert Mehrabian created the 7-38-55 rule. Only 7% of a message comes from the words, while 38% comes from the tone of voice and 55% comes from the body language and face of the person speaking.

Recognizing the incongruence and gently dealing with it through a label will make the other party feel respected, and trust will be improved.

Voss recommends three voice tones:

1. **The late-night FM DJ voice:** Use selectively to make a point. Inflect your voice downward, keeping it calm and slow. When done properly, you create an aura of authority and trustworthiness without triggering defensiveness.

2. **The positive/playful voice:** Should be your default voice to use 80% of the time. It's the voice of an easygoing, good-natured person. Your attitude is light and encouraging. The key here is to relax and smile while you're talking.

3. **The direct or assertive voice:** Use rarely. Will cause problems and create pushback.

Almost always, start with a positive, playful voice. This is the voice of a friendly, easygoing person. Relax and smile while you talk, even on the phone.

#3: The accusation audit

When you're in a negotiation and the other side is thinking bad things or you're about to give them bad news, the accusation audit is a great tool to use.

An accusation audit is an approach to communication where you begin by proactively defusing the negatives that might be floating around your prospects' heads. You know those moments when there's an elephant hiding behind the curtain, and no one talks about it but everyone knows it's there? It's a strategy in which you try to guess what the other side is thinking, then deal with those thoughts before the person can say them.

Example: The late checkout hack

Next time you want to chill out and stay a couple of extra hours at a hotel beyond the posted "checkout" time, try using an accusation audit.

It's as easy as 1-2-3:

Step 1: Put on your best late night DJ voice—slow and relaxed.

Step 2: Say, "You're probably going to hate me, and I know you have better things to do than deal with needy guests like me. Can I ask you a bit of an uncomfortable question?"

Step 3: Silence for two seconds. Let the intrigue of the moment sink in. In these few seconds, they will think of everything that could go wrong—from toilets overflowing to a sacrificial lamb being killed in your hotel room.

Step 4: Then say, "Would it be ridiculous to ask if I could stay in my room until 1:00 p.m.?"

Then wait. Since 2021, I have never failed to get a late checkout by using the accusation audit. Try it and enjoy having a couple more hours to relax.

Example: Airbnb and muddy feet

Two summers ago, I rented a great house in my home province that looked out over the ocean. It felt like the house was on the edge of the world. A few days later, the owner sent me a nasty email accusing us of leaving mud on the carpet.

You know when you're having a bad day and you get one of those emails that makes you go into "Karen mode"?

I was pretty sure we didn't make the mud stain because we always told my then-19-year-old daughter Olivia to take off her shoes whenever the front door opened.

So, there are two ways to deal with my reaction to this situation.

"The Rebel Yell"

Are you old enough to remember Billy Idol? If so, then "Rebel Yell" has some meaning. It really means I respond with an email that is just as harsh and uses highly inflammatory language and threatens to give them a one-star review. The Rebel Yell response would have sparked more tension and resistance.

But there's a second option that's less confrontational. This means you stand back and look at the situation from their point of view. In this instance, taking a calmer approach to the idea that it could have been Olivia who tracked mud.

The accusation audit, calibrated questions, and labeling are all used in the email I am about to share.

> I feel totally embarrassed. [Accusation audit]
>
> It sounds like my 19-year-old daughter Olivia has really messed up this time. [Label]
>
> What a careless first step inside your million-dollar view room, leaving that mud stain on the carpet.
>
> How can I make this right for you? [Calibrated question]

Here's his response:

> Kevin, I'm a parent of two teens and I feel your pain.
>
> I've got a teenage boy about the same age as your daughter. Now I'm wondering if Sam, not your daughter, brought the mud in. He has done it before. This can be fixed with a little hard work, but not by my elbow. Sam's.
>
> Anyways, I got this covered, and good luck raising your teen, it's not easy.

The accusation audit, the calibrated question, and the labeling all worked together to completely change the mood of the conversation. Try it next time you're in a dicey situation like this and need to defuse the tension.

#4: Mirrors

Mirrors are a ridiculously easy way to get a prospect to go beyond surface answers and reveal something deeper and more personal. Here's how easy it is to use a mirror: when the prospect is done talking, just repeat the last one to three words with a curious tone (upward inflection of your voice).

That's it.

Like labels, a simple mirror gets the other person's attention and lets them know *you* are paying attention. Using mirrors against even the most assertive people makes them talk more and reveal more about the same topic of conversation.

This gives you space and moves the conversation to the other side, which can help you find out more without having to ask a full question. To illustrate, imagine you forgot a receipt for a TV you purchased, and you want your money back, and the retail clerk says, "I'm sorry, but at this point, there's really nothing we can do."

Now, just use the mirror, which in this case is the last few words, and say, "Nothing you can do?" with a curious tone at the end. By repeating what people say to you, the other person will start to elaborate on what was just said. This keeps the conversation going without making the other person feel like they are being questioned.

Mirrors are one of my favorite tools to get me to stop talking and to get to what I call the "second truth," which gets below the surface of the first answer.

#5: No-oriented questions

Battering is a repeated action that hurts and wears down in a harsh way. Most salespeople are guilty of "yes battering" their prospects.

So many salespeople continue to go so hard for the forced yes because they're under pressure. Cash flow, the tax man, making payroll… If you don't get a yes, you don't get the sale, and you miss payroll.

But yes-seeking questions backfire, by causing prospects to be cautious and raising their anxiety levels. Your prospect's inner voice has a warning bell that goes off in milliseconds when they're getting backed into a corner.

The cure is "no-seeking" questions.

No-seeking questions help prospects feel safe and more willing to talk to you or meet with you and reduce sales resistance, because no one likes being told what to do, and that includes you.

It makes people fight back.

Here are a few situations where "going for no" questions lower the pressure:

Situation: Let's say you're at the end of a great meeting and you feel it's the right time to ask for an opportunity to earn their business.

✖ Yes-seeking: "Would you like me to quote you on that project?"

✔ No-seeking: "Would it be a ridiculous (or bad) idea if gave you a quote on this project to have in your back pocket—just in case?" or "Would you be opposed to…."

Situation: You're being ghosted by what you thought was an interested prospect and you just want to get to the truth and stop chasing.

✘ Yes-seeking: "I didn't hear back from you and wanted to follow up to see if you would still like to continue our chat?"

✔ No-seeking: "Are you against putting this project on ice?"

Situation: Asking the prospect for time on their calendar.

✘ Yes-seeking: "Would you have 30 minutes to grab a coffee?"

✔ No-seeking: "Would it be overstepping my bounds if we set up a quick 15-minute Zoom session to talk about cyber coverage for a company your size?" Or, "Feel free to say no, but would you be willing to schedule a demo so I can show you how those two things you mentioned work in real life?"

There are many kinds of "Go for No" questions, and the fact that 90% of salespeople do not have the courage to use them means they will sound new and different to the prospect:

◆ Have you given up on… ?

◆ Is it a terrible time to talk… ?

◆ Is it a ridiculous idea to… ?

◆ Is it a bad idea… ?

◆ Is it a bad plan… ?

◆ Would it be out of the question to … ?

◆ Would it be out of line to… ?

◆ Are you against… ?

♦   Are you opposed… ?

♦   Would it be out of your control to… ?

♦   Would it be out of the realm of possibility to... ?

♦   Is it impossible to… ?

♦   Do you disagree… ?

♦   Would it be inappropriate to ask... ?

And that is the shocking power of starting with no to increase the chances of getting a yes.

CHAPTER SUMMARY

You aren't dealing with terrorists, but in sales, you are dealing with another person who has their guard up.

The five techniques we talked about in this chapter, which came from Chris Voss's brilliant mind, helped me become a better listener and also made selling feel more like a conversation and less like a sales call.

You cannot learn these techniques just by reading about them and studying them. You need to start "Doing" not just "IQing." Starting tomorrow, try out some of these five techniques with a friend, your spouse, or even your kids as a safety net.

Start using labels and mirrors in your everyday conversations.

You'll be surprised at how much deeper the conversation goes, and how you will pick up on signals and feelings from the other person that you would have missed before because you'll be listening at a deeper level.

Just mix and match all the techniques. After a while it will become natural, and you won't even need to think about it:

♦ Label their emotions ("It seems like," "It feels like...")

♦ Ask calibrated questions, e.g., "What?" and "How?" questions

♦ Avoid asking "Why?" questions

♦ Mirror what they are saying to get to the deeper truth (repeat the last one to three words with upward inflection)

♦ Use "no-oriented questions" to ease the tension of asking for any kind of commitment or favor

♦ If you are about to ask a hard question, make a commitment, or need to talk about the elephant in the room, use the Accusation Audit ("Would it be a terrible idea… ?")

♦ Your tonality should be playful and easy—more TED-talker, less CrossFit instructor

Next, we'll get into the most common sales objections you'll face in the sales process. You'll discover a simple but powerful defusing strategy, so you'll never find yourself tongue-tied again.

CHAPTER

21

(Un)Stuck for Words: Defusing Sales Objections

In fourth grade I had a teacher named Ms Firth. She was a no-nonsense teacher who even the unruly kids wouldn't mess around with. To learn multiplication, we made homemade flashcards. I have to admit, though, the damn flash cards worked and I knew every answer. Enough about Ms Firth, I'm getting cold sweats as I type this.

Flashcards can similarly work for defusing sales objections. Objections aren't infinite and prospects are predictable in their actions.

There are only four types of objections:

1.   Money
2.   Time
3.   Fit
4.   And the dreaded "I'll think it over"

This chapter will only include my top 10 objection scripts. But it might be a clever idea for you to crack open a new pack of index cards and make your own objection flashcards after you digest the content in this chapter.

We'll use mirrors and label techniques from the last chapter to show you how to defuse the negative energy around objections elegantly and effortlessly.

Here we go.

Flash card-worthy objection scripts

#1 Objection: I'm not interested

Well, this is going to be a bitter pill to swallow, but if you're hearing a lot of "I'm not interested," it's probably because you aren't interesting. People are interested when you bring something to the table—a novel idea, a new angle—something they don't know that could make them do things better than they are today.

So, if you are lazy and aren't bringing an Illumination Hook to the table, you are pitching and pushing, and that'll get you a lot of "I'm not interested."

You could use a label, a mirror, or both.

Label: "Sounds like I butchered things up early on, didn't I?"

Mirror: "Sorry, not interested?"

#2 Objection: We have a vendor

It's not an objection; it's the truth.

"We have a vendor already, we're all set."

Mirror: "Sorry, a vendor?"

Label: "Sounds like you're in a really good place with those guys."

"Sounds like they're treating you pretty well over there?"

"Sounds like you've landed yourself the perfect partner?"

When you use that kind of label and show you understand how they feel, they will usually relax and no longer feel threatened. Don't be surprised if they open up and suddenly admit it's not all rainbows and unicorns. The pressure is created when they think you're trying to rip and replace someone with your solution and are attached to talking someone into things.

#3 Objection: We want the lowest price

Your job is to get to the truth. Do they only care about price? Is there anything else?

Mirror first: "Sorry, lowest price?"

Then label: "It sounds like you may be comparing us to someone else." Or "It seems like price is more important than coverage."

#4 Objection: Send me a proposal

Most salespeople see this as a buying signal, so they send a proposal. But the proposal might be leading you toward a false conclusion. In other words, the proposal might be a red herring.

You need a talk track that will tell you if sending a proposal is a buying signal or a red herring, so you don't waste your time writing proposals and chasing. Here's a *talk track* that will unlock the truth behind "Send me a proposal."

> Prospect: Can you send me a proposal?
>
> Salesperson: That's no problem. If you don't mind me asking, what specifically would you like to see in the proposal?

And then maybe a label: "It sounds like I might be pressuring you. Usually, when people ask for information, it's just a nice way of saying they're not interested, which is perfectly OK."

#5 Objection: Your price is too high

Again, your job is to understand what that means and get to "the truth."

Mirror: "Too high?"

> Prospect: Yes, you're too expensive.

> Salesperson: Sounds like you're comparing this to what you have, what you expected to pay, or to another solution. (Labeling)

> Prospect: It's more than I expected.

> Salesperson: Sounds like there's a cap to what you want to pay. (Labeling)

> Prospect: Well, we're not sure we want to switch right now.

Again, the price was a red herring.

#6 Objection: Call me back another time

It's either a way to escape the moment or the truth—you just don't know yet. So we have to get them to feel comfortable and open up.

Mirror: "Another time?"

Label: "Bob, it sounds like there is some hesitation in your voice."

"It seems like you might not be really interested, and you're being really nice. It's not a problem at all, I am OK if that's the case."

#7 Objection: I want to think it over

Change is scary. The status quo is safe. Get to the truth.

Mirror: "Sorry, think it over?"

Then label: "It seems like you have some real hesitations."

"It seems like this might not be a priority right now."

#8 Objection: We just switched vendors

It could be a truth or a brush-off. Unlock the truth.

Mirror: "Just switched?"

Then label: "Sounds like our timing is totally off. Would you be open to us reaching out closer to renewal? Maybe not to switch again, but just to have an option in your back pocket?"

#9 Objection: Call me next quarter

It's a polite way to get you off the phone or they have a valid reason why they need to wait. Truths have punch to them, brush-offs feel generic.

Mirror: "Sorry, next quarter?"

Label: "Sounds like this could be an option, but X and Y are more important right now. Would you be against me emailing you some of this stuff—maybe once a month—just to stay connected?"

"It seems like this isn't really a priority, which is totally OK."

"Can I ask a direct question? When people say 'Call me next quarter,' it's usually because they're just being nice to me and don't want to hurt my feelings. I'm a salesperson, so I'm used to hearing no. Am I wrong?" (Go for no).

#10 Objection: The timing is off

Mirror: "I'm sorry, the timing is off?"

Label: "Sounds like you have a lot on your plate."

"Looks like I called you at the worst possible time."

"Sometimes when people tell me the timing is off, it's just a polite way of saying 'Get away from me, you annoying salesperson, I'm not interested.' Would you like to fire me right now? It's OK; I've been fired three times this week."

Fighting objections won't work. But, defusing objections will.

I've prepared a two-part video series in my community that delves even further into this topic. If you're up for the challenge, follow this link: www.kevincasey.ca/objections or simply scan the QR code.

PART

5

(un)corking

CONCLUSION

Start More Conversations

We have reached the end of our journey together, but for you, it should feel like a new beginning. The main idea of this book is to help you start more conversations with people you want to meet, but in a way that makes you feel good and doesn't make you act in ways that go against who you are as a professional.

The things I constantly hear from entrepreneurs and even struggling salespeople who feel like daily imposters include:

"I'm afraid to pick up the phone."

"I get these pits in my stomach."

"I feel like selling is sleazy."

"I get off-balance when prospects put me on the spot."

"I hate the idea of closing; it makes my heart race."

By now, those icky feelings should be gone from your mindset. You now know that selling is just a casual conversation about how to solve a problem. It doesn't have to make you feel like you cannot breathe, as is often the case with sales.

If I have done my job right, this book has opened your eyes and given you the calm confidence to sell without having to sell out who you are as a professional.

Embrace the golden rule of selling, and sell in a way that you would like to be sold to. Your prospects are no different than you—they don't want to feel trapped, sold, or manipulated.

We have gotten rid of false beliefs that always seemed to trigger anxiety about selling.

CONCLUSION

Here's the truth:

◆ You don't have to be a back-slapping extrovert.

◆ You don't have to chase strangers around like a pest.

◆ You don't have to cold-call strangers in the middle of their day.

◆ You don't have to sell in a way that forces you to pretend to be someone you're not.

In the same way that George Costanza learned the power of "doing the opposite" that day in the diner on *Seinfeld*, this book is about celebrating the opposites to everything you thought you knew about sales. With each drop of the 14 Costanza-like opposites inside this book, your feelings of pressure and anxiety hopefully also dropped with every turn of the page.

We dealt with all the icky parts of selling that made you feel queasy, shaky, or uncomfortable together, by walking through real-life examples and backing them up by science and sales psychology about how people really behave and buy.

The escape route from the old-school selling to the (un)selling experience shifted us from ~~this mindset~~ to this mindset:

◆ ~~Always be closing (ABC)~~ Always be disqualifying (ABD)

◆ ~~Selling~~ Sifting

◆ ~~Seeking the sale~~ Seeking the truth

◆ ~~Pitching~~ Diagnosing

◆ ~~Winning more~~ Losing faster

◆ ~~Fearing the no~~ Celebrating the fast no

◆   ~~Being a pest~~ Being the welcome guest

The (un)selling experience is about letting go of the things we cannot control (like other people) and focusing on the one thing we can: ourselves. If you remember how we started things off in this book, I said it was never about conquering prospects, but rather about conquering yourself.

The era of talking people into things is over. Traditional sellers approach selling as if buying is a straight line: I'm ready to sell, there's nothing in the way, and that's my money.

But that's not how buyers really buy. It doesn't go in a straight line, and the hard truth is the sales process is full of stops, starts, delays, and stalls. Just because you are ready to sell doesn't mean the prospect is ready to buy. No wonder people are afraid of salespeople!

Selling is broken.

In traditional sales, you "talk" people "into" things. But prospects push back when they feel like they're being pushed and their freedom is being threatened. This is called sales resistance. Tell someone they can't drink coffee, and they'll drink more coffee.

When a prospect feels they're losing autonomy over their choices and behaviors, reactance kicks in. Reactance is an unpleasant motivational arousal that emerges when people experience a threat to or loss of their free behaviors. It's why "parental guidance" boosted sales for the music industry.

When people feel like they're being told to do something or warned away from something, they do the opposite. When you push, they pull away.

Prospects are afraid of you. They're afraid you're going to talk them into doing something they don't want to do. And since you made it this far, you now appreciate the irony that just doing more selling won't make your sales anxiety go away, it'll only make it worse.

The way out is, again, quite the opposite.

It's selling less. That's (un)selling.

Imagine how much less stressful selling will be if your only goal is to find the truth and not to make a sale. Imagine the calmness and confidence you will now have with a low-pressure, almost frictionless sales process you can repeat like clockwork. A process that's always about the next small step and never the outcome.

Plus, because you're only interested in seeking the truth and are detached from the outcome, you don't feel pressured or uncomfortable.

The result of the (un)selling sequence is a low-pressure exchange that is good for both the seller and the buyer. When you are comfortable, you act more comfortably. And when prospects feel more at ease, they are more honest and open up.

And the truth, even if it is a no, is all we want.

Selling is about qualifying softly, working more, and selling by accident. (Un)selling, on the other hand, is about disqualifying hard and working less, to sell more.

Sherlock Holmes tells us, "Once you eliminate the impossible, whatever remains… must be the truth."

No shit, Sherlock.

That's the 'plop-plop-fizz-fizz-oh-what-a-relief-it-is' you get from applying the principles of the (un)selling experience into whatever it is you sell:

✗ traditional selling = seeking the sale

High pressure, uncomfortable

✔ (un)selling = seeking the truth

Low pressure, comfortable

The 14 ~~Commandments~~ Costanzas of the (un)selling method are the guiding principles that are built into almost every page of this book.

As we put a bow on things around here, it's worth revisiting the "14 opposites" and why putting these into practice means you will show up differently than 95% of the common sellers out there:

The Conventional Way	The Costanza Way
Seek the sale	Seek the truth
Qualify prospects	Disqualify prospects
The money is the prize	You are the prize
Lead with solutions	Lead with problems
Be attached to the outcome	Be detached from the outcome
Be 5 stars	Be 4.2 stars
Be liked	Be respected
Be enthusiastic	Be "Aw shucks, whatever"
Use $50 words	Use five cent words
Buying is logical	Buying is emotional and logical
Fear the no	Celebrate the fast no
Humor is unprofessional	Humor is a sales superpower
Control is being manipulative	Control is about being a pro
Be a pest	Be a welcome guest

If you follow these Costanza opposites and get some serious reps in, it won't be long before selling won't ever feel like selling at all. Making this subtle shift from "seeking the sale" to "seeking the truth" is your superpower for overcoming your fear and anxiety about selling. You're a sifter, not a seller.

The shift lies in:

♦　　Surrendering control instead of being controlling

♦　　Provoking instead of pushing

You may have started this book with doubts and wondered whether your anxiety about selling could really be fixed. If you're still here, give yourself credit.

More than anything, it was your stubbornness and determination that helped you dance with resistance and open your mind to the reality that you *can* sell effectively and ethically at the same time.

Most of us have two lives. The life we live and the unlived life within us.

Between the two stands resistance.

The writer who doesn't write.

The painter who doesn't paint.

The entrepreneur that never sells.

That's the resistance.

Steven Pressfield, *The War of Art*

WHAT'S NEXT?

We uncovered a lot in this book together:

1. The best sellers are not born sellers, it's a learned skill.

2. Extroverts don't make the best sellers.

3. Everything I shared with you inside the (un)selling experience is a learnable skill.

4. As with all learnable skills, if you practice them, you will get better at them.

5. All other things being equal, the more you practice, the better you'll get and the better results you'll enjoy.

6. The only way these skills won't work for you is if you don't get good at them.

7. The only reason you won't get good at them is if you don't start putting them into practice in the real world.

8. If you don't practice because you don't want to mess up, look stupid, or care more about what other people think of you, you'll be stuck in neutral.

So, you have a choice: follow the majority and get "majority results," or show courage, confidence, and self-integrity and do things differently. You're free to make any choice you like, but each choice has consequences.

So, please, choose wisely. The only real mistake is to never make a mistake.

Reassurance is futile

There are sales books and ra-ra motivation books that will tell you everything will be OK. It's a soothing thing to say, but everything isn't going to be OK—at least not at first.

Here's what will happen when you begin trying some of the ideas in this book:

- You will get rejected.
- You will get hung up on.
- You will get barked at.
- You will get stuck for words.
- You will feel awkward.
- You will feel stuck.
- Your friends will tell you that what you are trying will make you look stupid.

And during those uncomfortable moments, it will make you search for more reassurance. But it will never be enough.

Reassurance doesn't scale, it stagnates. You have the blueprint and you are now on the hook to make change happen when it comes to how you sell—that's not on me.

Telling you that it will be perfect and easy is a lie. It wasn't easy for me, and I don't expect it to be easy for you.

So there's only one thing I know for sure to tell you:

"I'm afraid" is a normal way to start. "I'm afraid, and I'm going to start now" is an even better way to start.

In school, we're taught to wait until we are 100% sure before hitting the buzzer (raising our hands). But in the world of sales, that dangerous lesson means you'll conveniently give yourself an excuse to **never** hit the buzzer.

It becomes your armor against criticism and rejection. It's perfect protection, except it leaves you stuck. I need you to hit the buzzer.

Ask for the introduction from the happy client. Send that handwritten card. Front-load all the objections, don't pretend they don't exist. Invite people to tell you it's OK to tell you no. Confess to people you're not for everybody and you might not be for them. Do the right thing and point them to a better solution, even if it isn't you.

Start buzzing, even if it's not perfect. Get (un)stuck. Reading this book is good. Trying the principles is way better. If you follow the steps inside the (un)selling experience, you will become calmer and more confident about selling.

If you enjoyed this book, I'd love to hear about it. If you still feel like you need some extra help, drop me a line, there might be some options for you.

And yes, I read my own emails – kevin@kevincasey.ca.

I'm rooting for you.

KC

About the Author

Kevin is known for taking a no-nonsense approach to sales and marketing and has been named one of the Top 50 CEOs in Atlantic Canada. He was also named *Progress Magazine's* "Marketer of the Year," and won the prestigious Paul Harris Fellowship Award for his charity work for Rotary International.

Just as selling is uncomfortable for so many entrepreneurs, Kevin continues to push himself outside his own comfort zone, including getting kissed and mauled by Richard Simmons to raise $300,000 for Breast Cancer and deciding to rappel from a building to help raise money for Special Olympians.

ABOUT THE AUTHOR

Kevin has been an entrepreneur for over 23 years. He is the co-founder of The IDEA Factory, which started in a basement in 2001 and grew to $6 million.

Today, he is the co-owner of one of the region's largest B2B insurance brokers, and in under seven years, the value of the brokerage increased by $20 million.

Kevin is always reminding people that he didn't go to Harvard or Stanford and is quite proud that he graduated with a blistering 67% average from the Faculty of Business at Memorial University of Newfoundland, which proves that education should never be confused with success.

He isn't a book writer, he's an everyday entrepreneur.

And yes, he still sells.

Every. Single. Day.

Acknowledgements

Not only could I not have done this book alone, I wouldn't have wanted to. I stepped out of my comfort zone to write and publish this book, and along the way, you stepped out of your comfort zones for no other reason than to help me on this messy journey.

I thought finishing a book would take six to eight months, but it ended up taking three years.

Luckily for me, I was able to find some of the usual suspects, and then, as if by divine intervention, I met some amazing people who went from being strangers to being mentors—and now what feels like lifelong friends—who helped me get out of my own head and finish this thing called "a book."

As usual, my peculiar relationship with losing track of time and missing deadlines made life difficult for just about everyone involved. For those of you ready to tie me to a pole in the town square for an old-school public stoning, let me once again conveniently remind you and blame it on my ADHD.

So thanks and, in almost all cases, apologies are due to:

My wife, Linda, and my lovely daughter, Olivia. What is there to say? I still love you, and I hope you still love me. Over the last two and a half years, you both had to deal with more than a few first-time author breakdowns. No one signed up for the early morning wake-up calls, breaking cups, and knocking over tables while trying to make coffee at 4:30 a.m. in the dark. Luckily, it only took one year. Wait, sorry, it has been three years. I promise I will never write another book again.

ACKNOWLEDGEMENTS

To Seth Godin, the best teacher on the planet. Thank you for answering my email in 2021, even though I was a stranger. I showed up with 'hat in hand,' asking you to speak at a charity event in our province that brings Business and Arts people together. I'll never forget the moment when I saw a reply email ping in my inbox from Seth Godin (I had my IT guy check to see if it was a prank). It was real. You generously said yes because you believed in the cause, and words cannot describe how much you helped so many artists that evening. During our interview, I sweated more than the late Chris Farley did in his *SNL LIVE* Chippendale skits. People say you shouldn't meet your heroes, but this doesn't apply to you. Your wisdom that night helped me fight through so much of the resistance that was with me throughout this book journey. Thank you for being so generous to so many people all over the world.

To my dogs, Bella and Ben, who sat next to me every morning while I worked on my MacBook Air, without judging me or barking, "When the hell are you going to finish that thing?"

Charlie Oliver, Dean MacDonald, and Frank Coleman: I never asked any of you to be my mentors—because that would have been weird—but each of you has done more than your fair share to help me become a better version of myself. This meant being honest with me even when my ego didn't want to hear it. I appreciate having you in my life.

Dean, in 2003 you could have hired one of the big, proven safe ad agencies to lead a multimillion-dollar acquisition of a national company. But you didn't. You went against the grain and picked The IDEA Factory—five misfits with a massive chip on their shoulders ready to shake up the establishment of big agencies. You rolled the dice on us that day and we went from being a nuisance in the industry to legit players. But it's not just the good times. There have been lots of dips and missteps I've made along the way, and you always stood shoulder to shoulder with me for the past 20 years... well, not shoulder to shoulder—I'm 5'8" and you're 6'0, but you get my point.

Charlie, it's hard to know where to start here. You are an (un)common human and you keep me in check and tell me all the stuff I need to hear but I never want to. Tough love but completely sincere. But as tough as some of those bitter pills have been, each one is always out of love and kindness because you wanted to push me to be a better version of myself. Every big move in my life, you've been there working in the shadows, helping me find the path and never asking for anything in return. I want to punch you out sometimes, but thank you for being you. I'm still a work in progress, so don't stop now.

Frank, on paper, yes, you are a client. But off paper, you are a friend and mentor and in a strange way I feel like since my dad passed in 2019, you have been that surrogate dad giving me advice and peace along the way. I've never met someone who loves and cares for his family like you—and watching you operate as a dad, husband, and leader has helped me become better at all three.

To my faithful 8:30 a.m. Breakfast Club, which consists of Derm, John, Tommy, Scottie, Ed, and Jeff. For letting me try out some of this (un) selling stuff without hesitation and listening to me complain about the book over and over again.

The most important thing you did was bring the "Saturday Breakfast Club" to my dad's hospital room on the Saturday before he died. I know how much he loved that because he loved all of you.

The best gift you could have given me was to be there that day, when I needed friends like you the most. How lucky Dad was. How lucky I am.

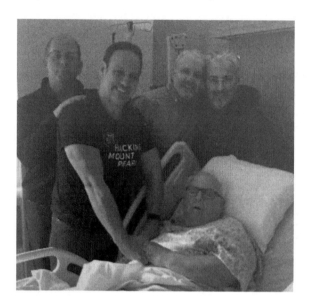

Then there is this strange place called LinkedIn—a community that was the testing ground for building my network and support around (un)selling. Along the way, I have met some of the smartest and nicest people. They helped me shape my message, always gave me support, and made me feel like the work I was doing was important. Mike Herberts, Pete Durand, Kyle Bell, Mike Bannister, Sam Dunning, Stuart Taylor, John Bissett, Nick Jeins, Danny Graf, David Rolls, Giulio Segantini Cimenis, Ben Browning, Flyn Penoyer, Kris Mulcahy, Fred Copestake, Tonya Whittle, Craig Tavenor, Jeff Molander, Dale Underwood, Dale Dupree, Ted Olson, Philipp Slappnig, and Derrick Swain—thank you for being so generous.

Then out of nowhere, a sales borg named Justin Michael came along. The creator of the JMM Method and a three-time author. Legend has it that Justin was abducted by a UFO and handed first-hand knowledge of the JMM Method, but this claim cannot be confirmed or denied. He is a massive name in the sales world, and to be blunt, there is no valid business case for him to connect with me and become such a mentor over the last 12 months of this journey. But he did, and never asked for anything in return. And that speaks volumes about his character. Justin, thank you for all you do.

Benjamin Dennehy calls himself the most hated sales trainer in the UK. He is, without a doubt, one of the toughest sons-of-a-bitch I have ever met. I wanted to punch him in the throat sometimes, but he lives in England and I live in Canada, so I couldn't get to him. Not only is he the best sales trainer on the planet, but he is also the most real. Without sparring sessions with Benjamin and his ability to perform an exorcism on "the needy Kevin" and expel that inner kid out of my sales life, the (un)selling may never have happened.

My business partners are Jeff LeGrow and Rod Vatcher. Thank you for seeing something in me in 2016 and bringing me into the world of insurance. For letting me bring my unconventional and sometimes very weird ways into a traditional model that doesn't usually welcome people like me. You always believed in me and were patient with me as I worked on this book. Without your kindness, this project would have died long ago. Friends first, partners second.

To Bill Dalton, another one of my amazing business partners, who is without a doubt the smartest insurance dude on planet Earth. But despite being a life-long insurance guy (hey, easy now, he really is a nice guy) he has always welcomed my weird sales style into his world and together we have enjoyed some incredible wins that no one gave us a chance at winning.

ACKNOWLEDGEMENTS

To my first business partner, Ed Roche, for being just crazy and stubborn enough in 2001 to start the ad agency we had talked about for 10 years but never did. And thank you for the 16 years we spent together. During my time at The IDEA Factory, I had some of the best times of my life. We did some amazing campaigns together and raised almost $500,000 for local charities with the "Toy Factory" idea.

Then there is Vicky Quinn Fraser of Moxie Books in the UK. When this whole damn book was still just a Google Drive of messy words with no flow, I invested in a seven-hour day with her on Zoom. Vicky ended the chaos and got me to finally believe I had a book inside of me. She helps rebels—misfits like me—find, write, and sell the story within. Vicky gets it. She has all these little tricks and tips to help get you unstuck. Writing a book can be lonely, and she made it less lonely.

And there's a special human by the name of Jackie Raymond, "the Corset for Flabby Writing." Jackie was the final set of eyes before I found the courage to hit "send to print" and, unlike my Grade Six English teacher, she never once put me in detention for typos and poor grammar and her feedback was always filled with empathy and a smile.

Thank you to Nada Orlic for making the 128 changes I asked her to make to the design of this book's cover. Even when scope creep was a real thing, you never made me feel bad about it. You nailed it.

Nicole Jobe. I don't even know what to say about this brilliant Word Wizard. I found her during the last year of this book, when the book was a "steaming hot pile of pages" and without her, I'm not sure you'd be reading this. She was like my GPS—taking this project from chaos to clarity. She cut this book from 85,000 words to 74,000 words like a world-class surgeon, without changing the tone or personality of any of the writing. When her final changes came through, I just clicked "accept all changes." I didn't need to double-check. I had that much faith in her. Nicole, thank you for sticking with me. If anyone needs an editor, I'll introduce you to Nicole. You'll thank me forever.

Jeremy Bennett is my unfair advantage. I can barely figure out how to use the TV remote at home, but he helped me figure out how to put together stuff around a book I had no clue about—from designing images to building out www.kevincasey.ca to help me build a community. He taught a middle-aged grown man how to use weird things like autoresponders, video sharing platforms, ClickFunnels, and a whole bunch of other things I still don't know the functions of but get monthly bills for anyway. He answered my calls at 6:30 a.m. and 9:30 p.m. during the week and on the weekends. He also answered more 911 calls than I care to admit. Jeremy, you have been a true friend and a great teacher.

To my Akimbo lab friends, Tania and Pegret, who got the very primal version of *(un)selling* and helped me believe it was worth sharing. I'll never forget you.

Gerry Carew, Lynn Hammond, Dee Cee, and Jesse Stirling for reminding me that my work matters, and taking the time to use their media platforms to share the (un)selling story.

Thank you to John Steele, Jim Mackey, Mark Dobbin, Amy Henderson, AnnMarie Boudreau, and Katrina Kum, who shared bits of wisdom and knowledge without even knowing I was even picking their brains.

Allison Blackburn. You have a remarkable book idea trapped in that head of yours that I can't wait for you to soon share to the world. I hope this book proves it to you, it's YOUR book next. If I can do this, you certainly can. Your support and kind words will never be forgotten.

ACKNOWLEDGEMENTS

To my mom for going first and showing me what it's like to take a chance and do something uncomfortable in life. When my mom was 42, she took off her apron, looked at my dad and my brothers and sister at the dinner table, and told us she was jumping headfirst to become a real estate agent and live her dream. We thought we would starve to death and be found dead in our dirty clothes. That didn't happen, but our mom went on to become one of the most successful real estate agents of her time. Mom, you don't need a cape, you are a superhero to me.

For my dad, who was my best friend and my travel buddy. I kept telling him until his last breath in 2019 that the $48 nachos he ordered from room service at the Royal York in Toronto weren't overpriced. They were a bargain and the best nachos ever, because they were with him, and I wish we could just have one more night like that.

I wish my dad could have seen this book come out, but I know he is waving at me and happy that I stuck with it. And if I am being honest, he wouldn't have read this book anyway because he hated books and liked newspapers.

And I am OK with that. Because he was with me all the way through every page.

I could go on and on, but I'm already way past the word count of this book.

K.C.

Share this book

Who else is stuck? Who else feels anxiety around selling? Who's hiding their gift from the world? Make a list of people you care about, and then circulate this book when you're done. Add a few names, and then pass it on. But don't forget to cross yourself off the list before you do.

1. _____

2. _____

3. _____

4. _____

5. _____

Please return this book to: _____

Printed in Great Britain
by Amazon

35368345R00234